INFINITE
HORIZONS

SCRIPTURE THROUGH
CARMELITE EYES

James McCaffrey OCD

First published 2013 by:

TERESIAN PRESS
Carmelite Priory
Boars Hill
Oxford OX1 5HB
priory@carmelite.org.uk

Copyright © James McCaffrey, OCD 2013

ISBN 978-0-947916-13-8

A catalogue record for this book is available from the British Library.

Quotations from the writings of the Carmelite saints
© Washington Province of Discalced Carmelites ICS Publications
2131 Lincoln Road, N.E. Washington, DC 20002-1199 U.S.A.
www.icspublications.org

Cover design by Bill Bolger

Typeset and printed by Joshua Horgan, Oxford

In memory of

BILL BOLGER

(1938–2013)

who designed the cover of this book just before he died

– a great friend to me personally
and to the Carmelite family

A loyal friend is something beyond price,
there is no measuring his worth.
(Ecclesiasticus 6:15)

I take up Holy Scripture. Then all seems luminous to me; a single word uncovers for my soul infinite horizons...

St Thérèse of Lisieux

CONTENTS

PREFACE

In two of my earlier books, *The Carmelite Charism* and *Captive Flames*, I have written at length on the link between Scripture and our Carmelite teachings on prayer. In the present book, I am to some extent exploring the same general theme. The stress is still on both Carmelite prayer and the Scriptures, especially the Gospels. But the perspective here is reversed. In *Captive Flames*, for example, I had examined themes from the writings of the Carmelite saints in the light of Scripture – that is, showing the saints' teachings to be rooted in biblical foundations. In the current book, however, I am taking instead themes from the Bible which teach us about the Christian life of prayer, and then exploring these themes in the light of the writings of the Carmelite saints.

The reason for this is that I have come to realise, over the years, the invaluable insights provided by the Carmelite prayer tradition as an aid to penetrating more deeply into the teaching of the Scriptures on prayer. The writings of our saints are teeming with practical help on how to read the Bible prayerfully, and this is in line with the instruction of Vatican II on the reading and praying of Scripture (cf. DV 11–26).[1] This book, then, is an invitation to read, ponder, pray and contemplate – following the teachings of Scripture and under the guidance of the great Carmelite masters of the spiritual life. We need only to keep our hearts open at all times, attentive to the workings of the Holy Spirit who is the ultimate guide on our prayer journey.

No Carmelite could fail to see Mary as *the* gospel woman of prayer. This is why, in the Prologue, we reflect on her prayerful attitude to the word of God. She is the great listener and is praised as such in the Gospels. A woman in the crowd raised her voice and said to Jesus, 'Blessed is the womb that bore you and the breasts that fed you' (Lk 11:27). When Jesus replied, however, he paid his mother an even greater compliment: 'Blessed rather are those who hear the word of God and obey it' (Lk 11:28). We know that Mary pondered the word of God and treasured it in her heart (cf. Lk 2:19.51). This is intimately linked with her response to God as she fulfilled her role, central to God's whole loving plan of redemption (cf. Jn 19:25–27).

By way of introduction to this book, then, the Prologue will be a reminder that to read the word of God in the spirit of Carmel is to pray it with the heart of Mary: it is to put on the dispositions of her inner life. A glance at her in the Gospels provides us with some aids on how to read the Scriptures in a way that is simple and easily accessible to all. Our primary focus here will be on Mary's dialogue with the angel at the Annunciation; this remarkable prayer scene invites all of us to listen, at one with the humble Virgin, open to the Spirit and surrendered entirely, like her, to the word of God as it speaks to us and challenges us.

Before we explore the biblical teachings on prayer, which form the essence of this book, Chapter 1 serves as an introduction to how deeply our Carmelite saints are rooted in the Scriptures. We see, too, how their burning love for the word of God provides us with so many varied ways of reading and listening to the Scriptures in a spirit of prayer; though inevitably, it would be impossible to record everything they have shared with us. Chosen here are five of the better-known saints, the first three of whom are Doctors of the Church: Teresa of Avila, John of the Cross, Thérèse of Lisieux, Elizabeth of the Trinity and Edith Stein. All their writings were born of prayer, and of a personal intimacy with the word of God in prayer. As their minds and hearts were steeped in the Scriptures, so their writings, too, are an abiding testimony to their passionate love for the Bible. No wonder their teachings teem with biblical references; at times, they even resemble mosaics of scriptural quotations, just like the *Rule* of Carmel itself.[2] These five outstanding Carmelites complement and enrich each other beautifully with the originality of their approaches, and with their own engaging ways of reading the word of God prayerfully. But ultimately, for all of them, the Scriptures are letters of love from God to his beloved children, and these saints respond to his word with that same love which is the very heart of Carmelite prayer.

In Chapter 2, we reflect on the mystery of Christian prayer, and also on the ways in which the Order of Carmel reflects in its special charism the Jesus of the Gospels as the teacher and model of all authentic Christian prayer. Everyone who is sincerely searching for light and support in prayer will be well advised to look to Teresa of Avila, the Doctor of Prayer, who is a perennial spring for all who wish to follow her teaching. Thomas Merton has so rightly said: 'There is no member of the Church who does not owe something to Carmel.'[3] The same can certainly be said of Teresa, who has enriched the whole Church with her teaching. So, in this chapter we look at how Teresian prayer can provide us with many deep and original insights into the gospel teachings on prayer. The Carmelite charism is deeply rooted in the Scriptures, and Teresa has stamped her message with an endearing human touch and the originality of her own creative genius. Ultimately, our Carmelite saints can open up for us deeper insights into the gospel teachings, and help us to penetrate ever more fully into the mystery of all Christian prayer.

It is surely fitting to give the priestly prayer of Jesus an entire chapter on its own. This prayer in John 17 stands apart in length and content and depth from all the other examples of prayer in the Gospels, and it provides a climax to the whole gospel prayer tradition as embodied in all four Gospels. It is also a replica in miniature of the teaching on prayer in the Fourth Gospel itself. The evangelist, almost unobtrusively, has woven the leading themes of his Gospel into the fabric of this prayer with remarkable and consummate skill. The priestly prayer is deeply embedded in the Carmelite tradition of prayer and kept alive in the writings of our saints, including the more recent ones such as Thérèse, Elizabeth and Edith. So the third chapter of this book is an invitation to look at this remarkable prayer through Carmelite eyes. In this way, we can begin to explore the unfathomable riches of the mystery which the priestly prayer both conceals and reveals. This discussion also provides a transition from the previous chapter, with its more general gospel teaching on prayer, to the following one on the passion of Jesus and the mystery of human suffering and its place at the heart of all Christian prayer.

Every true disciple is called to carry the cross while walking in the footsteps of Jesus. Christ's journey leads inexorably to his passion-resurrection and plunges his followers with him ever more deeply into the paschal mystery – a dying to selfishness and a rising to the joy of the risen Lord. Few spiritual writers have ever written of the wisdom and folly of the cross in the life of prayer as our Carmelite saints and blesseds have repeatedly done from personal experience. Chapter 4 of this book reminds us that those moments of darkness, failure, frustration, and the apparent absence of God on our spiritual journey have a special place and value in his loving plan of salvation. This chapter invites all of us to stand beside Mary in silent prayer at the foot of the cross and to fill up in our bodies, like her, what is still lacking in the sufferings of her Son for the sake of his body, which is the church (cf. Col 1:24). This fourth chapter should speak to all who embark on the demanding way of prayer and encourage them to keep their eyes fixed on the Crucified – to take up their crucifix, to listen like Mary on Calvary, and to 'gaze on him whom they have pierced' (cf. Jn 19:37; Zech 12:10).

The role of the Holy Spirit is fundamental to any understanding of the Scriptures and the mystery of Christian prayer. Our fifth chapter treats of the general gospel teaching on the Spirit with special emphasis given to the incomparable Paraclete passages in the Fourth Gospel. These sections in John are the supreme expression of a long and gradual development in the deepening understanding of the early church tradition; as such, they merit special consideration. At first sight, it may appear that our Carmelite saints have little to tell us about the hidden action of the Spirit in the depths of the human heart at prayer. Yet nothing could be farther from the truth, and when they do write about the action of the Holy Spirit, these are profound gems of spiritual teaching. Not just the writings of our saints but also their example help us enormously to enter into the deep mystery of the hidden presence of the Spirit, who comes to help us in our weakness and intercedes for us unceasingly with longings too deep for words and always according to the will of God (cf. Rm 8:26–27). It is only the Spirit, who breathes where it wills (cf. Jn 3:8), that can ultimately explain the flexibility, freedom and spontaneity that are such a distinctive mark of authentic Carmelite prayer.

In the sixth and final chapter, we reflect on the age-old monastic tradition of *lectio divina* worked out by saintly men and women of the past. Here, we see how this helpful method of reading the word of God is rooted in the teaching of the Scriptures themselves; and how it is perfectly in line with the teaching of Vatican II and, more recently, renewed and encouraged by Pope Benedict XVI. As the chapter shows, each of the four traditional divisions of *lectio divina* – reading and pondering, praying and contemplating – are enriched when understood with a Carmelite slant, supported by the perspectives of our saints. *Lectio divina* is no more or less than a practical and helpful unfolding of the central invitation of the Carmelite *Rule* to 'ponder the Lord's law day and night and to keep watch in prayer' (# 10). This precept is itself drawn from the Scriptures. Indeed, we read in the very first Psalm: 'Happy indeed is the man...whose delight is the law of the Lord and who ponders his law day and night' (Ps 1:2; cf. Jos 1:8). The four divisions of *lectio divina*, just mentioned, should not be understood as a straitjacket imposed in a fixed order indiscriminately on all who wish to engage with the word of God. Following the teachings of our Carmelite saints, we see that these four stages are a well-tested and helpful way of exploring the hidden depths of the Scriptures with ease, flexibility and freedom, in keeping with the lessons of the Bible and in the spirit of our Carmelite prayer tradition: 'Where the Spirit of the Lord is, there is freedom' (2Cor 3:17).

By way of Epilogue, Luke's Emmaus story translates the theory of *lectio divina* into practice, as we explore this concrete gospel example. Jesus takes the initiative: he speaks to the two disciples on the road to Emmaus and opens up the Scriptures for them while they listen and ponder in the light of their own life experience of shattered hopes. The story illustrates beautifully the four traditional phases of *lectio divina*, mentioned above; and to these we may add a fifth stage, 'action' – that is, allowing the word of God to bear in us the fruit of good works through an experience of conversion in our lives. This listening to Jesus leads us to reflect, like the two disciples, and in turn draws us with them to prayer in hearts burning with love, and finally to a silent gasp of wonder, awe and amazement in the blinding light of wordless contemplation. Before they encounter Jesus and listen to his word, the disciples are wandering away from Jerusalem which is the place of the passion-resurrection and the centre of salvation history; at the end of the story, they return to the centre in Jerusalem, transformed and changed by a complete conversion and, together with the other disciples, as witnesses proclaim their faith in the paschal mystery.

The Appendices to this book fall into two parts. The first provides four important texts from Scripture, as well as extracts from *Dei Verbum*, the document of Vatican II on reading the word of God, supported by a quotation from Pope Benedict XVI. The inclusion of the biblical texts – those of the Annunciation, the priestly prayer of Jesus, the Paraclete passages and the Emmaus story – should make it easier for the reader to consult these passages which are given extended treatment in the book; while the extracts from the Council document, with the additional passage from Pope Benedict XVI, will help to keep us always attentive to the official teaching of the Church on how to read the word of God.

The remaining Appendices comprise guidelines for practising *lectio divina*, whether alone or in a group. The first is a guided meditation, following the *lectio* stages, of a passage from John's Gospel which is rich in prayerful insights. The second, which is perhaps more suited for use in a group, includes those stages of *lectio divina* while simply inviting us to immerse ourselves in the word of God, in the tranquillity of silence, until the word 'moves us to bear fruit in an offering of praise and an offering of action' (HL, p. 16), to recall the words of Edith Stein.

I would like to add a brief word of thanks to all who have helped me by their encouragement and careful reading of this book, either in whole or in part, with special mention of Dr Joanne Mosley, my colleague as assistant editor of our Carmelite magazine *Mount Carmel*, and author of works on Edith Stein and Elizabeth of the Trinity. All who have read this book before its publication, or who have listened to my talks, have confirmed for me, through their interest and comments, the universal value and appeal of a prayerful reading of the Gospels through the eyes of our Carmelite saints and strengthened me in my calling, as a Carmelite, to a life of prayer.

Notes

1. DV = *Dei Verbum* (*Dogmatic Constitution on Divine Revelation*).
2. See the *Rule of Saint Albert* – with the numbering of sections as agreed in 1999, which is the numbering followed in this book – in John Malley, O Carm, Camilo Maccise, OCD & Joseph Chalmers, O Carm, *In Obsequio Jesu Christi: The Letters of the Superiors General O.Carm. and O.C.D. 1992–2002*, Rome: Edizioni OCD, 2003, pp. 133–9.
3. Thomas Merton, *The Ascent to Truth*, London: Hollis & Carter, 1951, p. ix.

Prologue
READING THE SCRIPTURES WITH MARY

To read the word of God in the spirit of Carmel is to pray it with the heart of Mary: it is to put on the dispositions of her inner life. She is a living witness to the quiet working of God's grace within her as she responds in concrete circumstances to the challenge of his word. A glance at her life provides us with some aids that we all need for a simple and renewed approach to reading the Scriptures in a way easily accessible to all, and drawing on the wisdom of *lectio divina*.[1]

There are no barriers when Mary listens to the word. There must be none for us either. She is at ease, relaxed with God – aware that she is the object of his special love. This awareness of his love for us must also be our own entry point into prayer for we, too, 'have found favour with God' (cf. Lk 1:30).[2] We must stand before God just as we are – like Mary who said to the angel, 'Behold, I am the handmaid of the Lord' (Lk 1:38). God looks on his servant 'in her lowliness' (Lk 1:48), and with this in mind we come as weak, frail, vulnerable and contrite sinners, unmasked before a God whose 'mercy is from age to age' (Lk 1:50). Mary comes before him, knowing that he who is almighty has done – and can still do – great things for her. We, too, must start with that same attitude of trust and be ready to risk everything on the truth of his word. Let us listen to the word, be challenged, and surrender ourselves to it. If we wish, we can do all this in an eloquently simple gesture with empty and upturned hands, waiting to receive whatever God wishes to say to us and ask of us.

Mary's faith unlocks the real secret of her approach to the word of God. Her cousin Elizabeth recognises this, saying:

1

'Blessed is she who believed that the word spoken to her by the Lord would be fulfilled' (Lk 1:45). We, too, must come to Scripture in a spirit of faith – a faith like Mary's, ever searching for a deeper meaning and understanding of what God is doing, here and now, in our lives. So, we come to Scripture making an act of faith, opening our inner eye to the action of the Spirit who will 'come upon' us as he did for Mary (cf. Lk 1:35).

We begin by invoking the Holy Spirit. For this, we may choose a prayer of our own liking. Perhaps it will be a traditional one such as: 'Come, Holy Spirit.' Or, if we prefer, we can of course formulate a prayer in our own words. Reading the Gospels, open with Mary to the action of the Spirit, will centre us directly on her Son. We must always bear in mind that the inspired texts, those of both the Old and the New Testament, *speak of Jesus*. So, we focus on Jesus, together with Mary who was the first to fix her eyes on the Word made flesh. As John of the Cross wrote so beautifully: 'The Mother gazed in sheer wonder' (R 9). He was contemplating with the eyes of Mary, and to see through her eyes is to see Jesus.

We now *read* the word. We select a short passage and repeat it slowly, more than once – reflecting on it and listening to it deep within our hearts. We wait for a word or phrase to stand out for us from the page. Like Mary, we then *meditate* on these words, 'pondering them in our heart' (cf. Lk 2:19.51). The word of God came to Mary: 'you will conceive in your womb and bear a son...' (Lk 1:31). Light begins to dawn as to what this might mean, when we call to mind other words of Scripture. When the angel says, 'the Lord God will give to him the throne of his ancestor David' (Lk 1:32), this refers back to the Old Testament prophecy that will now be fulfilled: Mary's Son will be the promised King-Messiah and Son of God, sprung from the house of David (cf. 2Sm 7:12–14). We, too, can be enriched and enlightened by pondering and reflecting on the word of God in this way: a word of Scripture will at times for us be sparked off and clarified by associations with other words of the Bible. We do not need to go in search of them; we let them come, spontaneously, unbidden.

The word of God must descend from our head to our heart. This is often a painful journey into the very core of our being. When we ponder the word, we also read it with our life's experience and let our life's experience be read by it in turn. Gradually, this will enable us, ourselves, to become a living word. This has nothing to do with sublime heights beyond our reach. Rather, it is the effect of direct contact with the power of God's saving love, released through the word by the Spirit. It is love, and love alone, that can change and transform us. The word touches our heart and we let our hearts go out in love.

We now begin to *pray* the word. We lay bare before the Lord whatever surfaces for us from it: our aspirations and longings, our disappointments and hopes, our concerns and gratitude, our joys and sorrows – all rising from the wellsprings of our heart. We tell him all our inmost thoughts and desires. Sharing with God our needs, and the needs of others, we can follow the example of the Virgin at Cana who merely stated the situation to Jesus, then trusted that God would provide the answer. 'They have no wine' (Jn 2:3), she said simply. We must not be shy about exposing to God our worries, our questions, even our doubts. Like Mary, we will surely feel bewildered and confused at times. 'How can this be?' (Lk 1:34), she asked the angel. And on another occasion we are told that she 'did not understand the saying' (Lk 2:50). Perhaps we may be wrestling with an urgent problem, seeking an answer that never seems to come. Then we can recall the words of Mary to Jesus: 'Why have you done this to us? Your father and I have been searching for you anxiously' (Lk 2:48).

As we walk in the light of the word, we will find a new self-knowledge, and we will be content, like Mary, in our 'lowliness' (Lk 1:48) as we discover a God of mercy who exalts the humble. How can we not find ourselves brimming with thanksgiving and praise, just like Mary who exclaimed: 'The Almighty has done great things for me, holy is his name' (Lk 1:49)? And we can give ourselves over to an inner current of joy, remembering Mary's cry of delight, 'My spirit rejoices in God, my Saviour' (Lk 1:47).

As our prayer continues, we may notice that it gives way to a deep stillness. Now is not the time to be *doing* things in prayer. In peace and confidence, we must let ourselves be drawn into this stillness – into what is nothing less than silent *contemplation*, a simple glance of love towards Jesus. In spirit we will stand with Mary, gazing on her Son – just as she herself stood at the foot of the cross, communing with him in love – and receiving into our open hearts the gift of Jesus himself. John of the Cross penetrates into the heart of the mystery here, when he writes: 'pure contemplation lies in receiving' (LF 3:36) and 'contemplation is nothing else than a secret and peaceful and loving inflow of God, which, if not impeded, fires the soul in the spirit of love' (1DN 10:6).

It is at such times that in a very subtle way God will inspire us with what he wants us to do. This again is like Mary who, gazing on her Son at the foot of the cross, received her mission to be mother of the church. To *accept the word* spoken to us in Scripture, or in the silence of contemplation, is to respond to God's personal invitation to us with Mary's *fiat* as we say, 'let it be done to me according to your word' (Lk 1:38). We must make our own Mary's response to the word of God, spoken to her by the angel, even when the page before us does not immediately 'speak' to us. It may be that the seed of the word is still sinking into the soil of our hearts. We have only to be patient: it will thrust up shoots at its proper time. This can be a slow, gradual, almost imperceptible process. The spiritual life is, in any case, a marathon, not a sprint: we must walk at God's pace, as Mary did when puzzling over the angel's enigmatic message and awaiting its unfolding in God's own time.

We must not anticipate God's action but remain always open to its fulfilment, even when he seems to be silent. We need constancy, determination and resolve in this desert experience – and we need to hold firm, as Mary did, when her initial *fiat* was finally tested on Calvary. All we have to do is to trust in the goodness of God and in the wisdom of his word which will bear fruit at the appointed time, as he reminds us through the words

of Isaiah: 'as the rain and the snow come down from heaven and
do not return without watering the earth, making it yield and
giving growth to provide seed for the sower and bread for the
eating, so the word that goes from my mouth does not return to
me empty, without carrying out my will and succeeding in what
it was sent to do' (Is 55:10–11).

The fruits of this prayerful openness and immersion in
Scripture – our *action*, in answer to God's word – may take many
forms. But Mary's experience shows that they will be essentially
the same for us as for her: *compassion* – hurrying to our neighbour in need, just as Mary 'arose and went with haste into the
hill country to a city of Judah' (Lk 1:39) so as to tend to her
cousin Elizabeth; *witness* – inviting others to come and listen to
Jesus, saying to them in the words of Mary at Cana, 'Do whatever
he tells you' (Jn 2:5), and announcing to the world the wonders
of God's goodness, as in this wonderful line of the *Magnificat*:
'My soul proclaims the greatness of the Lord' (Lk 1:46); and
solidarity with the community of believers – as we pray, for them and
with them, together with the mother of God and mother of the
church who was 'joined in continuous prayer' (Acts 1:14) with
the first disciples. We wait, like them, for the outpouring of the
Holy Spirit who will bring back to our memory the word we have
read, the word spoken by Mary's Son.

Ultimately, to listen to the word of God is to be conformed
to Jesus who 'went down with them to Nazareth and was obedient' (Lk 2:51) – 'obedient' in the radical sense of that word,
which is nothing other than 'listening'. Mary listened to Jesus
and he listened to her. That is what reading the Scriptures
should mean for us all: a perfect dialogue of love.

Notes

1. See Chapter 6, for an introduction to *lectio divina*. See also, for an
excellent study of the subject, Mariano Magrassi, OSB, *Praying the Bible: An
Introduction to Lectio Divina*, Collegeville, MN: The Liturgical Press, 1998.
2. For the text of the gospel account of the Annunciation, see Appendix 1a.

Chapter 1

A DEEP LOVE OF SCRIPTURE: THE EXAMPLE OF THE CARMELITE SAINTS

TERESA OF AVILA: *EMBRACING THE SCRIPTURES*

Unfathomable riches

'The force and power in the word of God,' Vatican II tells us, 'is so great that it remains the support and energy of the Church, the strength of faith for her children, the food of the soul, the pure and perennial source of spiritual life' (DV 21). Little wonder that Teresa of Avila, the sixteenth-century reformer of Carmel and foundress of the Discalced Carmelites,[1] steeped her mind and heart in the word of God and turned to it as the support of her charism: 'I would die a thousand deaths for the faith,' she said, 'or for any truth of Sacred Scripture' (*Life* 33:5); and for Teresa, the word of God was not only truth but also love. The *Rule* of Carmel, which she longed to restore in all its original force and beauty, calls on Carmelites to remain 'pondering the Lord's law day and night and keeping watch in prayer' (cf. # 10). It also reminded her of Paul's exhortation: 'the word of God must abound in your mouths and hearts' (cf. # 19; Col 3:16; Rm 10:8). The *Rule* itself, which Teresa inherited from the early hermits on Mount Carmel, is like a mosaic of biblical quotations, resembling a gospel discourse more than a legal document.

In view of the times and culture in which she lived, Teresa's understanding and love of the Scriptures was both profound and remarkable. As far as we know, she probably never had access to a complete Bible, at least not in her native Castilian language. She had no scriptural training, unlike John of the Cross, and she knew no Latin. Even the Spanish translations available to her were limited and restricted. Her knowledge of the word of God came mainly through means accessible to the ordinary, simple faithful of her day: the liturgy, partial translations, and some spiritual books teeming with biblical quotations like Francisco de Osuna's *Third Spiritual Alphabet* and Ludolph of Saxony's *Life of Christ*. Her writings contain about six hundred biblical quotations,[2] mostly from John, Paul, the Psalms and the Song of Songs.

This inspired love song was one of Teresa's favourite books of the Bible. She even wrote her own commentary on it, a work which she referred to as 'my meditations' (M 1:8) and which is now called *Meditations on the Song of Songs*.[3] She was keenly aware of the unfathomable riches concealed in this Old Testament book. She writes of it: 'these words must contain great things and mysteries since they are of such value that when I asked learned men...they answered that the doctors wrote many commentaries and yet never finished explaining the words fully... what a great Lord and God we have. For one word of His will contain within itself a thousand mysteries, and thus our understanding is only very elementary...' (M 1:8.2).[4]

The Song of Songs provided Teresa with her spousal imagery to describe the deepest form of prayer known to her: spiritual betrothal and spiritual marriage. The imagery is also deeply embedded elsewhere in the Scriptures and reflects the recurrent Old Testament theme of the marriage between God and his people: 'And in that day, says the Lord, you will call me, "My husband"... And I will betroth you to me forever' (Hos 2:16.19; cf. Jer 2:2; Is 61:10). This same imagery is also found in the New Testament – as, for example, when the Baptist designates Jesus as the Messianic *bridegroom* of Israel: 'He who has the bride is the bridegroom' (Jn 3:29; cf. Rv 19:7–9; Eph 5:23–32). 'O Jesus!' exclaims Teresa. 'Who would know the many things there must be in Scripture!' (IC VII:3:13). It was revealed to her in prayer that 'all the harm that comes to the world comes from its not knowing the truths of Scripture in clarity and truth; not one iota of Scripture will fall short' (*Life* 40:1).

Learning that gives light

Teresa herself knew just how much she needed to be enlightened: 'learning,' she said, 'is a great thing because learned men teach and enlighten us who know little; and, when brought before the truths of Sacred Scripture, we do what we ought' (*Life* 13:16). She held these *letrados*, the 'lettered', in highest esteem and great affection, constantly turning to them for light and help: 'I have consulted many learned men…,' she wrote, 'and I've always been a friend of men of learning' (*Life* 13:18; cf. IC V:1:7). Her preference for the learned director over the holy one, if a choice between them had to be made, is well known.

Teresa herself, though, was a woman of keen discernment, highly intelligent and with a mind of her own. She was not one to submit easily and blindly to any scholars who were narrow-minded. She had this to say in praise of Mary, who ceased her questioning upon hearing that the Holy Spirit would come upon her and the Most High overshadow her: 'She did not act as do some learned men…for they want to be so rational about things and so precise in their understanding that it doesn't seem anyone else but they with their learning can understand the grandeurs of God' (M 6:7). Like Mary, Teresa had made her own the lesson of the Psalmist: 'I have not gone after things too great nor marvels beyond me' (Ps 130:1).

Teresa was not easily led astray by the 'half-learned'. They 'cost me dearly' (IC V:1:8), she tells us. 'Half-learned confessors have done my soul great harm' (*Life* 5:3), she also said, having learned painfully, in the words of Alexander Pope, that 'A little learning is a dangerous thing'.[5] She was quick to warn against people who interpret the Scriptures with no reference to the humanity of Christ. Reflecting on the words of Jesus, 'anyone who sees me sees the Father' (Jn 14:9), she writes: '[People] will say that another meaning is given to these words. I don't know about those other meanings; I have got along very well with this one that my soul always feels to be true' (IC VI:7:6). An independent woman with great common sense and a brilliant sense of humour, she did not hesitate to tease playfully even her beloved soul-mate and the companion of her reform, John of the Cross, for his interpretation of the Lord's words to her, 'Seek yourself in me'. She found his interpretation too spiritual but consoled him gleefully: 'Nonetheless, we are grateful to him for having explained so well what we did not ask' (Sat Cri 7). In the last analysis, however, the *letrados* she trusted were, for her, 'those who give us light' (*Life* 13:21; cf. IC VI:8:8), those representatives of the Church 'in the place of God' (F 2:2).

Daughter of the Church

Teresa made it clear that a soul of strong, living faith 'always strives to proceed in conformity with what the Church holds' (*Life* 25:12). And the words 'in conformity with Sacred Scripture' run like a refrain through all her writings (cf. *Life* 25:13; 34:11; Sp Test 3:13; cf. IC VI:3:4). She was concerned to let herself be carried along by the living stream of the Church's teaching[6] – ancient, vast, rich, and ever deepening under the Spirit's action with the passage of time. She also encouraged great freedom and flexibility in our approach to the Scriptures, affirming the right of every believer to interpret the word of God prayerfully. But she always insisted on the necessity of remaining in communion with the Church: 'If I do not satisfy you,' she told her Carmelite sisters while sharing with them her thoughts on the Our Father, 'you can think up other reflections yourselves. Our Master will allow us to make these reflections provided that we submit in all things to what the Church holds' (WP 30:4).

Anticipating the teaching of the Church at Vatican II, Teresa knew, as though by instinct, that 'since holy Scripture must be read and interpreted according to the same Spirit by whom it was written, no less serious attention must be given to the content and unity of the whole of Scripture, if the meaning of the sacred texts is to be correctly brought to light' (DV 12). She strongly affirmed the basic necessity of believing in the truth and efficacy of God's word which, she said, 'cannot fail' (WP 27:2). Her faith embraced the whole range of the Scriptures, not just the parts that appealed to her. Importantly, this saved her from the fundamentalist view that would translate isolated passages into general rules.[7] Having decided to follow certain advisers, who were using Paul's words on the role of women in the Church (cf. 1Cor 14:34) so as to dissuade her from making new foundations, Teresa then received contrary advice direct from Jesus himself: 'Tell them they shouldn't follow just one part of Scripture but that they should look at other parts, and ask them if they can by chance tie my hands' (Sp Test 15).

Her surrender to the demands of God's word was the fruit of a 'living faith' (*Life* 19:5) in the *mysteries of the Church* and *the person of Jesus*. She felt no envy of those who had known the earthly Jesus – for, she says, referring to herself anonymously, 'the Lord had given her such living faith that when she heard some persons saying they would have liked to have lived at the time Christ our Good walked in the world, she used to laugh to herself. She wondered what more they wanted since in the most Blessed Sacrament they had Him just as truly present as He was then' (WP 34:6). Indeed, Teresa well knew that Jesus is now even more present by faith, and no longer restricted by time and space, through the power of the Spirit who continues to lead the community of believers through the word 'into all truth' (Jn 16:13).

The word in action

Teresa was never content to be a mere spectator in the story of salvation as it unfolded in the Scriptures. Eminently practical, she did not regard the Bible as simply a repertoire of sublime ideas and beautiful sentiments, or of episodes remote from her own life. Drawn into the drama, an actor in it, she 'wept with the Magdalene, no more nor less than if she were seeing [Jesus] with her bodily eyes in the house of the Pharisee' (WP 34:7). She could likewise identify with the more active Martha (cf. WP 17:5–6) and warned her sisters about 'wanting to be Mary before having worked with Martha' (*Life* 22:9; cf. Lk 10:38–42). The Samaritan woman was also one of Teresa's special favourites:

> Oh, how many times do I recall the living water that the Lord told the Samaritan woman about! And so I am very fond of that gospel passage. Thus it is, indeed, that from the time I was a little child, without understanding this good as I do now, I often begged the Lord to give me the water. I always carried with me a painting of this episode of the Lord at the well, with the words, inscribed: *Domine, da mihi aquam* ['Lord, give me to drink']. (*Life* 30:19: cf. M 7:6; Jn 4:7–26)

Little wonder that John's Gospel seems to have been a gospel specially dear to her. In so many subtle ways, the fourth evangelist constantly invites the reader to be one with the protagonists and to enter with them into dialogue with Jesus.

The gospel figure of the rich young man was also important for Teresa. He provided her with an embodiment of what she wished to teach us about a supremely important moment of transition in the life of prayer. She speaks of some 'upright and well-ordered' people (IC III:2:1), commenting: 'But since there is need of still more in order that the soul possess the Lord completely, it is not enough to say we want it; just as this was not enough for the young man whom the Lord told what one must do in order to be perfect. From the time I began to speak of these dwelling places I have had this young man in mind. For we are literally like him' (IC III:1:6; cf. Mt 19:16–30). Even from her early years, Teresa learnt to be 'a doer' not just 'a hearer of the word' (Jas 1:22). She was only sixteen and at boarding school when a nun there, Sr María de Briceño y Contreras, 'began to tell me,' she writes, 'how she arrived at the decision to become a nun solely by reading what the Gospel says: *many are the called and few the chosen*' (*Life* 3:1; cf. Mt 22:14). Teresa, again recalling her schooldays, speaks of 'the strength the words of God – both heard and read – gave my heart' (*Life* 3:5). Later in life, she affirms her readiness to use 'all my strength to carry out the least part of Sacred Scripture' (*Life* 40:2).

Teresa reminds us that the words of God are always efficacious, bringing into effect what they signify: they are 'both words and works' (*Life* 25:3) and a source and spring of action. She tells us that occasionally she also heard *interior words* from the Lord, not with her bodily ears but 'with the ears of the soul…in secret' (IC VI:3:12). These words are significantly linked with the words of Scripture, the truth of which is confirmed with greater clarity by Teresa's own experience. She writes: 'It also happens very quickly and ineffably that God will show within Himself a truth that seems to leave in obscurity all those there are in creatures, and one understands very clearly that God alone is Truth, unable to lie. What David says in a psalm about every man being a liar is clearly understood' (IC VI:10:5; cf. Ps 115:11).

So, too, when describing her deep experience of the Blessed Trinity, Teresa writes: 'When the soul is brought into that dwelling place, the Most Blessed Trinity, all three Persons, through an intellectual vision, is revealed to it through a certain representation of the truth… Here all three Persons communicate themselves to it, speak to it, and explain those words of the Lord in the Gospel: that He and the Father and the Holy Spirit will come to dwell with the soul that loves Him and keeps His commandments' (IC VII:1:6; cf. Sp Test 13:1; 65:9; Jn 14:23). But these words, received in such intimate depths, were exceptional favours granted to her later in life. However, the criterion for her of their truth was always their fruits: whether of fortitude and gentleness (cf. *Life* 25:13) or light and quiet (cf. *Life* 25:3), and especially their conformity to the word of God and the teaching of the Church.

A gospel prayer

'It is common knowledge,' Vatican II reminds us, 'that among all the Scriptures, even those of the New Testament, the Gospels have a special pre-eminence, and rightly so, for they are the principal witness of the life and teaching of the incarnate Word, our Saviour' (DV 18). They were certainly of prime importance for Teresa. The Council also tells us, using a quotation from St Ambrose, 'that prayer should accompany the reading of sacred Scripture, so that God and the person may talk together; for "we speak to Him when we pray; we hear Him when we read the divine sayings"' (DV 25).[8] No wonder that Teresa, Doctor of Prayer, directs all those in search of solid teaching on prayer to read the Gospels.

The Gospels also provided Teresa with a biblical foundation for her own incomparable understanding of prayer. She reassures us that they provide us with the ideal form of all prayer when they give us the Our Father. In it, Jesus shares with us his own prayer and invites us in turn to respond to God in his own words: 'Pray then like this: Our Father...' (Mt 6:9). When Teresa advises us on how to pray vocally – something which she links with her discussion of the Our Father – she provides us at the same time with a guide on how she herself read the Scriptures, and she invites us to do the same: 'being aware and knowing that we are speaking, with whom we are speaking, and who we ourselves are who dare to speak so much with so great a Lord' (WP 25:3; cf. 42:4). Indeed, Teresa gives us these requirements when she speaks about 'perfect contemplation and mental prayer' (WP 25:3).

In Teresa's day, suspicion about interior prayer was prevalent. It was often said: 'it's not for women, for they will be susceptible to illusions'; 'it's better they stick to their sewing'; 'the Our Father and the Hail Mary are sufficient' (WP 21:2). Strong woman that she was, and true champion of women's freedom and rights, Teresa was to counter these objections in her own subtle and ingenious way: 'indeed,' she asserts, speaking of these two prayers, 'they are sufficient! It is always good to base your prayer on prayers coming from the mouth of the Lord... No one will be able to take from you these books (the Our Father and the Hail Mary)... I have always been fond of the words of the Gospels [that have come from that most sacred mouth in the way they were said] and found more recollection in them than in very cleverly written books' (WP 21:3). So when Teresa writes her commentary on the Our Father, she invites us to read the Scriptures with an eye to this gospel prayer, and at the same time shares with us her love of reading the word of God and praying with its very words. In fact, she would have liked to write a commentary on the Hail Mary as well (cf. WP 42:4).

When Teresa shares with us her thoughts on the Our Father, she provides us with a masterly treatment of her understanding of the journey of prayer. For her, the Our Father is not a rigid formula of prayer to be recited by rote as we 'heap up empty phrases' (Mt 6:7)! Her approach to praying it is eminently flexible, just like her method of reading the Scriptures in general: 'no one can take vocal prayer from you or make you recite the Our Father hastily and without understanding it... It has seemed to me that...this prayer was intended for general use so that each one could petition according to his own intention' (WP 42:4; 37:2). For Teresa, reciting the Our Father is like reading all other words of Scripture: it is a kind of springboard or taking-off point when we want to enter profoundly into the depths of silent prayer. We repeat it with a quiet rhythm and a lingering pace, allowing the words to sink into our hearts and be sparked into love by the Spirit which 'breathes where it wills' (Jn 3:8). She exclaims: 'I marvel to see that in so few words everything about contemplation and perfection is included; it seems we need to study no other book than this one. Up to now the Lord has taught us the whole way of prayer and of high contemplation' (WP 37:1). Yes, the Our Father is for her a comprehensive 'book'.[9]

Jesus – the true book

Due to the *Index* published by the Inquisition in 1559, Teresa found herself deprived of many of her favourite books. But the Lord said to her: 'Don't be sad, for I shall give you a living book.' Recalling these consoling words, Teresa explains: 'His Majesty had become the true book in which I saw the truths' (*Life* 26:5).

For Teresa, the word of God was Jesus, living and present here and now. He was her all. As it happens, she was to discover the absolute centrality of Christ in the spiritual life through a painful experience which cost her dearly. She refers to the influence of certain harmful books which played down the central role of the sacred humanity, and she confesses that she was led astray by them: 'At no time do I recall this opinion I had without feeling pain,' she says; 'it seems to me I became a dreadful traitor – although in ignorance' (*Life* 22:3). Later, she was able to correct the imbalance and, evoking the words of Jesus 'I am the door' (Jn 10:7.9), she wrote:

> I see clearly…that God desires that if we are going to please Him and receive His great favours, we must do so through the most sacred humanity of Christ… Many, many times have I perceived this truth through experience. The Lord has told it to me. I have definitely seen that we must enter by this gate… desire no other path even if you are at the summit of contemplation; on this road you walk safely. This Lord of ours is the one through whom all blessings come to us… In beholding His life we find that He is the best example. (*Life* 22:6–7)

And she concludes her advice in characteristic style by directing our attention to the word of God in support of her advice:

> God is very pleased to see a soul that humbly takes His Son as mediator and that loves this Son so much that even when His Majesty desires to raise it to very lofty contemplation…, it is aware of its unworthiness, saying with St. Peter: *Depart from me, Lord, for I am a sinful man.* (*Life* 22:11; cf. Lk 5:8)

Teresa reminds us of the greatest criterion proving if a word received in prayer comes from God: it 'bears the credentials of being from God if it is in conformity with Sacred Scripture' (*Life* 25:13). No wonder she steeped her mind and heart in the Scriptures; and she encourages all of us, by her writings and by the example of her life, to do the same.

JOHN OF THE CROSS:
EXPLORING THE DEPTHS OF SCRIPTURE

An inexhaustible treasure

John of the Cross, faithful companion and unwavering support of Teresa in her great work of reform, speaks, like her, from the depths of his own personal experience of God, supported by a prayerful reading of the Scriptures and a deep knowledge of human nature. Both John and Teresa were steeped in the inexhaustible treasures of the word of God. But their approach to the Scriptures was understandably different. John was a theologian, artist, psychologist and incomparable spiritual director. So we could reasonably have expected from his pen works designed primarily for the learned, intellectual and more sophisticated reader. In one sense this is true. However, as John Paul II comments in his doctoral study: 'St. John of the Cross did not write his works with a view to the investigations of scholars or those engaged in higher studies'. John's works, the Pope reminds us, 'are written for the purpose of directing contemplatives toward union with God'.[10]

Nowhere, perhaps, is this more true than in John's use of the Scriptures.[11] They provided him with an inexhaustible source of inspiration for his work of guiding and directing others to intimacy with God. 'Every scribe who becomes a disciple of the kingdom of heaven is like a householder who brings out from his storeroom things both new and old' (Mt 13:52). John was no exception. As Newman observes so well: 'the whole Bible... is written on the principle of development. As the Revelation proceeds, it is ever new, yet ever old.'[12] Today, we are privileged to have our understanding of the Bible enormously enriched by a variety of new approaches and ways of penetrating the depths of the sacred text.[13] But these were largely unknown to John. All indications, however, are that he would have been completely at ease with the developments of recent biblical research in the wake of Vatican II. In his own day, John was familiar with the lively controversy about the interpretation of Scripture in the University of Salamanca where he studied. Gaspar Grajal was a prominent figure among the so-called 'scripturists', who sought the literal sense of Scripture through scientific methods and the study of languages.[14] He was probably John's professor and was later imprisoned by the Inquisition for these ideas. John, however, did not have a general theory or method of explaining the Scriptures.[15] He had a thorough familiarity with the Bible, he had reason, and he had faith.

John would insistently extol the value and importance of human reason. This might come as a surprise to some. He also categorically affirms that faith is 'the only proximate and proportionate means to union with God' (2A 9:1). For John, there is no opposition between faith and reason. His is the celebrated maxim: 'One human thought alone is worth more than the entire world, hence God alone is worthy of it' (SLL 35; cf. 116). He is an uncompromising champion of the dignity of the human person. 'What a piece of work is a man,' wrote Shakespeare, his contemporary, 'how noble in reason'.[16] And the Psalmist: 'you have made [man] little less than a god' (Ps 8:6). These are sentiments affirmed by John himself, as his maxim shows. But John well knew that reason – with its lights and limitations – is at its noblest and best when it remains always open to God in mystery. He insists: 'one can get sufficient guidance from natural reason'. But he qualifies this by continuing: 'and from the law and doctrine of the Gospel' (2A 21:4). This is something we can 'understand' only in faith – and, John might add, through faith in the teachings of the Church.

The Bible and the Church

'Whether I deduce [some point] from Scripture or not,' John tells us, 'I will not be intending to deviate from the true meaning of Sacred Scripture or from the doctrine of our Holy Mother the Catholic Church' (A Prol. 2). Repeatedly, he affirms that his entire teaching is based on the Bible and the teachings of the Church. He writes, for example, in the Prologue to *The*

Spiritual Canticle: 'I desire to submit...entirely to Holy Mother the Church... I want to explain and confirm at least the more difficult matters through passages from Sacred Scripture' (SC Prol. 4). John will also draw on his own experience and knowledge, but always insists: 'my help in all that, with God's favour, I shall say, will be Sacred Scripture' (A Prol. 2). This is confirmed by Thomas Merton who highlights this same point in his discussion of John's works: 'even though he draws upon his experimental knowledge of mysticism, he does not attempt to prove anything by that experience alone. All that he says of the graces of prayer serves him as an occasion to seek out the final theological answer, the true Catholic doctrine on each point, in the revealed word of God. Saint John of the Cross does not merely *illustrate* his doctrine by a literary use of Scripture, he *proves* it by Scripture. More than that, he finds his doctrine in the Bible.'[17] So, even John's incomparable familiarity with the ways of the Spirit and his own intimate communion with God in prayer remain always secondary to the Bible and to the teachings of the Church.

The word of God is ever 'alive and active' (Hb 4:12) through faith and the power of the Spirit. John knew only too well that Scripture is 'not the word of any human being, but God's word, a power that is working among believers' (cf. 1Th 2:13). 'Taking Scripture as our guide,' he says, 'we do not err, since the Holy Spirit speaks to us through it' (A Prol. 2) – that is: speaks and is still speaking to us, here and now. John is constantly reminding us that the words of the Bible are the actual words of the Holy Spirit (cf. 2A 16:9; 22:2).

The same Spirit is at work in both the Bible and the Church. We must always remember that the Bible was born in the heart of the Church, the community of believers.[18] So, John tells us, 'we must be guided humanly and visibly in all by the law of Christ...and that of his Church and of his ministers' (2A 22:7). In his understanding of the Scriptures, John remains always in communion with the Church and open to the action of the Spirit. Therein lie the inspiration and perennial value of all that he has left us in his writings.

A deeper exploration

'[God's words] embody an abyss and depth of spirit,' John writes, 'and to want to limit them to our interpretation and to what our senses can apprehend is like wanting to grasp a handful of air' (2A 19:10). He was fully aware of the literal sense of the Scriptures which could be grasped by reason. But his preference was clearly for the 'spiritual' sense. This latter is intelligible only in the darkness of faith, and it unfolds under the action of the Spirit. It is a deeper meaning which incomparably exceeds the literal sense. This spiritual meaning, writes John, is 'much richer and more plentiful, very extraordinary and far beyond the boundaries of the letter' (2A 19:5).[19]

John's emphasis on the deeper spiritual meaning of the word of God might easily perplex readers familiar with modern tools of biblical interpretation.[20] But for John this deeper, 'spiritual' sense has a solid basis in the Scriptures. He rightly finds support for it in the promise of the Paraclete who will guide the Church into 'all truth' (Jn 16:13; cf. 14:26; 2:22; 12:16). When John writes about the 'comparisons of the divine Song of Solomon and other books of Sacred Scripture', he does not hesitate to explain that 'the Holy Spirit, unable to express the fullness of his meaning in ordinary words, utters mysteries in strange figures and likenesses... the abundant meanings of the Holy Spirit cannot be caught in words' (SC Prol. 1). Here, the Mystical Doctor is in line with an ancient Carmelite tradition. Witness the words of one anonymous thirteenth-century Carmelite writer:

> Within these secret words, held captive beneath images, are hidden meanings that are subtle and mystical, like treasures in the ground. To discover these secrets, by separating the spirit from the letter, is to draw up life, the life of the Spirit. Happy is the person who in the misery of exile devotes all his spirit and all his love to the delights of these mysterious meanings![21]

Lectio in the spirit of Carmel[22]

John's approach to the sacred text is akin to *lectio divina* – a way of reading the Scriptures prayerfully. It is a method deeply embedded in the monastic tradition. God's word emerged spontaneously in the saint's writings from his retentive memory shaped in large measure by the Bible. His mind was constantly echoing to parallel, contrasting, qualifying and explanatory texts, and his works are teeming with scriptural quotations.

John therefore urges us to savour the sacred text as he did, to the exclusion of all else present: 'leave as well all these other things,' he writes, 'and attend to one thing alone that brings all these with it (namely, holy solitude, together with prayer and spiritual and divine reading), and persevere there in forgetfulness of all things' (SLL 79). And in an expansion of one proverbial gospel text, 'seek, and you will find; knock, and it will be opened to you' (Mt 7:7), he invites us to explore the Scriptures deeply and prayerfully as he suggests a relationship between the four stages of *lectio divina*: 'Seek in reading and you will find in meditation; knock in prayer and it will be opened to you in contemplation' (SLL 158).[23]

John himself would read Scripture again and again in order to relish its deeper meaning. This method of constantly repeating it in a slow and prayerful reading allows the word of God to seep into the heart 'as the rain and the snow come down from the heavens and do not return without watering the earth' (Is 55:10; cf. 55:11). One of his companions on his journeys, Jerónimo de la Cruz, testifies that the saint used to repeat the sacred text, quietly and with great devotion.[24] Here, John was praying in the monastic tradition of reading the word of God aloud or, for greater personal impact, *sotto voce*. The testimony of other witnesses also speaks volumes. His secretary for many years, Fray Juan Evangelista, testifies that John knew almost all of the Bible by heart;[25] while another friar, Pablo de Santa María, made this equally astounding comment: 'I am sure he knew the whole Bible.'[26] Little wonder that Fray Agustín de los Reyes could confide to a friend how he found John one day leaning against a wall, 'with a Bible in his hand, absorbed, as usual,' he said, 'in contemplation'.[27] Edith Stein sums up well: 'Our Holy Father John...educates us to read the Scriptures. He is said to have had, at the end, only the New Testament in his cell' (SP, p. 218).

As we have seen earlier, Vatican II reminds us that 'prayer should accompany the reading of sacred Scripture, so that God and the person may talk together; for "we speak to Him when we pray; we hear Him when we read the divine sayings"' (DV 25). It is hardly surprising, then, to find *lectio* and prayer inseparably entwined in John's interpretation of the Bible and embodied in the saint's own works. His incomparable descriptions of the inner life – whether in magnificent verse or in what he calls his 'awkward style' of prose (A Prol. 8) – draw their substance from John's intimacy with God's word and from the drama of the Bible: the love story between God and his people.

Flexibility and originality

John's writings are, unsurprisingly, rich in biblical imagery. One image of paramount importance for his overall outline of the spiritual journey is that of the exodus: the passage of God's people out of Egypt across the desert and into the promised land, a journey out of slavery and into freedom. References to this event, explicit and implicit, recur throughout John's works. He compares the cravings of unruly desires – our slavery to sin and temptation – to the way the Israelites were still hankering, in the wilderness, after the food of their captivity (cf. 1DN 9:5). John's words of advice to those who guide contemplatives also contain echoes of the exodus experience and again highlight the aspect of the desert (cf. LF 3:38).

This same imagery of Israel's desert experience enriches and gives added depth to John's exquisite lyrical poetry. In the opening verse of his poem 'The Dark Night', he writes: 'fired with love's urgent longings... / I went out ['salí'] unseen, / my house being now all stilled' (DN, stanza 1). This poem ends, too, with the imagery of departure: 'I went out from myself ['dejéme'], /

leaving my cares / forgotten among the lilies' (DN, stanza 8). In 'The Spiritual Canticle', the restless bride voices an anguished cry for her absent Lover, just like the distraught lover of the Song of Songs: 'I went out ['salí'] calling you, but you were gone' (SC, stanza 1; cf. Sg 3:1–2; 5:6). Here, too, the bride longs to journey out – out of this life into glory and the spiritual marriage of the beatific vision: 'Let us rejoice, Beloved, / and let us go forth to behold ourselves in your beauty' (SC, stanza 36).

John finds much of his inspiration in the wanderings of the chosen people. He alters, amplifies and superbly adapts the psalm 'By the rivers of Babylon...' (Ps 136). The resulting poem (P 10) was written while he was imprisoned in a dark dungeon during his captivity in Toledo. There, his mind and heart could echo more easily to the sobbing music of God's captive people, longing in their exile for a second exodus. His words give passionate expression to the thirst of every human heart reaching out in pain and waiting on God to lead us, like his banished people, out of slavery and into the freedom of the promised land.

It was this same imagery of the exodus that enabled John to discover in the first two commandments a biblical foundation for his understanding of the ascetical basis on which to build his spiritual edifice. These two commandments constitute the heart of God's covenant with his people in the desert and contain the radical and absolute demands of a 'jealous' God (Ex 20:5), an 'unrivalled' God (Is 45:5), who wants to take first place in his people's hearts (cf. Ex 20:3–4). But before giving his commandments, God first reminds his people of their exodus experience: 'I am the Lord your God, who brought you out of the land of Egypt, out of the house of bondage' (Ex 20:2; cf. Dt 5:6). John sees that the first two commandments are central to the whole biblical message and provide the conditions for entering the promised land. Without necessarily following these two commandments as a preconceived plan for his own works, John simply opened himself to the word of God which yielded its riches to him with its radical and absolute demands. In this light, he wrote the three books of *The Ascent of Mount Carmel*.

Newman reminds us of the value of this kind of originality and flexibility in our personal exploration of the unfathomed riches and possibilities in the Bible: 'There is no greater mistake, surely, than to suppose that a revealed truth precludes originality in the treatment of it... a reassertion of what is old with a luminousness of explanation which is new, is a gift inferior only to that of revelation itself.'[28] Inspired by the Scriptures, John's writings invite us on an exodus journey into freedom, withdrawing us from all that is not God in order to focus us entirely on God's love.

Story of a love

The Bible contains the whole narrative of salvation history. John read it as a love story. In his *Ballads*, a series of nine poetic scenes also known as the *Romances*, he invites us to do the same, and these love songs are also his way of explaining to us the Jesus he discovered in the Scriptures. Here, John does not refer to 'Jesus' or 'Jesus Christ' – titles quite rare in his writings – or to 'Christ', 'Word', 'Son' or 'Lord' which are somewhat more common in his works. Instead, he speaks of Jesus as 'Bridegroom' and 'Lover', terms which he borrows from the Song of Songs which is arguably the greatest love song ever written. Just as for Teresa of Avila, these names are far more personal and speak to us of a relationship of love. They occur about five hundred and fifty times in John's writings and are the only terms used of the Son in the *Ballads*.[29]

The *Ballads* are not the finest fruit of John's poetic genius. They are simple and uncluttered in style, creations in harmony with a popular literary form prevalent in John's day. But the poignancy of their message of love is heightened considerably, since they were born of John's harrowing experience in the darkness and privation of his Toledo prison cell. They are shining examples of the flexibility with which John read the word of God and assimilated it: expanding and adapting it; penetrating its meaning and finding revealed in it the inspiration of his deep personal relationship of love with God in prayer. Again, his approach is a lesson for all of us on how to read the Scriptures and how to ponder them leisurely and prayerfully with the same freedom and ease.

The *Ballads* show us, in a particularly striking way, how deeply John's mind was steeped in the Scriptures, how faithful he was to their meaning at the deepest level, and how relevant they were for him in the concrete circumstances of his lived experience. They comprise nine scenes chosen designedly from all four Gospels. They are not a 'harmony' (or compilation) of the Gospels, but they are in perfect harmony with them. For John, as they can be for us, the Gospels are a window opening onto the beauty and intensity of God's everlasting love lavished upon us and revealed to us in the person of Jesus.

An eternal dialogue of love

At the outset, we are plunged into the timeless life of the Trinity before the world was made, as John reflects on the opening lines of the Prologue to the Fourth Gospel: 'In the beginning was the Word…' (Jn 1:1). The dynamism of the personal relationship of the Word 'turned towards God' the Father (cf. Jn 1:1.18) is translated for us in the *Ballads* as a reciprocal sharing of love between the three divine Persons: 'One love in them all / makes of them one Lover, / and the Lover is the Beloved / in whom each one lives' (R 1). Here, John is both faithful to the meaning of the gospel words and also expands them. For in the loving dialogue between the Three, we are told, the eternal plan of salvation is conceived: 'My Son, I will give myself / to him who loves you / and I will love him / with the same love I have for you, / because he has loved / you whom I love so' (R 2). The intimate dialogue of love continues with the Father's promise to his Son of a bride who, her heart burning with love, will love him and will share the company of the Three (cf. R 3).

We are later told how the deepest desires and loving prayers in expectation of the promised Messiah are fulfilled: 'when the aged Simeon / burned with longing, / and begged God that he / might see this day / …he took God himself / into his own hands / and holding him in his arms, / pressed him to himself' (R 6). It is also a loving embrace that we find in God's advance of love to his own people (cf. R 4).

After this, the inner dialogue of love between the Father and the Son continues, as the Father speaks tenderly of love as the meaning of the Word made flesh: 'In perfect love / this law holds: / that the lover become / like the one he loves' (R 7). The Son replies: 'I will go [and] seek my bride / and take upon myself / her weariness and labours / in which she suffers so' (R 7). There is no mention of sin as such, only of the effects of sin and the Son's willingness to be one with the weakness of broken humanity in the flesh. It is the loving and tender union of a marriage between Bridegroom and bride, the church, with the Son 'embracing his bride, / holding her in his arms' (R 9).

John leaves us to contemplate the weakness of a transcendent, omnipotent and incomprehensible God who incredibly is lying in tears on a bed of straw. With this, John gives us a lesson on how to read the story of salvation history in the Scriptures, through the eyes of Mary brimming with quiet love at the wonder of it all. On her feast as Mother of God, the Church cries out: 'O wonderful exchange!'[30] So, too, does John with his parting words, describing Mary as gazing 'in sheer wonder' at a God taking on our pain and our tears, in exchange for his love and joy: 'in God, our weeping, / and in us, gladness, / to the one and the other / things usually so strange' (R 9).

ELIZABETH OF THE TRINITY: *IMMERSED IN THE SCRIPTURES*

Openness to the word

All the Carmelite saints and blesseds practised what they preached, as we have seen again and again. We can learn from the way they prayed, and from their advice to others, how much they loved the Scriptures and how carefully they read them. Elizabeth of the Trinity is certainly no exception. John Paul II writes: 'Elizabeth gives the witness of a perfect openness to the Word of God which she assimilated to the point that...she found in it all her reasons for living'. And he calls her 'a brilliant witness to the joy of being rooted and grounded in love' (cf. Eph 3:17).[31] Elizabeth's openness to the Scriptures challenges us to read the Bible as she did, and to make her 'openness' to the word of God our own, in our search for meaning and in our need to satisfy the deepest longing of our hearts for love.

Almost all of Elizabeth's writings are full of biblical texts, drawn from her retentive memory and aptly applied to concrete situations in her own life and the lives of others; she frequently handles them with remarkable flexibility, and always with deep reverence for the inspired text. Elizabeth was no scholar, though. Her approach was typically Carmelite like the true contemplative that she was: she prayed her way more and more deeply into the mystery of God's love, revealed to her as she steeped herself in his word.

Into the depths

Elizabeth distilled the essence of her spirituality into her great *Prayer to the Trinity*, written in November 1904, and we can find in it the key to how she read the word of God. Even a cursory glance at this spontaneous outpouring of her heart shows how deeply she loved the Scriptures and how immersed she was in them, mind and heart. She evokes the sacred texts both implicitly and explicitly and weaves them skilfully and adroitly into the fabric of her *Prayer*, while revealing at the same time her own special way of reading Scripture with deep faith. For Elizabeth, faith was not something lifeless and static. It was powerful, dynamic and life-giving: 'alive and active, more penetrating than any two-edged sword' (Hb 4:12).

Her *Prayer* is addressed to the Blessed Trinity – the centre of her spirituality. 'O my God, Trinity whom I adore... may each minute carry me further into the depths of Your Mystery,' she prays. 'May I...be wholly present, my faith wholly vigilant... and wholly surrendered to Your creative Action.' This is how Elizabeth read the Scriptures: she allowed herself to be drawn by faith into the mystery of God and to be entirely transformed by their power. This is how she teaches us to read Scripture as she did – journeying in faith ever more deeply into the riches of God's word.

Focused on Jesus

The *Prayer* continues: 'O my beloved Christ, crucified by love...' Jesus is always the focus for Elizabeth in her reading of the Scriptures. She first discovered him in the Gospels, and there too she recognised him as love – as love crucified. 'Take your Crucifix, look, listen' (L 93), she wrote to her sister in one of her earlier letters from Carmel.

But it was her beloved St Paul who would later lead Elizabeth more deeply into the mystery of Jesus (cf. LR 29–31). So it is hardly surprising that the *Prayer* now turns to speak of Jesus in language characteristic of St Paul: to 'be clothed with' or to 'put on' Christ (cf. Gal 3:27; Rm 13:14; Eph 4:24; Col 3:10). 'I ask You to "clothe me with Yourself",' she writes. She then continues her prayer to Jesus, following Paul's train of thought: 'identify my soul with all the movements of Your Soul'. This is Elizabeth's longing for a closer and greater intimacy and oneness with Jesus; it is a longing for incorporation in Christ which is a lesson typical of St Paul, deeply embedded in his letters and characteristic of his teaching (cf. Eph 1:3–10).

Listening to the word

For Elizabeth, there is one disposition of paramount importance for praying and reading the Scriptures as she did: *to listen to God speaking.* And so her *Prayer* continues with echoes of John's Gospel, beginning with Jesus as 'the Word' (Jn 1:1): 'O Eternal Word,' she prays, 'Word of my God, I want to spend my life in listening to You'. The lesson of silent listening in response to the words of Jesus runs almost like a refrain throughout the Gospels and especially the Gospel of John. It is the mark of every true disciple of Jesus. 'Whoever is of the truth listens to my voice' (Jn 18:37), Jesus tells us as he recalls his words about himself as the Shepherd of his flock: 'the sheep hear his voice, and he calls his own sheep by name and leads them out... the sheep follow him, for they know his voice' (Jn 10:3–4).

But why listen silently to the word? Elizabeth explains her reason as her *Prayer* continues: 'to become wholly teachable that I may learn all from [Jesus]'. As Edith Stein would express it: 'We need hours for listening silently and allowing the Word of God to act on us until it moves us to bear fruit in an offering of praise and an offering of action' (HL, p. 16). To be docile or 'teachable' is not weakness in Elizabeth, it is flexibility: readiness to respond humbly to the action of the Spirit, and to discover and accept God's will for herself and for others. Elizabeth was no starry-eyed dreamer. She knew darkness and aridity in her experience of God's absence. So she continues by pleading for perseverance in prayer – words which apply also to her reading of the Scriptures, to which she would turn for help when she was suffering in her night of faith and painful illness: 'through all nights, all voids, all helplessness,' she prays, 'I want to gaze on You always and remain in Your great light. O my beloved Star...' She read the Scriptures with typical Carmelite perseverance (cf. WP 21:2). Her example invites us to do the same.

Assimilating the word

Always faithful and without ever losing heart, Elizabeth read the word of God in order to assimilate it, to identify with it entirely, and to make it her own. In fact, the words of Scripture surface spontaneously and unexpectedly in the very expression of her *Prayer to the Trinity*. In the words of the angel to Mary at the Annunciation, 'The Holy Spirit will come upon you' (Lk 1:35), Elizabeth implores the Spirit to do the same for her: 'O consuming Fire, Spirit of Love,' she prays, '"come upon me", and create in my soul a kind of incarnation of the Word: that I may be another humanity for Him in which He can renew His whole Mystery.' *His whole mystery*: that is, every aspect of his life, embodied in the church. Elizabeth prays in union with Jesus and with his body, the church.

Elizabeth wrote her prayer on the feast of the Presentation of Mary in the Temple, which also happened to be the end of a retreat in which the preacher had spoken inspiringly about the Annunciation. It is hardly surprising, then, that the words of the gospel story of Mary were ringing in her ears. They surface a second time as Elizabeth invites the Father to 'cover her with [His] shadow', just as the angel promised that the Spirit would 'overshadow' Mary (cf. Lk 1:35).

A hymn to the Trinity

Anyone familiar with the Fourth Gospel cannot fail to notice how strikingly Elizabeth has assimilated the very movement of John's hymn to the Word, living forever in the bosom of the Trinity (cf. Jn 1:1–18). John's Prologue begins in eternity: 'In the beginning was the Word'; it descends like the swing of a pendulum and touches earth at the centre with the 'Word made flesh'; and it swings back again, at the end, into the timeless life of the Trinity where 'the only Son who is in the bosom of the Father' dwells forever in the eternal life of God. So, too, Elizabeth's *Prayer* begins in the timeless life of the Blessed Trinity: 'O my God, Trinity whom I adore'; it descends to the centre and touches earth in the person of Jesus: 'O my beloved Christ, crucified by love'; and at the end it ascends once more to immerse us with Elizabeth in the eternal Trinity: 'my Three, my All, my Beatitude, infinite Solitude, Immensity in which I lose myself...'

Indeed, the *Prayer to the Trinity* is a shining example of how to pray in the spirit of the Gospels: 'true worshippers will worship the Father in spirit and in truth' (Jn 4:23), John tells us. That is authentic Trinitarian prayer directed to the Father under the action of the Spirit in the risen Jesus, who is the Truth and the centre of all true Christian prayer. This is not to say that Elizabeth was designedly or even consciously thinking of this as she wrote her *Prayer*. But reading the word of God, she was drawn to explore and penetrate it ever more perfectly in silent prayer – at one with the action of the Spirit who is the inspiration and the primary author of all the Scriptures.

Letters of love

It was in Paul's Prologue to Ephesians that Elizabeth discovered her vocation as 'Praise of Glory': 'We who first hoped in Christ,' she read, 'have been destined and appointed to live for the praise of his glory...and have believed in him, were sealed with the promised Holy Spirit...to the praise of his glory' (Eph 1:12–14). Here, Paul is describing the call of every believer to be a praise of glory, sealed with the promised Holy Spirit and 'destined in love to be his children through Jesus Christ...to the praise of his glorious grace' (Eph 1:5–6). So it is hardly surprising that Elizabeth would explain her vocation in terms of love, and at the same time would recall the action of the Holy Spirit who is the Spirit of love. She writes, at the end of her work *Heaven in Faith*: 'A praise of glory is a soul of silence that remains like a lyre under the mysterious touch of the Holy Spirit... In the heaven of her soul, the praise of glory...is under the action of the Holy Spirit who effects everything in her'; 'A praise of glory is a soul that lives in God, that loves Him with a pure and disinterested love,...[has] passed into praise and love in her passion for the glory of her God' (HF 43–44). Elizabeth shows us how to read the Scriptures in depth, with her and like her, in order to be 'rooted and grounded in love' (Eph 3:17). She took St Paul – the 'father of her soul',[32] as she called him – and St John, the Beloved Disciple, to be her unerring guides on her journey of exploration. We, too, can do no better than follow her example.

We can hardly exaggerate the influence of St Paul on Elizabeth in her search for love: 'there is a phrase from Saint Paul that is like a summary of my life,' she says, 'and could be written on every one of its moments: "Propter nimiam charitatem" ["because of his exceeding love"]' (L 280; cf. Eph 2:4). Or, as Elizabeth expresses it here, adapting it to herself: 'because He has loved me too much'. She often expresses this phrase in the French as: 'because of "His *too great love*"' (GV 11; cf. L 319) – something ultimately inexplicable, which left her lost in wonder at the unfathomable abyss of God's folly and wisdom (cf. 1Cor

1:23–25). 'In his magnificent epistles,' she writes, 'Saint Paul preaches nothing but this mystery of the charity of Christ' (L 191). She cherished his words as love letters from God, addressed to her personally. She had no qualms in adapting them to herself with great flexibility and originality: 'Who will separate me [not 'us'],' she writes, 'from the love of Christ?' (HF 26; cf. Rm 8:35). She applied herself to studying Paul's letters, making indexes of her favourite quotations so that choice texts, ever ready at her fingertips, surfaced spontaneously when she wrote.

Elizabeth had an enquiring mind. She questioned the meaning of Paul's words and probed them continually for a deeper understanding. She was always open to discovering hidden meanings beneath the surface; she was not a doubter but someone searching with a living faith, like Mary at the Annunciation who asked, 'How can this be...?' (Lk 1:34). Elizabeth went to Scripture, and especially to St Paul, for an answer to the burning question of how to understand and live out her vocation to be a 'praise of glory' (LR 37). Her *Last Retreat* is punctuated with phrases like: 'how [do we do this]?', 'I think', 'St Paul...teaches me this' (LR 37), or 'St Paul gives me light on this' (LR 20). Light on what? On, as St Paul expresses it, being 'rooted and grounded in love' (LR 20; cf. Eph 3:17). Elizabeth's writings are full of such lessons, teaching us how to read the word of God while at the same time exploring the riches of Paul's teaching on God's love. She exhorts us: 'Believe in His love, His *exceeding* love' (GV 11). A few days before her death, she said to her sisters in Carmel: 'Everything passes!... At the [evening] of life love alone remains...'[33]

Sharing love

Elizabeth did not hesitate to share with others the fruits she gained from reading the letters of St Paul. What she says is invariably a lesson on love. She was both a teacher and a witness, or rather a teacher who was a transparent witness to the depths of God's love which she discovered in Paul's writings. She was no mere listener of the word – she was a doer (cf. Jas 1:22): 'it is not enough just to listen to this word,' she reflects in her *Last Retreat*, 'we must keep it!' (LR 28). The lesson of God's love was alive for Elizabeth: she knew that it was addressed to people here and now, that it was always reaching out to them, all-embracing. Her family, friends and relatives were ever close to her heart. She was ready at all times to give them practical advice whenever she read something in St Paul that was relevant to them about love. She spontaneously thought of them, and then shared with them the fruits of her intimacy with his writings.

Examples abound. Elizabeth referred to a passage from Paul that was relevant to her sister's life: 'I have just been reading in Saint Paul some splendid things on the mystery of the divine adoption. Naturally, I thought of you – it would have been quite extraordinary if I hadn't, for you are a mother and know what depths of love God has placed in your heart for your children, so you can grasp the grandeur of this mystery' (L 239; cf. Eph 1:5). She always seemed to choose the right message of love to encourage the person in question. When writing to priests, Elizabeth often put an epigraph from Paul in Latin, such as: 'Mihi vivere Christus est' – 'For me, to live is Christ' (L 219; cf. Ph 1:21). In a New Year's letter to a friend, Elizabeth said, 'let us be only the "praise of His glory", according to the Apostle's beautiful expression' (L 220; cf. Eph 1:12). These words are also a lesson on love. For Elizabeth is reminding us here that this vocation, which she discovered in Ephesians, is everyone's vocation and shared by every believer: 'A praise of glory is a soul that lives in God,' she explains, 'that loves Him with a pure and disinterested love' (HF 43).

Praying the word

John the evangelist was another of Elizabeth's favourite authors. Again, it was the mystery of God's love that fascinated her and drew her to explore his teaching in depth. She did it with characteristic originality and flexibility. She read his Gospel to deepen her life of prayer, and she invites us to do the same. We can see how seriously she did so from her treatment of the Johannine phrase 'Remain in me' (Jn 15:4), which she expanded for her sister Guite.

The word 'remain' runs all through the Fourth Gospel, and Elizabeth draws out the fundamental meaning of the term. To 'remain' does not refer to a one-off action but to a permanent or abiding one; it speaks of continuity. Elizabeth captures the meaning in John exactly when she writes, in the person of Jesus: 'Remain in Me, not for a few moments, a few hours which must pass away, but *"remain..."* permanently, habitually' (HF 3). The term speaks to Elizabeth of continual prayer. It sparks off for her an association with another biblical text, 'The kingdom of God is within you' (HF 5; cf. Lk 17:21). Moreover, Elizabeth invests the words of John with an added dimension by combining the two quotations. She then explains this fuller meaning (cf. HF 5): we can 'remain' in God (cf. Jn 15:4) by dwelling in him who dwells 'within' us (cf. Lk 17:21).

This is a prayer-filled pondering, in that it takes us ever more deeply into the word of God. For Elizabeth, reading the Scriptures cannot be separated from prayer. It draws her into the indwelling presence of God. She was a master at teasing out the implications for prayer of God's word. She specifies, expanding on Jesus' words 'Remain in Me': 'Remain in Me, pray in Me, adore in Me, love in Me, suffer in Me, work and act in Me' (HF 3). Elizabeth leads us through God's word into the prayer of recollection, silence and peace. This is the purpose of *lectio divina* brought to fulfilment.

Communion in love

It is a short step from Jesus' phrase, 'Remain in me... remain in my love' (Jn 15:4.9–10), to the words of Elizabeth's farewell letter to her prioress, now known as *Let Yourself Be Loved*. This was a variation on the words of Jesus to Peter, 'Do you love me more than these?' (Jn 21:15). Both phrases complement each other beautifully, for love is a two-way relationship: it is our response to a God who first loved us (cf. 1Jn 4:10.19). It is a communion in love.

In the First Letter of St John, Elizabeth discovered a word for 'communion' (1Jn 1:3): 'société', in the French version she used.[34] The original Greek term is 'koinōnía', and it refers to 'fellowship' with the Father and the Son. Although 'society' – the near equivalent of 'société' – is not a word we would use in our English rendering of that term in John, fortunately we get an insight into what it meant for Elizabeth from what she says about it in her writings. This is one of the first appearances of the term: 'Yet even here below, He lets us live in His intimacy, and in some way we begin our eternity, living in communion with the three Divine Persons' (L 223); here, we see her speaking of 'communion' as intimacy and as an anticipation of the life of heaven. Often she mentions it in the same breath as God keeping her company (cf. L 327; 329), and once as a sharing in God's life (cf. HF 14). This is essentially what prayer is for Elizabeth: living a life of friendship and intimacy with God. It is ultimately Carmelite prayer: the life of eternity already begun, here on earth, in our communion with God in love.

Biblical witnesses to love

So far, we have been speaking of biblical *writers* who were inspirational for Elizabeth. But there were also certain biblical *figures* who had an impact on her life. As she read the Scriptures, she seems to have engaged directly with the biblical characters as with people who were instructing and guiding her, just as she does with Paul and John who were teaching her directly. For Elizabeth, all these figures were living people in their own right, and she was particularly drawn to those who symbolised prayer and the spirit of Carmel.

Elizabeth refers to Elijah, for example, as 'our first Father' (L 136) – that is, in his role as father of all Carmelites. Even before she herself was clothed with the religious habit, she had longed to receive from him both the mantle and the 'double spirit' of Carmel.[35] Elizabeth's yearning, here, evokes the biblical scene of Elijah's heritage being passed on to Elisha, who literally took up the mantle of the fiery prophet (cf. 2Kgs 2:9.13–14).

It is an episode deeply embedded in the Carmelite tradition. Elizabeth also describes herself as 'the little Moses on the mountain' (L 218), referring to the gesture of the great prophet and law-giver, his arms raised to heaven in prayer for the victory of God's armies (cf. Ex 17:8–13). It was a posture dear to St Teresa herself. She used it to describe the contemplative as a standard-bearer, supporting in prayer the army of those who are apostles (cf. WP 18:5).

Elizabeth was especially drawn to Mary Magdalen, on whose feast day she had been baptised; at the time, the Magdalen was associated with the Mary who sat at the feet of Jesus and listened to his words (cf. Lk 10:39) – an attitude of silent prayer and listening which inevitably struck a deep chord with the contemplative Elizabeth (cf. Pm 83; 94). She also speaks of the Beloved Disciple whom, in her first few days in Carmel, she named in the postulant's questionnaire as her favourite male saint: her reason being that he 'rested on the Heart of his Master' (IN 12; cf. Jn 13:23). In both cases, as with Elijah and Moses, we have a gesture, a physical posture, that fired Elizabeth's imagination. It expressed the intimate love of a person for Jesus and was admirably designed to touch the heart of Elizabeth, called by her Carmelite vocation to a life of loving attention to Jesus. Moreover, the Beloved Disciple teaches Elizabeth about God's love, as we see from her words: 'in Him who is "charity", according to the beautiful definition of the disciple of love' (L 223; cf. 1Jn 4:8.16). The disciple who rested his head on the heart of Jesus was, then, especially qualified to speak of the mystery of God's love. All the writings of Elizabeth are like variations on the theme 'God is love' (1Jn 4:8.16).

Both the Magdalen and the Beloved Disciple affirm this truth, each in their own way. The Magdalen, searching for Jesus in the garden, is like the distraught lover of the Song of Songs in search of her absent lover: 'I will seek him whom my soul loves' (Sg 3:2; cf. Jn 20:2.13). The Beloved Disciple, running to the empty tomb, is also the wounded lover in search of the absent Jesus (Jn 20:1–10). They are both a reminder of the priority of love in our quest for God. Ultimately, the discovery of all who read the Scriptures with Elizabeth as guide is this: 'God is love'.

EDITH STEIN:
THE OLD REVEALED IN THE NEW

Her Jewish heritage

Vatican II highlights for us the importance of the Old Testament. 'In carefully planning and preparing the salvation of the whole human race,' we read, 'the God of supreme love, by a special dispensation, chose for Himself a people to whom He might entrust His promises' (DV 14). Edith Stein was one of this chosen race. It is hardly surprising, then, that she read the Scriptures with a mind and heart steeped in the writings and teachings of the literature sacred to her people. 'Are they Hebrews? So am I. Are they Israelites? So am I. Are they descendants of Abraham? So am I' (2Cor 11:22) – words of St Paul which Edith could have applied equally to herself.

Like Paul, Edith was to discover that the gospel of Christ 'is the power of God for the salvation of everyone who has faith, of the Jew first and also of the Greek' (Rm 1:16). But even after their respective conversions – and for these committed Christians, everything was 'regarded as loss because of Christ' (cf. Ph 3:7) – their writings were always visibly permeated by Jewish ideas, brimful of Old Testament references, and rich with the traditions of Israel. For Edith, like Paul, retained immense respect for Judaism and for those who remained faithful to it. As her new-found Catholic faith developed, she never felt that she had to renounce her Jewish heritage. Rather, she found that she was steeping herself more and more in the Jewish roots of the Christian faith. Her niece has these surprising words: 'Edith Stein tells us that by becoming a Catholic she felt truly Jewish for the first time in her life' (SEL, p. 117).

But while her conversion and later entrance into Carmel appeared to distance her from her Jewish people, her method of reading the Scriptures was in fact to lead her into an ever deeper rediscovery of her Jewish roots. How thrilled Edith must have been, as a Carmelite, to find the core of Carmel's *Rule* expressed with echoes of her beloved Old Testament: the call to remain 'pondering the Lord's law day and night' (#10; cf. Ps 1:2; Jos 1:8). We can only surmise what her joy would have been, had she known that the two greatest figures of the reformed Carmel, Teresa of Avila and John of the Cross, shared her Jewish blood.[36] In her search for the truth of God's word, Edith was to discover that 'the books of the Old Testament... written under divine inspiration, remain permanently valuable... God, the inspirer and author of both testaments, wisely arranged that the New be hidden in the Old and the Old be made manifest in the New' (DV 14.16).[37] The writings of Edith are an abiding witness that she read the Scriptures in the light of this teaching of Vatican II: the New is hidden in the Old, and the Old revealed in the New.

Jesus – the fulfilment of the law

Edith Stein's search for truth led her inexorably, like the first disciples, to the person of Jesus as the promised Messiah of her rich Jewish heritage. She must surely have found her quest reflected in theirs. Edith, like the first disciples, was already searching for Jesus without even knowing it; or, as she would later write: 'God is truth. All who seek truth seek God, whether this is clear to them or not' (SP, p. 272). 'What are you seeking?' (Jn 1:38), Jesus asks his disciples. In Jesus, they find the Messiah of Jewish expectations. 'We have found the Messiah' (Jn 1:41), Andrew says to his brother Simon Peter. This expression of Andrew's faith is followed by another one, even more explicit, on the lips of Philip: 'We have found him of whom Moses in the law and also the prophets wrote, Jesus of Nazareth, the son of Joseph' (Jn 1:45).

The Torah, or the law, was God's special *gift* to his people:[38] 'the law was given through Moses; grace and truth came through Jesus Christ' (Jn 1:17). The law serves as a 'pedagogue' leading to Christ (Gal 3:24); or, as Paul explains elsewhere: 'Christ is the fulfilment of the law' (Rm 10:4). Matthew's expression of the same truth is more nuanced, explaining that Jesus did not come 'to abolish the law and the prophets…but to complete them', and in order that the purpose of the law might be 'achieved' (Mt 5:17–18). In a significant gesture, Paul 'called together the local leaders of the Jews' (Acts 28:17), we are told, 'to convince them about Jesus both from the law of Moses and from the prophets' (Acts 28:23). Edith Stein knew the Hebrew Scriptures well – but it was only after her discovery of Christ that she immersed herself in them, to fathom the depth of the true reality of the Messiah.

'The truth will set you free'

In the end, it was not arguments of philosophy or theology that convinced Edith, this outstanding intellectual, to become a Christian. The moment of discovery came for her when she chanced on the autobiography of Teresa of Avila, the reformer of Carmel.[39] The story goes that Edith read all night until she finished the book. Then, with the first streaks of daybreak, the inner light also dawned. 'That,' she exclaimed, 'is the truth.'[40] Through reading the *Life* of Teresa, Edith had found a *Person* who claimed to be, and was, *Truth* (cf. *Life* 40:1–4). Edith was to discover, in the very opening of John's Gospel, this great secret of the Christian faith: 'The Word was made flesh…, full of grace and truth' (Jn 1:14). Again, during the Last Supper, Jesus claims that he himself is the truth in person: 'I am the way, the truth and the life; no one can come to the Father except through me' (Jn 14:6). Edith had always been, in gospel terms, 'of the truth' (Jn 18:37). Now, having discovered *the* truth, she would henceforth reread and rediscover her Jewish traditions made manifest in the New Testament. There, like every true disciple of Jesus, she would 'listen to [his] voice' (Jn 18:37) and respond to it everywhere in the Scriptures.

In Jesus, Edith would rediscover the law of her own people that was now fulfilled. For them, the Torah was the highest source of wisdom. She well knew, like the first disciples, that it occupied a central place in the Jewish Scriptures: it was God's word to his people, the revelation of his will, a lesson not just for Israel but for all the nations of the world (cf. Dt 4:6). A devout Jew is one 'whose delight is the law of the Lord and who ponders his law day and night' (Ps 1:2). Edith Stein's continuing love of that law was to be fulfilled and completed, and its purpose achieved (cf. Mt 5:17–18) as she contemplated, in the Gospels, the person of Jesus.

Later, writing as a Carmelite in the light of her Jewish tradition, Edith asks the question: 'What is meant by "the Law of the Lord"?' (HL, p. 4). She draws on her intimacy with the Scriptures to explain. She describes Psalm 118 as 'entirely filled with the command to know the Law and to be led by it through life', and she comments: 'The Psalmist was certainly thinking of the Law of the Old Covenant.' 'But,' she adds, 'the Lord has freed us from the yoke of this Law.' And she continues: 'We can consider the Saviour's great commandment of love, which he says includes the whole Law and the Prophets, as the Law of the New Covenant... But we understand the Law of the New Covenant, even better, to be the Lord himself' (HL, p. 4). Here, we are already close to Edith's life-long focus on the person of Jesus – hidden in the Old Testament and revealed in the New.[41]

Models of inspiration

Edith read the Scriptures with an eye to some of the great characters of the Old Testament. It was to them that she looked for light and inspiration, so as to give meaning to the disconcerting experiences in her life. Among those biblical figures, Elijah and Esther must surely hold pride of place in Edith's spirituality. They strengthened and enlightened her by their example. She read their lives and words in response to the concrete circumstances and challenges of her own life.

In the prophet Elijah, known as the father of all Carmelites, Edith found a great model of prayer within the Jewish tradition.[42] He was her shining exemplar of someone in a personal relationship, and loving communion, with God. When she writes, 'Prayer is looking up into the face of the Eternal' (HL, p. 3), she is thinking here of how Elijah is introduced in the First Book of Kings, where he says, 'As the Lord the God of Israel lives, before whom I stand...' (1Kgs 17:1). So Edith explains her own words, just quoted, in terms of this great prophet: 'Elijah stands before God's face because all of his love belongs to the Lord... He stands before God's face like the angels before the eternal throne' (HL, p. 2). She further relates this to her life of prayer in Carmel – her own life and that of her Carmelite sisters: 'To stand before the face of God continues to be the real content of our lives' (HL, p. 4).

But Elijah is also a reflection of the figure of Jesus at prayer. For Jesus, writes Edith, 'stands, always and everywhere, before the face of God' (HL, p. 12). It is to Jesus as supreme model that she turns for her last word on the Carmelite vocation of 'pondering the Lord's law day and night and keeping watch in prayer' (*Rule*, # 10; cf. HL, p. 3): 'We thus fulfil our Rule when we hold the image of the Lord continually before our eyes in order to make ourselves like him' (HL, p. 4), she writes. And for that reason, she concludes, speaking from personal experience, 'We can never finish studying the Gospels' (HL, p. 4).

Paul was willing to be branded 'accursed' (Rm 9:3) for the sake of his people. With Edith it could be no different. She was willing to face the risk of expulsion from her own home because of her conversion, as well as exile from her family through her entrance into Carmel – like a new Esther removed from her people, all the better to plead on their behalf (cf. SP, p. 291). Little wonder that the Book of Esther, in particular the pleading of the exiled Esther for the lives of her people, is one of the readings of the liturgy of the Mass on Edith's feast day. Edith identifies herself with this Old Testament queen: 'I keep having to think of Queen Esther,' she says, 'who was taken from among her people precisely that she might represent them before the king' (SP, p. 291).[43] Edith, like Esther, would step into the presence of her King; and, like Esther, she would stand before him for her people.

But Edith also knew the truth of her own vulnerability and loved to see her weakness in terms of Esther: 'I am a very poor and powerless little Esther,' she writes, 'but the King who chose me is infinitely great and merciful. That is such a great comfort' (SP, p. 291). This knowledge of her own littleness led Edith to an ever greater trust in God. Even when writing as a philosopher, she sums up the confidence that sustained her at all times: 'In my own being, then, I encounter another kind of being that is not mine but that is the support and ground of my own unsupported and groundless being' (FEB, p. 58).

Hidden meanings of the word

Edith's discovery of Mary in the Scriptures was little more than a rediscovery, continuation and gradual deepening of her own biblical roots. It is a reminder for all of us of how Edith read the Scriptures, with a mind and heart ever open to new lights and the hidden mysterious meanings of God's word. Faithful to her Jewish origins, she went back to the first pages of Genesis to learn about the mystery of Mary. For Edith, Eve was the prototype of Mary, who is herself in turn the prototype of all women. This derives from the two names, significant in meaning, given to Eve in Genesis, and of which Edith reminds us: as 'Woman' (Gn 2:23), she is a *companion*; as 'Eve' (Gn 3:20), she is named a *mother* – 'mother of all the living'. Edith, conscious of her own role as a woman, advised women to look at Mary in the Scriptures as she herself did – contemplating Mary as a caring mother and as a woman of deep compassion.

We can see, from talks she gave on the role of woman, how Edith read the Scriptures with an eye to the minutest details of Mary's life and always with a view to assimilating their lessons. She writes: 'In the centre of [Mary's] life stands her Son. She awaits His birth in blissful expectation; she watches over His childhood; near or far, indeed, wherever He wishes, she follows Him on His way; she holds the crucified body in her arms; she carries out the will of the departed. But not as *her* action does she do all this: she is in this the Handmaid of the Lord; she fulfils that to which God has called her. And that is why she does not consider the child as her own property: she has welcomed Him from God's hands; she lays Him back into God's hands by dedicating Him in the Temple and by being with Him at the crucifixion' (W, p. 47).

In the light of her own life experience of struggle and painful events, Edith would also look to Mary and write: 'Everywhere the need exists for maternal sympathy and help,… *motherliness*…; in accordance with the model of the Mother of Mercy, it must have its root in universal divine love for all who are there, belaboured and burdened' (W, p. 264). Here, Edith is discovering her own lifelong apostolate of compassion in imitation of Mary at Cana, practical and sensitive: 'Mary at the wedding of Cana in her quiet, observing look surveys everything and discovers what is lacking. Before anything is noticed, even before embarrassment sets in, she has procured already the remedy' (W, p. 51). Edith is not thinking here merely of the housewife confined to the kitchen and busy among the pots and pans. She is also reading the life of Mary with a message for herself as a professional woman engaged in the exacting demands of writing and teaching. So she adds (perhaps surprisingly for some!): 'Let [Mary] be the prototype of woman in professional life' (W, p. 51) – as she certainly was for Edith.

Pondering the mysteries of Mary

Less surprisingly, though, Edith also sought to understand her own personal calling in the light of Mary in the Scriptures. Pondering still more deeply on Mary as the new Eve in Genesis (cf. Gn 2:23; 3:20), she discovered in greater depth the significance of her own place in God's loving plan: to be a bride of Christ. Again, Edith turned to the Old Testament, as well as the witness of Mary's life, for light on her call to Carmel. Still pondering the word of God in the first pages of Genesis, Edith discovered that Eve was created as a 'helpmate' to man – expressed as 'Eser kenegdo' in the Hebrew.[44] She explains the meaning: it designates a helper, a *counterpart* to man as if face-to-face with him: 'they complement each other as one hand does the other' (W, p. 61).

For Edith, Mary as the new Eve was the bride of Christ. Edith writes: 'there was woven between the soul of the divine Child and the soul of the Virgin Mother the bond of the most intimate unity, which we call betrothal' (HL, p. 98). Edith's calling as a consecrated woman was to walk, like Mary her model, by the side of Jesus – a side-by-side companion with him at all times, standing 'beside' him just as Eve stood 'by the side' of Adam (W, p. 200). When Edith looked to Mary, she saw her taking on the role of Eve as 'co-redeemer by the side of the Redeemer' (W, p. 199), sharing in the work of redemption, engendering souls for the kingdom – a spiritual maternity in which Edith herself would be called to share. Edith would offer her whole life for this, carrying her cross faithfully, longing to walk with Christ even to Golgotha; 'the Lord will never allow His consecrated bride to stray from His side' (W, p. 123), Edith had foretold – relevant and prophetic words, later to be realised with Edith's death in the gas chambers of Auschwitz.

Writing about the mystery of Christmas, Edith tells us that the 'mysteries of Christianity are an inseparable whole. If one becomes absorbed in one, he is drawn to all the others. Thus the road from Bethlehem leads inexorably to Golgotha, from the manger to the cross' (MC, p. 22). This is how the Gospels themselves were written: with hindsight, under the full light of the passion-resurrection of Jesus. Edith herself shows us how to read the mysteries of Mary's life in the same way: as an indivisible whole and inseparably linked in the Scriptures.

The new Eve and the Church

Edith directs us to penetrate the deepest mystery of Mary: the new Eve. She writes: 'The original cell of all redeemed humanity is Mary... Before the Son of Man was born of the Virgin, the Son of God conceived of this very virgin as one full of grace, and He created the Church in and with her' (W, p. 238). This is the initial grace bestowed by God on Mary in her Immaculate

Conception. It is the beginning in her of the Church – redeemed humanity. This, ultimately, is why this woman, untainted by sin, is the *new* Eve. Edith explains: 'by that is meant Mary, but, at the same time, also the whole Church' (W, p. 239). In this way, the mystery of Mary is inseparably linked with the originality of Edith's insights into the mystery of the Church. Mary as the new Eve is not just *by* the side but *from* the side of Jesus: 'The creation of Eve from the rib of the first Adam becomes a prefigurement for the emergence of the new Eve...from the opened side of the new Adam' (W, p. 239), she writes. Near the new Adam on the cross, blood and water flowing from his side, the new Eve stands by his side as mother of the Church – born, like the Church, from the pierced side of the Saviour (cf. Jn 19:34).

Jesus and Mary were present on Calvary as head and heart. Edith explains: '[Mary] is also a unique organ of the Church, that organ from which the entire Mystical Body, even the Head itself, was formed. She might be called, and happily so, the heart of the Church in order to indicate her central and vital position in it' (W, p. 240). Edith had no hesitation in calling her this. She laid bare her own heart to Mary in these words: 'you are now always present because you are the heart of the Church.'[45]

This is surely the spirit of Carmel speaking through Edith, at one with Mary as the praying heart of the Church – Mary, the model for Edith and for every Carmelite called to a life of prayer. Clearly, Edith's teaching on how to explore the mystery of Mary derives from a mind and heart steeped in the rich Jewish tradition and its Scriptures. Her writings remind us that the New Testament cannot be understood fully except in the light of the Old Testament (cf. DV 16). They reaffirm the vigorous spiritual ties that unite the church of Christ to the Jewish people. 'You don't know what it means to me when I come into the chapel in the morning,' Edith said one day to a priest, 'and looking at the tabernacle and the picture of Mary, say to myself: they were of our blood.'[46] Directing us on how to ponder and read the Old Testament in the light of the New must surely rank among one of Edith's most original and valuable contributions to the spirituality of our time.

THÉRÈSE OF LISIEUX:
THE HUMAN FACE OF CHRIST

Rediscovering the Scriptures

Long before Vatican II, Thérèse discovered for herself, and in a personal way, this important lesson of the Council: 'It is common knowledge that among all the Scriptures, even those of the New Testament, the Gospels have a special pre-eminence' (DV 18). This is not, of course, surprising: for the Gospels are, to quote the Council once more, 'the principal witness of the life and teaching of the incarnate Word, our Saviour' (DV 18). Thérèse once wrote: 'as yet I had not discovered the treasures hidden in the Gospels' (SS, p. 102); but later she could say: 'I have only to cast a glance in the Gospels and immediately I breathe in the perfumes of Jesus' life' (SS, p. 258). Only the Gospels could satisfy her fully. She was always discovering in them, as she expressed it, 'new lights, hidden and mysterious meanings' (SS, p. 179). One sentence says it all: 'with the exception of the Gospels, I no longer find anything in books. The Gospels are enough' (LC, p. 44). Thérèse can teach us how to read them with fresh eyes, and to rediscover them for what they really are. As Jesus says to us: 'The words that I have spoken to you are spirit and they are life' (Jn 6:63).

Vatican II also stresses the perennial value of the Old Testament, reminding us that 'these books, therefore, written under divine inspiration, remain permanently valuable' and that 'Christians should receive them with reverence' (DV 14.15). Thérèse was also to discover for herself 'the true word of God in the books of the Old Testament' (DV 14), as the Council expresses it. It was in fact in the Old Testament that she found reassurance for the truth of what she terms her '*little* doctrine' (SS, p. 189). As Thérèse writes, quoting from three Old Testament books in support of her 'Little Way': 'Whoever is a *little one,* let him come to me [Pr 9:4]... *For to him that is little, mercy will be shown* [Wis 6:7]... *God shall feed his flock like a shepherd; he shall gather together the lambs with his arm, and shall take them up in his bosom* [Is 40:11]... *As one whom a mother caresses, so will I comfort you; you shall be carried at the breasts and upon the knees they will caress you* [Is 66:13.12]' (SS, p. 188; cf. p. 208).

Attention to detail

As Thérèse pondered the Scriptures, she came to the point where she could say: 'a single word uncovers for my soul infinite horizons' (LT 226).[47] So it is not surprising that the example of her writings encourages us to read Scripture carefully and with due attention to detail. The evangelists, for example, often describe the same incident but with significant differences. Thérèse had a keen eye to these variations and often noticed details given by one evangelist that are omitted by the others in their description of the same scene. She mentions, for instance, Jesus' '*look of love*' which pierces into the heart of the rich young man (LT 247; cf. Mk 10:21). She draws attention to the '*pillow*' on which Jesus rests his head during the storm at sea – one of her favourite scenes – and here she observes explicitly: 'The Gospel gives us this detail' (LT 144; cf. Mk 4:38). She reminds us of how Jesus, at prayer, gave thanks to the Father 'in a transport of joy' (SS, p. 209; cf. Lk 10:21). And even the homely presence of Tobias' dog, following faithfully behind his master, will not escape her observant eye (LT 18a; cf. Tb 11:4). Such attention to detail is indeed striking. Thérèse invites us to reflect like her on these details, however minute, and to explore their significance.

To the heart of the Gospels

While Thérèse found support in the Old Testament for her 'Little Way', there is no doubt that it was in the Gospels that she found the overall basis of her spirituality, for it is there that she encountered, and responded to, the human face of Christ as portrayed by each of the four evangelists.[48] Generally speaking, we are closer in Mark to the human Jesus than in any of the other Gospels. Thérèse focuses repeatedly on his scene of Jesus *asleep* in the storm-tossed boat with his disciples (Mk 4:35–41).[49] Here, she finds a Jesus after her own heart who fully accepts the human condition. He is weak, tired, and eminently human.

A few weeks before she died, Thérèse asked her sister to read the Sunday gospel for her. Pauline replied, 'It's the Gospel where Our Lord warns us against serving two masters.' In response, Thérèse went on to repeat the whole passage by heart, from beginning to end (cf. LC, pp. 188–9). A reassuring message runs through this passage from Matthew like a refrain: 'Do not be anxious about your life...' (cf. Mt 6:25.34). It contains the kernel of Thérèse's 'Little Way' of surrender and confidence.

Luke, in turn, is the gospel of God's mercy. His Jesus is a compassionate and merciful Saviour, with a gift of forgiveness for all. Some of Thérèse's favourite gospel characters like Mary Magdalen, the public sinner and the father of the prodigal son spoke to her of the Lord's mercy and forgiveness (cf. SS, pp. 258–9). They are all found in Luke (cf. Lk 7:36–50; 18:9–14; 15:11–32). God's merciful love is the core of Thérèse's teaching. She introduces her autobiography with these words: 'I shall begin to sing what I must sing eternally: "*The Mercies of the Lord*"' (SS, p. 13; cf. p. 205; Ps 88:2).

So, too, Thérèse pierces straight to the heart of John's Gospel: 'It seems to me that the *word* of Jesus is *Himself*... He, *Jesus*, the *Word*, the *Word* of *God!*' (LT 165; cf. Jn 1:1). Jesus is the revelation of God's abiding love in the weakness of human 'flesh', 'full of grace and truth' (Jn 1:14). The Word truly became weakness for Thérèse (cf. Hb 4:15; 5:2). This is the Jesus she found when she went to the Gospels in search of love. She could identify with this Jesus. We all can.

In search of love

Reading the Scriptures with Thérèse, we will find the true face of God in the person of Jesus. The experience of her weakness drove Thérèse to the Gospels. She had a tremendous need for love. 'The Spirit of Love sets me aflame with his fire,' she writes in one of her poems; 'I want to be set on fire with his Love' (PN 17:2.15). She had to find someone to love who was weak, frail and vulnerable like herself; and, like herself, passionately in need of love. She did: it was none other than Jesus.

Jesus sleeps through a storm – which, as we have seen, is one of Thérèse's favourite gospel scenes (cf. Mk 4:35–41); and he stops to rest by Jacob's Well, tired and thirsty (cf. Jn 4:5–42). She needs a God like this: weak, needy – quite simply, human. She can walk with this Jesus at her side, and even run, for he is a companion and a friend. Jesus, she writes, is the 'only Friend whom I love' (PN 23:5).[50] In this poem to the Sacred Heart, her thirst for love becomes one with the thirst of the Magdalen. Thérèse does not dwell on the symbol of the pierced heart so popular in her day but lingers with the Magdalen who wept as she searched for the one she loved. Thérèse cries out:

'I need a heart burning with tenderness,
Who will be my support forever,
Who loves everything in me, even my weakness...
And who never leaves me day or night.'...
I must have a God who takes on my nature
And becomes my brother and is able to suffer! (PN 23:4)

Unrequited love

Thérèse draws our attention especially to the fact that Jesus himself is in search of love. Reflecting on his unrequited love revealed in the Gospels, she writes sadly: 'On every side this love is unknown, rejected... Is Your disdained Love going to remain closed up within Your Heart?' (SS, pp. 180–1). Her *Act of Oblation to Merciful Love* ends with her own painful cry of love to God, asking him to allow 'the waves of *infinite tenderness* shut up within [him] to overflow into [her] soul' (SS, p. 277).

Thérèse was profoundly struck by the cry of Jesus, '*I thirst!*' (SS, p. 99; Jn 19:28). His 'thirst' was a thirst for love, reaching out for love when he said to the Samaritan woman, 'Give me to drink' (Jn 4:7). She comments: 'it was the *love* of His poor creature the

Creator of the universe was seeking. He was thirsty for love' (SS, p. 189). This love of Jesus had all the feminine qualities of a caring mother's tender love: patience, understanding, always the readiness to forgive. In Isaiah, as we have seen, Thérèse read with joy that God cares for us like a mother (cf. Is 66:12–13). And it was in Jesus that she discovered the maternal heart of God – eternal, merciful love shining through human weakness and thirsting for her love. She says: 'I felt at the bottom of my heart that...God is more tender than a mother' (SS, p. 174).

At ease with the Scriptures

Thérèse went to Scripture in search of answers to her own needs, and she interprets it with the freedom of the children of God. She is uninhibited in her approach to the Bible. She will not hesitate to fuse texts, even from different Gospels. She asks a question in the words of John, 'Master, where do you live?', and gives Jesus' reply with a variation of Luke: 'I have no place to rest my head' (LT 137; cf. Jn 1:38; Lk 9:58). She recalls the words of the Fourth Gospel, 'Lift up your eyes and see how the fields are already white enough to be harvested', but then continues in the words of Matthew: 'the harvest is abundant but the number of labourers is small' (LT 135; cf. Jn 4:35; Mt 9:37).

Moreover, Thérèse does not hesitate to interpret the silences of the Gospels. When Jesus speaks of 'things' that are 'hidden from the wise and prudent and revealed to little ones' (Mt 11:25), he does not tell us what they are. Thérèse shares with us her intuition: they are 'the *things* of His *love*' (SS, p. 105), she says. She will even change the words of Jesus himself: 'you will find rest for your souls' (Mt 11:28), he says in Matthew, in the version used by Thérèse – and she recounts this as: 'you will find rest for your *little* souls' (LC, p. 44). Again, Jesus gives no indication of who will 'sit at my right or at my left' (Mt 20:23) in the kingdom; but Thérèse interprets this, saying that these places are 'reserved to little children' (LC, p. 215). In the First Letter to the Corinthians, St Paul speaks of the different members of the church, using the image of different parts of the body (cf. 1Cor 12:14–26). He does not use the word 'heart', but Thérèse infers it from his hymn to love in his next chapter: 'I understood that the Church *had a Heart...BURNING WITH LOVE*' (SS, p. 194), she writes. She adds to the meaning of the sacred text without betraying it.

Thérèse even reads Scripture with a sense of humour. Her superior spoke of her as one 'whose head is filled with tricks... a *comedienne*'; and the prioress added: 'She can...make you split your sides with laughter' (LC, p. 16). This sense of humour saved Thérèse from taking herself too seriously, even in her approach to the Scriptures. 'It's a curious thing,' she said, 'when I open the Gospels, I nearly always come across the phrase "little children"' – then she added, tongue in cheek: 'Unless it's..."brood of vipers"!'[51] Even on her deathbed, she read the story of the Good Samaritan with a touch of humour: 'I'm like this "half-dead" traveller,' she said, 'half-dead, half-alive' (LC, p. 174). At times, she was conscious of even shocking those around her with her daring, with her free and easy approach.

Praying in the Spirit

Thérèse's prayer seems to have been mainly a prolonged meditation on the Gospels, listening to them prayerfully under the action of the Holy Spirit. On one occasion, she retired in silence to her room and asked herself what Jesus thought of her many failings. This is how she recounts it: 'I recalled these words He addressed one day to the adulterous woman: "Has no one condemned you?" And I, tears in my eyes, answered Him: "No one, Lord"' (LT 230; cf. Jn 8:10–11). The Spirit would often bring a word of Scripture to Thérèse's mind and in this way recall it for her.[52] She repeated it and let it seep into her mind and heart, as she tells us in *Story of a Soul*: 'I repeated to myself these words of St. Paul: "It is no longer I that live, it is Jesus who lives in me!"' (SS, p. 79; cf. Gal 2:20). Her method of 'repetition' is as old as the *lectio divina* of the Desert Fathers and the monastic tradition. Again, she writes: 'I repeated over and over the words of love burning in my heart' (SS, p. 103).

But the Spirit does not recall the word of God to her with a lesson only for Thérèse herself. He also shows her how it may be effective in others, too, through her reading of Scripture. She says of herself and a companion: 'in us was realised this passage from Scripture: "*A brother who is helped by a brother is like a strong city*"' (SS, p. 236; cf. Pr 18:19). Her sister Céline once wrote to her with a problem and Thérèse replied: 'After having read your letter, I went to prayer, and taking the gospel, I asked Jesus to find a passage for you, and this is what I found: "Behold the fig tree... the kingdom of God is near." I closed the book, I had read enough' (LT 143; cf. Lk 21:29–31). A year before her death, Thérèse was still meditating, pondering, praying the word of God: 'This evening, during my prayer,' she wrote to a priest friend, 'I meditated on some passages from Isaiah which appeared to me so appropriate for you' (LT 193).

'Patience obtains everything'

Thérèse was no stranger to the difficulties of reading the word of God. She shares with us, in vivid terms, her own experience: 'this *vast field* [of the Scriptures] seems to us to be a desert,' she says, 'arid and without water... We *know no longer* where *we are*; instead of peace and light, we find only turmoil or at least darkness...' (LT 165). It seems that the Lord kept her waiting in darkness, often for a long time. She needed patience, just as we all do if we want to read the Scriptures as Thérèse did. Or, to quote the words of Teresa's 'bookmark' on prayer: 'patience obtains everything'. We must wait on the Lord's time for the light to dawn.

As Thérèse pondered the biblical words again and again, this passage from her *Act of Oblation* could well apply to her experience of reading the Scriptures: 'a single day is like a thousand years. You can, then, in one instant prepare me...' (SS, p. 277; cf. 2Pt 3:8). Something similar happened when she heard the gospel message of confidence in God. She had already spent three years in Carmel, but still she agonised over her 'faults' and worried constantly about offending God.

Then, during a retreat, the visiting priest spoke no more than a few words to her – but words imbued with the message of the Gospels – and he 'launched me full sail,' she says, 'upon the waves of *confidence and love* which so strongly attracted me, but upon which I dared not advance' (SS, p. 174). This is the power of the word of God.

'Loving in deed and truth'

Thérèse read the Scriptures with an eye to the demands of daily living in community. Keenly aware of her own weakness, she found, in the Fourth Gospel, how to respond to that same human frailty in others. The key was the 'new commandment': Jesus' command that we should love one another as he has loved us (cf. Jn 13:34; 15:12). Thérèse exclaims: 'Ah! how contrary are the teachings of Jesus to the feelings of nature!' (SS, p. 229), and she sums everything up so well: 'I understand now that charity consists in bearing with the faults of others, in not being surprised at their weakness, in being edified by the smallest acts of virtue we see them practise. But I understood above all that charity must not remain hidden in the bottom of the heart' (SS, p. 220). And so, Thérèse goes on to say: 'it isn't enough to love; we must prove it' (SS, p. 225).

As always, Thérèse is inspired by the words of Jesus in the Gospels. He is the perfect exemplar. And the example of his life points to Calvary. There, Thérèse finds the full and complete revelation of Jesus' pure and selfless love for others – sacrificial and redemptive. The thought-pattern of Thérèse is often the same as that of the fourth evangelist, and her words echo clearly the teaching of his Gospel. She writes: '[Jesus] wills to die on the cross, for He said: "*Greater love than this no man has than that he lay down his life for his friends*"' (SS, p. 220; Jn 15:13; cf. 13:34). In each day of our lives, we are called to give ourselves to others as he did. So, for Thérèse, the words of Scripture were not a mere repertoire of beautiful thoughts and sentiments – a mirror to look into, only to forget later what manner of person one is (cf. Jas 1:23–24). She reiterates the lesson of Teresa of Avila

on the criterion of authentic prayer, 'good works, good works'
(IC VII:4:6): 'The most beautiful thoughts are nothing,' Thérèse
tells us, 'without good works' (SS, p. 234).

Thérèse would recall this when she felt challenged to put
it into practice. 'Not wishing to give in to the natural antipathy
I was experiencing,' she writes – about relating to one sister
with a very difficult character – 'I told myself that charity must
not consist in feelings but in works' (SS, p, 222); and again:
'I understood my love was not to be expressed only in words'
(SS, p. 219). Once more, her thinking is along the mind of John:
'Little children, let us not love in word or speech but in deed
and truth' (1Jn 3:18).

Is this love possible?[53]

Thérèse is aware of the exalted and radical demands of fraternal love: not just to love one another, but to love in the same way
that Jesus himself has loved us (cf. Jn 13:34; 15:12). So she asks
if this love is actually possible. In one of the deepest and loveli-
est passages she ever penned, she records her discovery of the
truth of Jesus' teaching, inspired in her by her reading of his
new commandment in John's Gospel: 'Ah! Lord,' she exclaims,
'I know you don't command the impossible' (SS, p. 221).

Thérèse is still aware of her weakness and imperfection,
always conscious of the elusive 'beam' in her own eye. 'You know
very well,' she says to Jesus, 'that never would I be able to love my
Sisters as You love them'. Then immediately comes the solution:
'unless *You*, O my Jesus, *loved them in me*. It is because You wanted
to give me this grace that You made Your *new* commandment...
it gives me the assurance that Your Will is *to love in me* all those
You command me to love!' (SS, p. 221). Ever practical, Thérèse
goes on to draw out the implications of her teaching: 'it is Jesus
alone who is acting in me, and the more united I am to Him,
the more also do I love my Sisters' (SS, p. 221). That is how real
community grows. We can so easily miss the reality beneath the
surface, a truth open only to the eyes of faith: 'Remain in me...
remain in my love' (Jn 15:4.10).

Few have ever lived the new commandment as fully as Thérèse. Ultimately, she speaks of God's vast plan of salvation and of her – and our – place in it, as channels of his love. Again, it is Scripture that helps her to express her thoughts – or indeed, to express the thoughts of God himself: '*therefore have I raised you*,' she quotes, '*that I may show* MY POWER *in you, and my name may be spoken of throughout all the earth*' (SS, p. 234; Ex 9:16). Thérèse goes on to explain: 'Century has followed on century since the Most High has spoken those words, and since then His conduct has undergone no change, for He is always using His creatures as instruments to carry on His work in souls' (SS, pp. 234–5). *All* believers have a mission from God: to be channels of his love. Yes, Christ the Word is present in us, spread out everywhere, until the end of time. Like Thérèse, we are Christ's love 'let loose in the world'.[54]

Notes

1. Significantly, Edith Stein comments: 'Our Holy Mother strenuously denied that she was founding a new Order. She wanted nothing except to reawaken the original spirit of the old Rule [of St. Albert]': see HL, p. 1.
2. See Emmanuel Renault, OCD, *Reading the Bible with St Teresa*, Darlington Carmel, n.d., pp. 2–3.
3. This is the title used in the standard translation by ICS Publications. The translation by E Allison Peers has the title, *Conceptions of the Love of God*.
4. Cf. John of the Cross, SC Prol. 1–2.
5. Alexander Pope, *An Essay on Criticism* (1711), l. 215.
6. This is, in theological terms, *sentire cum Ecclesia*: see Christopher O'Donnell, O Carm, *Ecclesia: A Theological Encyclopedia of the Church*, Collegeville, MN: The Liturgical Press, 1996, p. 423.
7. An excellent treatment of fundamentalism and its dangers can be found in Pontifical Biblical Commission, *The Interpretation of the Bible in the Church*, Boston, MA: Pauline Books & Media, 1993, pp. 72–5.
8. Cf. St Ambrose, *On the Duties of Ministers*, I, 20, 88.
9. For a concise discussion of Teresa's commentary on the Our Father, see Miriam Vaughan, OCD, 'A Prayer that Gives us Everything: The "Our Father" through the eyes of St Teresa', in *Mount Carmel*, vol. 60/4, 2012, pp. 55–63.

10. Karol Wojtyla, *Faith according to St John of the* Cross, San Francisco: Ignatius Press, 1981, p. 35.

11. For an excellent treatment of John's reading and use of Scripture, see Terence O'Reilly, 'St John of the Cross and the Traditions of Monastic Exegesis', in Margaret A Rees (ed.), *Leeds Papers on Saint John of the Cross: Contributions to a Quatercentenary Celebration*, Leeds: Trinity and All Saints College, 1991, pp. 105–26; see also the revised version of this article, 'From Reading to Contemplation: John of the Cross and the Monastic Study of Scripture', in *Mount Carmel*, vol. 60/4, 2012, pp. 31–43.

12. John Henry Newman, *Essay on the Development of Christian Doctrine*, London & New York: Sheed & Ward, 1960, p. 48.

13. For an outline and critical assessment of methods of interpretation of the Bible, see the following two documents by the Pontifical Biblical Commission: *The Interpretation, op. cit.* and *The Jewish People and their Sacred Scriptures in the Christian Bible*, Vatican: Libreria Editrice Vaticana, 2002, especially # 19–22, pp. 42–51.

14. See *The Collected Works of Saint John of the Cross*, Washington, DC: ICS Publications, 1991, p. 12.

15. See Federico Ruiz Salvador, OCD, *Introducción a San Juan de la Cruz: El escritor, los escritos, el sistema*, Madrid: Biblioteca de Autores Cristianos, 1968, p. 85.

16. *Hamlet*, Act II, Scene 2.

17. See Merton, *The Ascent to Truth, op. cit.*, p. 91.

18. For an expansion of this theme of the origin of the Gospels in the community of believers, see my earlier work *The Carmelite Charism: Exploring the Biblical Roots*, Dublin: Veritas, 2004, pp. 60–1.

19. Note this interesting observation in a recent Church document: 'As a general rule, we can define the spiritual sense, as understood by Christian faith, as the meaning expressed by the biblical texts when read, under the influence of the Holy Spirit, in the context of the paschal mystery of Christ and of the new life which flows from it... While there is a distinction between the two senses, the spiritual sense can never be stripped of its connection with the literal sense. The latter remains the indispensable foundation.': see Pontifical Biblical Commission, *The Interpretation, op. cit.*, p. 85.

20. See n. 13 above.

21. In Henri de Lubac, SJ, *Exégèse médiévale: Les quatre sens de l'Écriture*, vol. 4, Paris: Aubier-Montaigne, 1964, pp. 498–9.

22. For a more extended treatment of *lectio divina* in the Carmelite spirit, see my *The Carmelite Charism, op. cit.*, pp. 31–5 and my *Prayer – The Heart of the Gospels*, Dublin: Columba Press, 2008, pp. 12–20.

23. Here, John is quoting from Chapter 2 of the *Scala paradisi* (*Ladder of Paradise*) by the Carthusian Guigo II.

24. See *The Collected Works of Saint John of the Cross*, *op. cit.*, p. 624, n. 1; cf. Ruiz Salvador, *Introducción*, *op. cit.*, p. 82. This testimony concerns in particular John's reading of the priestly prayer of Jesus (Jn 17).

25. See Colin P Thompson, *The Poet and the Mystic: A Study of the Cántico Espiritual of San Juan de la Cruz*, Oxford: Oxford University Press, 1977, p. 3.

26. See Crisógono de Jesús, OCD, *Vida de San Juan de la Cruz*, Madrid: Biblioteca de Autores Cristianos, 1982, p. 301, n. 46.

27. See Ruiz Salvador, *Introducción*, *op. cit.*, p. 83.

28. John Henry Newman, *Historical Sketches*, vol. II, London: Pickering & Co, 1881, pp. 475–6.

29. For an excellent discussion of the *Ballads*, see Iain Matthew, OCD, *The Impact of God: Soundings from St John of the Cross*, London, Sydney & Auckland: Hodder & Stoughton, 1995, pp. 119–22.

30. In *Divine Office*, vol. I, p. 257.

31. In Conrad De Meester, OCD, 'Elizabeth in the Words of the Pope: "A new guide – certain and sure"', in *Mount Carmel*, vol. 55/2, 2007, p. 18.

32. In [Mother Germaine de Saint-Seine, OCD], *The Praise of Glory: Reminiscences of Sister Elizabeth of the Trinity, A Carmelite Nun of Dijon, 1901–1906*, London: R & T Washbourne / New York: Benziger Brothers, 1914, p. 149. See also L 240, n.1 for a list of the terms of affection and admiration given by Elizabeth to St Paul and his writings.

33. In [Mother Germaine de Saint-Seine, OCD], *The Praise of Glory*, *op. cit.*, p. 212.

34. For a fuller treatment of this theme and of the biblical witnesses to love considered below, I am indebted to the discussion in Joanne Mosley, *Elizabeth of the Trinity: The Unfolding of her Message*, vol. 1, Oxford: Teresian Press, 2012, pp. 380–1 & 375–7.

35. See [Mother Germaine de Saint-Seine, OCD], *The Praise of Glory*, *op. cit.*, p. 75.

36. On Teresa's lineage, see Teófanes Egido, OCD, 'The Historical Setting of St Teresa's Life', in John Sullivan, OCD (ed.), *Carmelite Studies*, vol. 1 (*Spiritual Direction*), Washington, DC: ICS Publications, 1980, pp. 122–82 (see especially pp. 132–49); on John, see Richard P Hardy, *John of the Cross: Man and Mystic*, Boston, MA: Pauline Books & Media, 2004, p. 3.

37. These words on the Old and the New are a saying taken from St Augustine, *Quaestiones in Heptateuchum*, 2, 73.

38. For a splendid treatment of the relationship between the Torah and the law of the Spirit according to St Paul, see the discussion by Stanislaus

Lyonnet, SJ, in his book co-authored with Ignace de La Potterie, SJ, *The Christian Lives by the Spirit*, Staten Island, NY: Alba House, 1971, pp. 145–74. See also, for an insightful article on the Torah, Kurt Hruby, 'The Torah', in Roger Le Déaut, CSSp, Annie Jaubert & Kurt Hruby, *The Spirituality of Judaism*, Wheathampstead: Anthony Clarke, 1977, pp. 59–67.

39. As mentioned earlier, Edith followed Teresa in placing the emphasis on the saint as the *reformer* of Carmel rather than as the *foundress* of the Discalced Carmelites: cf. HL, p. 1.

40. In Teresia Renata Posselt, OCD, *Edith Stein: The Life of a Philosopher and Carmelite*, Washington, DC: ICS Publications, 2005, p. 63. For a discussion of how Edith first came to read the *Life* of Teresa, as well as a suggested alternative account of the episode, see the article by Benjamin Gibbs, '"My long search for the true faith": The Conversion of Edith Stein', in *Mount Carmel*, vol. 60/3, 2012, p. 39.

41. Edith's writings are permeated by both the Old and the New Testaments: see Francisco Javier Sancho Fermín, OCD, *La Biblia con ojos de mujer: Edith Stein y la Sagrada Escritura*, Burgos: Editorial Monte Carmelo, 2001.

42. On Elijah in the Carmelite tradition, see my *The Carmelite Charism*, *op. cit.*, pp. 38–59. See also the extended study: Jane Ackerman, *Elijah: Prophet of Carmel*, Washington, DC: ICS Publications, 2003; and *Mount Carmel*, vol. 51/3, 2003, an issue devoted entirely to the many aspects of Elijah's story in relation to the Carmelite charism. For a treatment of Elijah specifically in the writings of Edith Stein, see Joanne Mosley, *Edith Stein – Woman of Prayer: Her Life and Ideals*, Leominster: Gracewing, 2004, pp. 113–20.

43. For a discussion of Queen Esther's intercession in relation to Edith Stein, see Mosley, *Edith Stein, op. cit.*, pp. 96–111.

44. The Hebrew expression also has an adversarial meaning, as a 'helper over and against him': see Jonathan Sacks, *Radical Then, Radical Now: The Legacy of the World's Oldest Religion*, London: HarperCollins, 2000, p. 79.

45. From Edith Stein's retreat notebook *Gedanken zur Karwoche 1938* (*Thoughts on Holy Week 1938*), in '*Wandle den Weg dem Glanze zu': Dokumentation zur Heiligsprechung von Edith Stein am 11. Oktober 1998 in Rom*, Speyer: Edith Stein-Gesellschaft Deutschland e. V, 1999, p. 91.

46. In Waltraud Herbstrith, OCD (ed.), *Edith Stein: Ein Lebensbild in Zeugnissen und Selbstzeugnissen* (*Edith Stein: A Picture of a Life in Testimonies by Others and by Herself*), Mainz: Matthias-Grünewald-Verlag (Topos Taschenbücher), 1998, p. 134; the priest in question was Johannes Hirschmann, SJ.

47. For an excellent and succinct introduction to Thérèse as a reader of Scripture, see Aloysius Rego, OCD, *Holiness For All: Themes from St Thérèse of Lisieux*, Oxford: Teresian Press, 2009, pp. 50–64.

48. For an account of the different approaches of each of the four evangelists, in their portrayal of Jesus and their teachings on prayer, see my *Prayer – The Heart of the Gospels, op. cit.*, pp. 9–10 & 21–131.

49. For a complete list of the many texts in Thérèse's writings which refer to this scene in Mark, see Sr Cécile, OCD & Sr Geneviève, OP (eds.), *La Bible avec Thérèse de Lisieux*, Paris: Cerf & Desclée De Brouwer, 1979, pp. 187–90.

50. Thérèse engraved the words, 'Jesus is my only love!' on the lintel of her door: see Pierre Descouvemont & Helmuth Nils Loose, *Thérèse and Lisieux*, Toronto: Novalis / Grand Rapids, MI: Eerdmans, 1996, p. 261, which also contains a photograph of it.

51. In Sr Cécile, OCD & Sr Geneviève, OP (eds.), *La Bible, op.cit.*, p. 32.

52. On the 'recalling' action of the Holy Spirit who brings the word of God back to our memory, see my *The Carmelite Charism, op. cit.*, pp. 18–20.

53. See the discussion, 'An Impossible Commandment', in my booklet *St Thérèse: The Gospels Rediscovered*, Darlington Carmel, n.d., pp. 43–52; see also my 'Saint Thérèse and the New Commandment', in Thomas M Curran, OCD (ed.), *The Mind of Saint Thérèse of Lisieux*, Dublin: Carmelite Centre of Spirituality / Bury, Greater Manchester: Koinonia, 1977, pp. 26–36.

54. This last phrase comes from John Masefield's play, *The Trial of Jesus*, London: William Heinemann, 1925, p. 96.

Chapter 2

JESUS – WITNESS TO PRAYER

'Come to me'

The following of Christ is the foundation of all Christian life. The call of Jesus, 'Follow me', is addressed to all believers. The response of the first disciples was *radical*: 'they left their nets' (Mk 1:18; Mt 4:20), embarked on a whole new way of life, and embraced a whole new world of gospel values. In fact, 'they left everything' (Lk 5:11), we are told. There could be no half measures. It was a challenge to total commitment.

'What are you looking for?' (Jn 1:38), Jesus asked his first disciples before inviting them to embark on a life of faith. 'Come and see' (Jn 1:39), he also said, calling them to experience a personal encounter with himself, which in turn would lead them to share with others their own experience of meeting him (cf. Jn 1:40–51). The call to follow Jesus is not primarily about the observance of rules, regulations and laws; it is an invitation to enter into a deep, personal relationship with him: 'follow *me*... come to *me*... learn of *me*' (Mk 1:17; Mt 11:28–29; cf. Jn 1:39).

Reflecting the light of Christ

Each of the evangelists has his own particular slant on the mystery of Jesus: for Mark, he is the Suffering Messiah; for Matthew, he is the obedient Israelite; for Luke, he is the Spirit-filled prophet; for John, he is the revelation in person of the Father. All these facets of the mystery of Jesus complement each other beautifully (cf. DV 19). The manifestation of God in his Son is like a splendid chandelier: we can walk around it, admire it, contemplate it and marvel at it with a side-long glance from different angles – but we cannot take it all in with a single sweep of the eye.

The church is the whole mystery of Christ spread out in the world, reflecting his light to all people: 'I am the light of the world' (Jn 8:12; 9:5), says Jesus of himself. And we are all called to shine with the reflected light of Christ: 'You are the light of the world,' says Jesus also of every believer. 'A city set on a hill cannot be hidden... No one lights a lamp and puts it under a bushel' (Mt 5:14–15).

Carmel – *the* Order of prayer

'Thus it has come about that various forms of solitary and community life,' Vatican II tells us, 'as well as different religious families have grown up [in the Church]... these groups have been like branches sprouting out wondrously and abundantly from a tree growing in the field of the Lord from a seed divinely planted' (LG 43).[1] Each of these religious families reflects some aspect of the mystery of Jesus; and like the image of the chandelier, all together they enrich, enhance and complement each other to help radiate ever more fully the inexhaustible and dazzling light of the Church, pointing to Jesus as the light of the world.

The Order of Carmel is no exception. Teresa of Avila, reformer of Carmel, reminds us that all Carmelites are called to a life of 'prayer and contemplation' (IC V:1:2). She directs us back to the first Carmelites, the hermits on Mount Carmel 'who in such great solitude and contempt for the world sought this treasure, this precious pearl of contemplation' (IC V:1:2). They are the inspiration of all her sons and daughters and the first witnesses to the charism and spirit of Carmel still alive and active in the world today. *Carmel reflects the mystery of the person of Jesus as a witness to prayer*: it radiates his prayer life and, as a teacher of prayer like Jesus, Carmel proclaims it everywhere for all to see.

Teresa expressed the core of her teaching in her celebrated description of prayer: 'mental prayer in my opinion is nothing else than an intimate sharing between friends; it means taking time frequently to be alone with Him who we know loves us' (*Life* 8:5). Her faithful sons and daughters continue the rich

Carmelite tradition of prayer, though of course each with their own special and original slant and emphasis, while always in total fidelity to the spirit of Teresa. Even a cursory glance at the teachings of some of the better-known and more recent Carmelites reveals the unmistakable Teresian touch. Edith Stein writes these words: 'The only essential is that one finds, first of all, a quiet corner in which one can communicate with God as though there were nothing else, and that must be done daily' (SP, p. 54). Or, to quote Thérèse of Lisieux, a Doctor of the Church: 'I think that the Heart of my Spouse is mine alone, just as mine is His alone, and I speak to Him then in the solitude of this delightful heart to heart, while waiting to contemplate Him one day face to face...' (LT 122). We need outstanding witnesses and teachers like these. They guide our exploration in greater depth into the mystery of Jesus as the true witness and teacher of prayer in the Gospels.

'Abba! Father!'

There is one word on the lips of Jesus that underlies the inestimable value of what is known as 'vocal prayer': the word 'Abba' (Mk 14:36), the Aramaic address spoken by Jesus in Gethsemane. There are many other beautiful words spoken by Jesus in prayer, not least his great priestly prayer, when 'he lifted up his eyes to heaven and said, "Father"...' (Jn 17:1); his recitation of the Hymn of Praise or 'Hallel' (Ps 112–117) with his disciples at the Last Supper – 'And when they had sung a hymn, they went out to the Mount of Olives' (Mk 14:26); his prayer of thanksgiving to the Father, 'I thank you, Father, Lord of heaven and earth...' (Mt 11:25; Lk 10:21); and again at the grave of Lazarus, 'Father, I thank you that you have heard me...' (Jn 11:41); his prayer in Gethsemane, when he 'offered up prayers and supplications, with loud cries and tears' (Hb 5:7).

In a real sense, every word that Jesus speaks in the Gospels reveals to us his continual inner relationship with his Father, summed up for us in this one great vocal prayer, 'Abba'. It speaks to us of the most intimate, loving and filial attitude of a child and projects onto the stage of time the eternal relationship between Son and Father in the inner life of God – an intimate relationship with God in prayer unheard of until the coming of Jesus. When we pray as Jesus did, we relate to God in the same way as he did: 'God has sent the Spirit of his Son into our hearts, crying, "Abba! Father!"' (Gal 4:6; cf. Rm 8:15).

'Pray like this…'

But it is not just by his example that Jesus is a witness to the value of vocal prayer. He also teaches us that it is necessary, when he tells us that it must be recited not in some off-hand or cursory fashion but in a meaningful way: 'And in praying do not heap up empty phrases as the Gentiles do; for they think that they will be heard for their many words. Do not be like them, for your Father knows what you need before you ask him. Pray then like this: "Our Father…"' (Mt 6:7–9).

It is highly significant that just before Matthew gives us his version of the Our Father, Jesus warns us of the danger of routine, as when we sometimes repeat prayers parrot-like or gabble them with little or no attention to their inner depth of meaning. We can so easily rattle off our prayers glibly and carelessly, with scant attention to our need of them to support and sustain us in our difficulties on the spiritual journey. Steeped as his mind was in the Old Testament, Jesus himself would surely have been fully aware of the prayer of the false prophets of Baal (cf. 1Kgs 18:26–29). It provides a striking example of how precisely *not* to pray.[2] Howling and shrieking, they hurl empty phrases at the silent heavens, prattling on through noon till evening: 'they raved on…but there was no voice; no one answered, no one heeded' (1Kgs 18:29). Vocal prayer is not about striving to overwhelm God or change his mind with an avalanche of words and pious formulas. Quite the opposite: it is for *us* to be overwhelmed and changed! Hence, right at the heart of Matthew's version of the Our Father, we have the petition 'Thy will be done' (Mt 6:10). Vocal prayer, all prayer, is a child's cry of surrender echoing the cry of Jesus, 'Abba! Father!'

Setting free the wings of prayer

If we turn now to Teresa's writings on prayer, at first sight it may seem strange that such an accomplished teacher of mystical prayer would feel the need to treat of vocal prayer. More astonishing still is that she does not admit any real distinction between vocal and mental prayer.[3] But Teresa had learned well the lesson of Jesus on the importance and value of vocal prayer. Moreover, she invites us to explore more deeply with her the depth of his words and their practical implications. She demands three essential things: awareness of who we are; awareness of whom we are addressing; and awareness of what we are saying (cf. IC I:1:7). Without this heightened attention, there can be no authentic prayer, vocal or otherwise. 'My words fly up, my thoughts remain below; / Words without thoughts never to heaven go,' says the King at prayer in *Hamlet*.[4] Teresa endorses this lesson, and with a touch of humour: 'if you are to be speaking, as is right, with so great a Lord, it is good that you consider whom you are speaking with as well as who you are, at least if you want to be polite' (WP 22:1). Then, if we are faithful to her prerequisites – engaging our minds and hearts *as well as* our lips – she reassures us: 'This is mental prayer' (WP 22:8; cf. 21:10; IC I:1:7).

Teresa also insists on proper respect and due reverence while reciting our vocal prayers. After all, that is how Jesus prayed (cf. Jn 11:41; 17:1). We can only surmise the awe and admiration of his followers as they watched him rapt in prayer. 'He was praying in a certain place, and when he ceased, one of his disciples said to him, "Lord, teach us to pray"' (Lk 11:1). Enthralled, they did not even dare to interrupt him but waited until he had ceased before they asked him to teach them how to pray. He was such a witness to prayer in his whole being that they wanted to pray as he himself prayed. Jesus may well have been praying in silence, but his answer gives voice to his relationship with his Father and invites us to express it in words. 'When you pray,' he replied, 'say "Father..."' (Lk 11:2).

The Our Father, Teresa reminds us, is always at hand to support us in our prayer; it is of all the more inestimable value 'for it comes from the mouth of Truth itself' (WP 42:5). And she explains: 'no one can take vocal prayer from you or make you recite the Our Father hastily and without understanding it' (WP 42:4). Here, she is anticipating the words of Paul VI who urges us to pray the rosary with 'a quiet rhythm and a lingering pace' (MC 47).[5]

For Teresa, the Our Father provides a kind of springboard or taking-off point when we want to set free the wings of prayer. One petition, one phrase, one word can launch us into silent communion with God, and then the ever deepening silence can draw us further into the stillness of perfect contemplation. Teresa says that the Lord's Prayer contains 'the entire spiritual way...from the beginning stages until God engulfs the soul and gives it to drink abundantly from the fount of living water, which He said was to be found at the end of the way' (WP 42:5).

Eminently practical as always, she illustrates this teaching from her own experience of 'many persons who while praying vocally...are raised by God to sublime contemplation' (WP 30:7). One such person who could only pray vocally came to her in great distress. Teresa asked her about her prayer and then observed: 'I saw that though she was tied to the Our Father she experienced pure contemplation and that the Lord was raising her up and joining her with Himself in union' (WP 30:7). Teresa then applied the acid test of all authentic prayer – the kind of life this sister was leading: 'from her deeds it seemed truly that she was receiving such great favours, for she was living a very good life' (WP 30:7). It is the gospel lesson: 'You will know them by their fruits' (Mt 7:16).

The prayer of a child

Like Teresa, who herself was plagued for years with distractions, Thérèse also knew this experience, which is common to all who pray. She was no stranger to the inability to concentrate, or to various other difficulties in prayer: unanswered requests, aridity, loss of fervour, emptiness, and the apparent absence of God. She often slept during prayer. At times, we have all suffered such disappointments and frustrations. We, too, know what it is to struggle as she did. But for Thérèse, weakness is not an obstacle to communion with God: it is a stepping-stone to closer intimacy with him. In this, she has lessons for all of us on how to deal with our difficulties and struggles in prayer.

So, what did she do? Powerless and weak like a little child, she related to God exactly as a child: 'I do like children who do not know how to read,' she tells us, 'I say very simply to God what I wish to say, without composing beautiful sentences, and He always understands me' (SS, p. 242). In fact, rather like a child who cannot read, she says: 'I do not have the courage to force myself to search out *beautiful* prayers in books... it really gives me a headache!' (SS, p. 242). When Thérèse speaks of her powerlessness to pray, she confesses to sometimes finding it 'impossible to draw forth [from prayer] one single thought to unite me with God' (SS, p. 243). So, in the spirit of Teresa,[6] she teaches us by her own example to elicit the help of vocal prayer: 'I *very slowly* recite an "Our Father",' she writes, 'and then the angelic salutation [Hail Mary],... they nourish my soul much more than if I had recited them precipitately a hundred times' (SS, p. 243). As Teresa herself had discovered (cf. WP 30:7), so Thérèse, too, found that the Our Father could lead into deep prayer and contemplation. One day, her sister found Thérèse alone in her room, 'lost in profound contemplation'. Céline asked what she was thinking about, and Thérèse replied with tears in her eyes what a wonderful thing it was 'to call God our Father'; she was, she explained to Céline, 'meditating on the *Our Father*'.[7]

Jesus, our friend

'The invisible God,' Vatican II tells us, 'out of *the abundance of His love* speaks to people *as friends* and lives among them, so that He may invite and take them *into friendship with Himself*' (DV 2; italics mine). Pope Benedict XVI echoes this lesson of the Council and points us directly to the person of Jesus as the

friend of all believers: 'If we let Christ into our lives, we lose
nothing, nothing, absolutely nothing of what makes life free,
beautiful and great. No! Only in this friendship are the doors of
life opened wide. Only in this friendship is the great potential
of human existence truly revealed. Only in this friendship do
we experience beauty and liberation'.[8]

These few words evoke the image of Jesus in the Gospels
as our true friend. At the Last Supper, he speaks to us as his
friends: 'You are my friends... No longer do I call you servants...
I have called you friends...' (Jn 15:14–15). The intimate sharing
between Jesus and his Father is the perfect model of friendship for every follower of Jesus. It plunges us into the heart of
the mystery of the inner life of God: 'The only Son, who is in
the bosom of the Father, he has made him known' (Jn 1:18).
This image is used of the closest and most tender of human
relationships: that of mother and child (cf. Ps 130:2; Nb 11:12),
of husband and wife (cf. Dt 13:6), and also of friends, like the
Beloved Disciple reclining on the 'breast' of Jesus at the Last
Supper (cf. Jn 13:23). It describes an intimate friendship of
love. The exact meaning of John's original words, just quoted
(Jn 1:18), is quite stunning. The phrase is not strictly '*in* the
bosom' of the Father but '*into* the bosom' ('eis') – combining, as
it were, rest and motion, a timeless relationship between Father
and Son already accomplished, and at the same time a ceaseless
and dynamic thrust between the two.

This deep friendship within the mystery of God finds expression throughout the Gospels in various, complementary ways.
They all help to expand, in biblical terms, the meaning of friendship in the gospel sense of the word. The companionship between
Father and Son is *uninterrupted*: 'I am not alone, for the Father
is with me' (Jn 16:32). In fact, it is a unique fellowship, involving
perfect *oneness*: 'I and the Father are one' (Jn 10:30; cf. 17:11). It
is a union of minds and hearts, a deep *mutual knowledge and love*:
'the Father knows me and I know the Father' (Jn 10:15). This is a
reciprocal self-disclosure: 'no one knows the Son except the Father,
and no one knows the Father except the Son...' (Mt 11:27).

This deep relationship in God is ultimately a question of *love*: 'the Father loves the Son, and has given all things into his hands... The Father loves the Son, and shows him all that he himself is doing... For this reason the Father loves me, because I lay down my life...' (Jn 3:35; 5:20; 10:17). Jesus reciprocates that love. As he enters into his passion, he tells us: 'I do as the Father has commanded me, so that the world may know that I love the Father' (Jn 14:31). This mutual love between the Father and the Son is the Spirit of love, and it is a love that expresses itself in a *harmony of wills*: 'I seek not my own will but the will of him who sent me' (Jn 5:30; cf. 4:34; 6:38; Mt 26:39; Hb 10:7).

'He first loved us'

All through the Scriptures we are reminded that God constantly takes the initiative with the free gift of his love. In this way, the God of Israel created for himself a people to be his own: 'It was not because you were more in number than any other people that the Lord set his love upon you and chose you, for you were the fewest of all peoples; but it is because the Lord loves you' (Dt 7:7–8; cf. Hos 11:1–4). He led them in love through the desert into the promised land 'for his great love is without end' (Ps 135:1–26). In Mark's Gospel, we are told that Jesus 'went up onto the mountain and summoned those he wanted...and he appointed twelve, to be with him' (Mk 3:13–14). This is a free choice of his love: 'he appointed twelve'.

God's love is creative: literally, Jesus '*made* twelve' ('epoíēsen'), in order that they should 'be *with* him'; that is, he 'summoned' or called them into a close, personal fellowship with himself as his *companions*. By the power of his love, God has transformed us, too, into his friends. This choice is God's initiative – an advance of love centred on Christ: 'The God and Father of our Lord Jesus Christ...chose us in [Christ] before the foundation of the world... He destined us in love to be his children through Jesus Christ' (Eph 1:3–5).

Love and friendship go hand in hand. When Jesus called his disciples 'friends' at the Last Supper, he said to them, 'You did not choose me, but I chose you' (Jn 15:16). Jesus was about to lay down his life for us, *not because* we were *already* his friends, but *in order that* we might *become* his friends. Paul expresses the idea well: 'God shows his love for us in that while we were yet sinners Christ died for us' (Rm 5:8). Jesus is offering us a closeness and intimacy with himself, and an invitation to respond: 'We know and believe the love God has for us. God is love... We love, because he first loved us' (1Jn 4:16.19).

Jesus goes even further. That same eternal love of God 'has been poured into our hearts through the Holy Spirit who has been given to us' (Rm 5:5). It is a love already promised as a 'new heart' and a 'new spirit' (Ez 36:26), as a 'law within' (Jer 31:33), 'written...with the Spirit of the living God...on tablets of human hearts' (2Cor 3:3). It is a God-given love in response to the prayer of Jesus, 'that the love with which you [Father] have loved me may be in them' (Jn 17:26). Jesus invites his disciples at the Last Supper to 'remain' in this love (Jn 15:9–10) – permanently and intimately united to him in a covenant of friendship that is deeper even than the love of Jonathan for David: 'The soul of Jonathan was knit to the soul of David... Then Jonathan made a covenant with David, because he loved him as his own soul' (1Sm 18:1.3). When Jesus calls his disciples 'friends', he explains: 'for all that I have heard from my Father I have made known to you' (Jn 15:15).

Friendship foreshadowed

This self-disclosure of Jesus is 'an intimate sharing', to recall Teresa's words (*Life* 8:5), and it was already foreshadowed in the Old Testament: 'The Lord used to speak to Moses face to face,' we are told, 'as a man speaks to his friend' (Ex 33:11). 'With him,' God said, 'I speak mouth to mouth, clearly and not in obscure speech' (Nb 12:8). To speak 'face to face' and 'mouth to mouth' is to communicate person to person in an intimate and deep relationship. True friendship requires this trusting and open sharing in close intimacy. Without friendship, there is no true love; and without love, there is no true friendship.

An 'intimate sharing' also demands entire surrender in service of the other. Jesus has given the perfect example: 'The Son of man came not to be served but to serve' (Mk 10:45); 'No one has greater love than this, to lay down one's life for one's friends' (Jn 15:13). He requires no less of his disciples: 'You are my friends if you do what I command you' (Jn 15:14). Again, the Old Testament provides a beautiful illustration of the friendship between God and Abraham, who surrendered in faith to God's command. He obeyed and was called 'my friend' by God himself (Is 41:8). The Letter of James expands on this: 'the scripture was fulfilled, which says, "Abraham believed God, and it was reckoned to him as righteousness"; and he was called the friend of God' (Jas 2:23; cf. Gn 15:6). But it was not just Abraham who as a true friend had to prove his love for God: 'Remember that our fathers were put to the test to prove their love of God. Remember how our father Abraham was tested and became the friend of God after many trials and tribulations. The same was true of Isaac, Jacob, Moses, and all those who met with God's favour. They remained steadfast in the face of tribulations of every kind' (Jdt 8:21–23).[9]

The portrait of a true friend in Ecclesiasticus is an inspiring and sensitive foreshadowing of what Jesus' friendship can mean for those who wish to enter into a communion of friendship and fellowship with God in the inner life of the blessed:

> A loyal friend is a powerful defence:
>> whoever finds one has indeed found a treasure.
> A loyal friend is something beyond price,
>> there is no measuring his worth.
> A loyal friend is the elixir of life,
>> and those who fear the Lord will find one.
> Whoever fears the Lord makes true friends,
>> for as a person is, so is his friend too. (Ecclus 6:14–17; cf. 1Jn 1:14)

Love responding to love

God, then, advances in love to meet us and find us. He is a God who is always coming into our lives: 'The true light which enlightens everyone was coming into the world... He came to his own people, and his people did not receive him' (Jn 1:9.11). At the Last Supper, Jesus tells his disciples that he will come again; but he speaks of his future return as an abiding presence, a coming of himself that is always taking place in the Church: 'I will not leave you orphans; *I am coming* to you' (Jn 14:18; cf. 14:3). Jesus is the good shepherd who is always ready to leave the ninety-nine sheep and go in search of the one who has strayed. God is the prodigal father who scans the horizon for the return of his wayward child and receives him with open arms and a welcoming kiss.

Our response to the God who is already searching for us, always reaching out to us in love, must be to love him in return and allow him to come into our lives at all times. Jesus asks his first disciples: 'What are you looking for?' (Jn 1:38). They are already searching for God, unwittingly, before they ever encounter him in Jesus. Theirs is the heart that is always restless until it rests in God. At the Last Supper, Jesus says, 'Those who love me will be loved by my Father, and I will love them and manifest myself to them' (Jn 14:21). Jesus reveals himself to us in response to our love: 'Whoever does not love does not know God, because God is love' (1Jn 4:8). The story of John outrunning Peter to the empty tomb illustrates this priority of love so well: it was *not* Peter, it was John, the Beloved Disciple, we are told, who 'saw' and 'believed' (Jn 20:8). The disciples failed to recognise the risen Jesus as he stood by the lakeside. It was again John, the disciple whom Jesus loved – and he only – who recognised him, crying out: 'It is the Lord!' (Jn 21:7). Paul, too, emphasises the overriding importance of love when he prays that his first converts might 'know the love of Christ, *which is beyond all knowledge*' (Eph 3:19).

A special meeting place of friends

Friends can meet in many places. Those who are friends with Jesus are no exception. We can meet him in the hearts of the poor, the outcast, the marginalised, and in all whom we are privileged to serve: 'as you did it to one of these, the least of my brothers and sisters, you did it to me' (Mt 25:40). We can meet him in the community at prayer: 'Where two or three are gathered in my name, there am I in the midst of them' (Mt 18:20). We can meet him in every event of our lives: 'We know that all things work together for good for those who love God' (Rm 8:28). We can meet him in the Eucharist: he invites his disciples – and us with them – to seek and find him in *the breaking of bread* (cf. Lk 24:30–31). And we can of course meet him in the Scriptures: where 'it is the Lord who speaks' (Ez 16:8.14.58.63; cf. Is 52:6). God is always coming to meet us and is searching for us in so many different ways, and we likewise respond by going out to meet him and searching for him in so many different ways.

There is, however, one place where we can meet God at every moment: in the solitude of our hearts. It is precisely the place where God asks us to encounter him whenever we are at prayer: 'When you pray, go into your [inner] room and shut the door and pray to your Father who is in secret' (Mt 6:6). This is an invitation to go deep into our own heart where we will meet God. It is there also that Jesus wants his friends to experience the intimate sharing of love between himself and his Father, and the love that they will give us: 'Those who love me will keep my word,' he tells us, 'and my Father will love them, and we will come to them and make our home in them' (Jn 14:23).

It is in this infinite and eternal union of love in the heart of the Blessed Trinity that we meet God in quiet prayer. Jesus prayed to his Father that all believers might experience this union: 'that they may all be one; even as you, Father, are in me and I in you, that they also may be in us' (Jn 17:21); 'that they may be one, even as we are one, I in them and you in me, that they may become perfectly one' (Jn 17:22–23); 'that the love

with which you have loved me may be in them, and I in them'
(Jn 17:26).

John describes this communion and fellowship of love as
being centred in the Word made flesh: 'Our message concerns
that Word, who is life; what he was from the first, what we have
heard about him, what our own eyes have seen of him; what
it was that met our gaze, and the touch of our hands. Yes, life
dawned; and it is as eyewitnesses that we give you news of that
life, that eternal life ever abiding with the Father and which
has dawned, now, on us. What we have seen and heard we proclaim to you so that you too may have fellowship with us; and
our fellowship is with the Father and with his Son Jesus Christ'
(1Jn 1:1–3). Here, fellowship, companionship, friendship – and
ultimately love – are one.

An intimate dialogue of love

Teresa herself strongly stresses this fundamental truth of God's
love for us when, as we have seen, she speaks to us of prayer as
friendship with God: 'mental prayer in my opinion,' she tells
us, 'is nothing else than an intimate sharing between friends;
it means taking time frequently to be alone *with Him who we
know loves us*' (*Life* 8:5; italics mine). Moreover, she refers to the
'inner room' (cf. Mt 6:6), where prayer takes place, as the 'little
heaven of our soul' (WP 28:5). When John of the Cross asks the
question about *where to find God* (cf. SC, stanza 1), he explains: 'It
should be known that the Word, the Son of God, together with
the Father and the Holy Spirit, is hidden by his essence and his
presence in the innermost being of the soul. Individuals who
want to find him should leave all things through affection and
will, enter within themselves in deepest recollection, and let all
things be as though not' (SC 1:6).

John continues by quoting these words from the *Soliloquies*,
attributed in his day to St Augustine: 'I did not find you without,
Lord, because I wrongly sought you without, who were within'
(SC 1:6). Teresa was struck by a similar thought about the indwelling of God in the soul, which she read in either the *Confessions*

or the *Soliloquies*: 'Consider what St Augustine says,' she writes, 'that he sought [God] in many places but found Him ultimately within Himself' (WP 28:2; cf. *Life* 40:6; IC IV:3:3). And in her great and final masterpiece, *The Interior Castle*, Teresa invites us to 'consider our soul to be like a castle...in which there are many rooms,...where the Lord says He finds His delight... and in the centre and middle is the main dwelling place where the very secret exchanges between God and the soul take place' (IC I:1:1.3).

Prayer, the door of entry

After Teresa introduces the image of the soul as a castle in which God is present, she adds: 'Insofar as I can understand the door of entry to this castle is prayer and reflection' (IC I:1:7). It is there in the depths of the human heart that she, like Jesus, invites us to commune with God in 'an intimate sharing', an exchange and dialogue of love:

> Those who...can enclose themselves within this little heaven of our soul, where the Maker of heaven and earth is present, and grow accustomed to refusing to be where the exterior senses in their distraction have gone or look in that direction should believe they are following an excellent path and that they will not fail to drink water from the fount; for they will journey far in a short time. Their situation is like that of a person who travels by ship; with a little wind he reaches the end of his journey in a few days. But those who go by land take longer. (WP 28:5)

The call of the first disciples in John reaches its climax with the words of Jesus: 'You shall see greater things... you will see heaven opened, and the angels of God ascending and descending upon the Son of man' (Jn 1:50–51). Here, we have an Old Testament scene by way of background: that of Jacob's ladder, pitched between heaven and earth, with the angels of God ascending and descending on it (cf. Gn 28:10–17). Edith Stein sees this unceasing communication between heaven and earth as a significant image of prayer within her Jewish tradition. She writes: 'Prayer is the communication of the soul with God... Prayer is a Jacob's ladder on which the human spirit ascends to God and God's grace descends to people' (HL, p. 38). The human spirit, like that of angels, is in an unbroken link between heaven and earth. It is able, Edith explains, 'to receive God's love with understanding and to return it freely' (HL, p. 38).

The 'intimate sharing between friends' is expanded throughout all Teresa's writings as a communion with God in love. She reminds us repeatedly that prayer 'does not lie in thinking much but in loving much' (cf. F 5:2; IC IV:1:7). This is the very heart of Teresa's teaching on prayer. It is a dialogue of love, a loving exchange. Her teaching is faithfully captured by Thérèse on her deathbed. Asked by her sister how she was praying, Thérèse replied quite simply, 'I love Him!' (LC, p. 228). The same simple but profound lesson was repeated by Elizabeth of the Trinity when asked what she managed to say to God during her long hours in prayer. She, too, replied quite simply: 'we love each other'.[10]

A painful experience shared

Teresa is eminently practical. Her life was an adventure in prayer, so when she writes about prayer she does not speculate: she communicates her own experience and freely invites us to share it. Her prayer journey was not a smooth passage from first fervour to the heights of mystical prayer. Her youthful spontaneity, her ease with God, and her fascination with 'the truth I knew in childhood' (*Life* 3:5) were soon to disappear. For some time, however, she experienced and enjoyed the stimulation of 'good [spiritual] books' (*Life* 3:7), such as Osuna's *Third Spiritual Alphabet*, and remained faithful to her nightly appointment with Jesus in Gethsemane (cf. *Life* 9:4). But growth in prayer eventually became a long and painful struggle for her. To converse with God as with a friend did not come easily to Teresa for many years. In fact, this was the fruit of nearly two decades of intense aridity – although these years were relieved, at intervals, by brief periods of deep mystical prayer. Teresa's thoughts wandered uncontrollably 'like little moths at night, bothersome and annoying' (*Life* 17:6) and she was unable to reason, think or meditate, or picture things to herself in God's presence. She felt powerless for 'eighteen years' and writes:

> In all those years, except for the time after Communion, I never dared to begin prayer without a book... For the dryness...was always felt when I was without a book. Then my soul was thrown into confusion and my thoughts ran wild. (*Life* 4:9)

She confesses how, during these years of crisis, she used to wait anxiously 'for the striking of the clock' to end the hour of prayer, and how she had to 'force' herself to persevere (*Life* 8:7).

During this troublesome period, Teresa was to experience an additional crisis. She was becoming ill at ease with some friendships and disturbing infidelities in her life. She realised that her prayer and lifestyle were not in harmony. This discrepancy began to disturb her greatly and discouraged her from praying: 'I was then ashamed to return to the search for God,' she wrote, 'by means of a friendship as special as is that found in the intimate exchange of prayer' (*Life* 7:1). So, at some time in 1543, Teresa fled the battlefield and gave up prayer; she was now twenty-eight and halfway through her long years of struggle. She did, however, return to wrestle with God in prayer after 'a year and a half', or at any rate after 'at least...a year' (*Life* 19:4). She describes this infidelity as the beginning of the temptation of Judas (cf. *Life* 19:11). Afterwards, she would continue in her earlier resolve. But her unhappy experience was to leave a lasting impression. She would repeatedly caution others against the dangers of abandoning prayer. Her method for perseverance during her trials was simple but effective. It is also highly beneficial for those who are eager to understand the Teresian way of communing with God and to advance in it.

Re-presenting Christ within

During her long years of wrestling with wandering thoughts, Teresa followed a helpful device: what she calls *representing* Christ as near, or within her, where she could speak to him. It grew out of frustrating beginnings: the inability to represent Christ in the Gospels with either her intellect or her imagination. She explains:

> I had such little ability to represent things with my intellect that if I hadn't seen the things my imagination was not of use to me, as it is to other persons who can imagine things and thus recollect themselves. I could only think about Christ as He was as man, but never in such a way that I could picture Him within myself... (*Life* 9:6)

This was a painful experience for Teresa, as she longed to establish a real personal relationship with Jesus as her friend and to commune with him, near or present within her. She therefore pressed into service every ruse she could conceive of, such as reading a book or identifying with gospel scenes and her favourite biblical characters. Eventually, she discovered the key – *she represented Christ within*:

> I tried as hard as I could to keep Jesus Christ, our God and our Lord, present within me, and that was my way of prayer. If I reflected upon some phrase of His Passion, I represented Him to myself interiorly... God didn't give me talent for discursive thought or for a profitable use of the imagination. In fact, my imagination is so dull that I never succeeded even to think about and represent in my mind – as hard as I tried – the humanity of the Lord... This is the method of prayer I then used: since I could not reflect discursively with the intellect, I strove to represent Christ within me... (*Life* 4:7; 9:4)

The phrase, 'to represent Christ within', can have a twofold meaning. It denotes either picturing him with the imagination;

or *re*-presenting him, in the sense of *making him present again*. At prayer, Teresa did not 'imagine' Christ, nor could she ever do so. She strove to 're-present' him to herself, to make him present to herself *in faith* as Someone real within herself:

> I was like those who are blind or in darkness; they speak with a person and see that that person is with them because they know with certainty that the other is there (I mean they understand and *believe* this, but they do not see the other)... (*Life* 9:6; italics mine)

There is nothing here resembling the Ignatian method, however valuable in itself, of setting a scene and imagining what the incarnate Word looked like, for example. Teresa just makes space within herself for Jesus in his sacred humanity and invites him to enter her own 'inner room' (cf. Mt 6:6). There, we might say, she can be 'with him' and 'in him', and he in turn be 'with her' and 'in her', so that they can talk and commune together in that 'intimate sharing between friends' which is Teresian prayer. Teresa's attempt to make Jesus, in his mysteries, present again through faith is what Jesus himself describes as the 'recalling' action of the Spirit (cf. Jn 14:26).[11] The Spirit makes Jesus present again, alive and active here and now in the heart of the believer, and relevant to the challenge of living gospel values in the concrete circumstances of every Christian life.

'Come away to a lonely place...'

Jesus provides us with an example of what he invites his disciples to do when he says, 'pray to your Father who is in secret; and your Father who sees in secret will reward you' (Mt 6:6). All through the Gospels, we see Jesus slipping off into the seclusion of the mountainside and the silence of the night, to pray in solitude away from the crowd and the busy demands of proclaiming the good news. Already in the first chapter of his Gospel, Mark describes a typical day in the life of Jesus: 'In the morning, a great while before day, he rose and went out to a lonely place, and there he prayed. And Simon and those who were with him followed him, and they found him,' we are told, 'and said to him, "Everyone is searching for you"' (Mk 1:35–37). We can almost feel the disappointment of Jesus as the disciples want to entice him out of his solitude and tempt him to popularity, telling him that everyone is searching for him.

At so many of the great turning-points in the unfolding of God's plan of salvation, we again see Jesus withdrawing from the crowds to commune with his Father in secret. Before he chose the Twelve, we read: 'In these days, he went out into the hills to pray; and all night he continued in prayer to God. And when it was day, he called his disciples, and chose from them twelve, whom he named apostles' (Lk 6:12–13). Later, when Jesus asked his disciples the vital question, 'Who do the people say that I am?', we learn that it happened 'as he was praying alone' (Lk 9:18). Jesus went up Mount Tabor to pray, we are told, and it was 'as he was praying' (Lk 9:29) that he was transfigured and shone like the sun. These were not just isolated moments in the life of Jesus. He used to withdraw into solitude when the pressure mounted and his popularity began to grow: 'But so much the more the report went abroad concerning him; and great multitudes gathered to hear and to be healed of their infirmities. But he withdrew to the wilderness and prayed' (Lk 5:15–16). Even as he went to pray alone in Gethsemane, 'he went, *as was his custom*, to the Mount of Olives' (Lk 22:39). Jesus in turn invites his disciples to withdraw like himself into solitude, and he explains why: 'Come away by yourselves to a lonely place, and rest a while.' For many, we are told, were coming and going, and they had no leisure even to eat. 'And they went away in the boat to a lonely place by themselves' (Mk 6:31–32).

Listening to the word

The story of Mary of Bethany, 'who sat at the Lord's feet and listened to his word', illustrates the value of silence for every follower of Jesus (cf. Lk 10:38–42). Elizabeth of the Trinity captures this aspect of the Carmelite charism of prayer when she prays, 'O Eternal Word, Word of my God, I want to spend my life in listening to You, to become wholly teachable that I may learn all from You' (PT). She also writes of this Mary as one whose listening is an example of loving:

> To love is…
> Never to leave the Lord
> But to remain in the fullness of peace
> At the feet of this divine Saviour.
> She listened in great silence to
> 'The word which He spoke to her'.
> So as better to savour His presence
> Ah, everything in her was silent. (Pm 94)

Elizabeth concludes by saying that this Mary, buried in Jesus' love, 'gave herself irrevocably' (Pm 94).

Jesus does not invite us to withdraw from the hectic pace of modern living in order to escape the challenges of today's world. He calls us into solitude so that we might *listen* more intently in silence to the word of God. This was God's first command to his people: 'Hear, O Israel: The Lord our God is one Lord; and you shall love the Lord your God with all your heart, and with all your soul, and with all your might' (Dt 6:4–5). The Lord calls his people on their desert journey to an experience of listening in quiet communion with himself: 'I am going to seduce her and lead her into the desert and speak to her heart' (Hos 2:14). The Psalmist expresses the longing of the Lord to his exiled people: 'O that today you would listen to his voice! "Harden not your hearts as at Meribah"' (Ps 94:7–8). Jesus reminds us that the members of his family are 'those who hear the word of God and do it… those who hear the word of God and keep it' (Lk 8:21; 11:28).

Moreover, the Gospels speak to us of God himself listening. The Son listens to the Father: 'everything that I have heard from my Father,' he tells his disciples, 'I have made known to you' (Jn 15:15). Likewise, the Spirit listens to Jesus: '[the Spirit] will not speak from himself, but whatever he hears he will speak' (Jn 16:13). Indeed, every praying disciple of Jesus is drawn into this communion of listening in the inner life of God: 'Everyone who is of the truth,' Jesus says, 'listens to my voice' (Jn 18:37). And as we shall now see, Teresa shows us a wonderful way in which we can learn to listen.

In the 'little heaven of our soul'

'I confess that I never knew what it was to pray with satisfaction,' Teresa tells us, 'until the Lord taught me this method' (WP 29:7). She is speaking here about the *prayer of recollection*,[12] a form of silent prayer of listening in the presence of God, often considered to be independent of – and even superior to – vocal prayer. Yet, as Teresa shows, vocal prayer is intimately linked with it: 'With [recollection],' she assures us, 'we shall pray vocally with much calm, and any difficulty will be removed... get used to praying the Our Father with this recollection, and you will see the benefit before long' (WP 29:6).

We can readily understand the importance and value of this kind of prayer for Teresa. As we have seen, she experienced a great obstacle on her long and painful prayer journey: an inability to concentrate. The prayer of recollection provided her with the perfect solution. Teresa gives the essence of her teaching on recollection in three chapters of *The Way of Perfection* (WP 26.28–29). Here, she is perhaps at her most practical and helpful. Her advice is designed to help those who cannot practise, or who are entangled in, 'discursive meditation' – a reflection with the intellect on God and the truths of faith – and to calm the distraction of too much thinking.

With recollection, everything becomes simplified. Christ is really present. We have only to look at him or see him looking at us, and to listen to what he has to say to us. To *look at him* with a simple and intuitive gaze of faith is the kernel of Teresa's advice. This is what she advises beginners: 'one should...just remain there in His presence with the intellect quiet... occupy ourselves in looking at Christ who is looking at us, and...speak, and petition, and humble ourselves, and delight in the Lord's presence' (*Life* 13:22). Communing like this with Jesus in prayer is rooted in what Teresa has called 'an intimate sharing between friends' (*Life* 8:5). 'Believe me,' she tells us, 'you should remain with so good a friend as long as you can' (WP 26:1).

The prayer of recollection implies withdrawing from externals that dissipate the energies. Teresa calls it entering within oneself 'to be with [one's] God and close the door to all the world' (WP 29:4). Or, in gospel terms, it is to 'shut the door' (Mt 6:6) on all unnecessary distractions and idle wanderings of the mind. Teresa explains: 'This prayer is called "recollection", because the soul collects its faculties together and enters within itself to be with its God' (WP 28:4). She further assures us that this way of prayer is well suited to those 'who cannot engage in much discursive reflection with the intellect or keep [the] mind from distraction' (WP 26:2) – a description that probably applies to most people at one time or another. This prayer can also be called the 'prayer of presence' or the 'prayer of companionship': a peaceful and simple gazing in love, through the eyes of faith, at God present within. The place 'within' is, as we have seen, 'this little heaven of our soul':

> Do you think it matters little for a soul with a wandering mind to…see that there is no need to go to heaven in order to speak with one's Eternal Father or find delight in Him? Nor is there any need to shout. However softly we speak, He is near enough to hear us. Neither is there any need for wings to go to find Him. All one need do is go into solitude and look at Him within oneself… Those who…can enclose themselves within this little heaven of our soul, where the Maker of heaven and earth is present,…should believe they are following an excellent path and that they will not fail to drink water from the fount; for they will journey far in a short time. (WP 28:2.5)

Teresa uses a vivid image to illustrate this centring of the faculties: 'the bees are approaching and entering the beehive to make honey' (WP 28:7). And she is careful to point out that this recollection is not something entirely beyond our power, 'but that it is something we can desire and achieve ourselves with the help of God' (WP 29:4). That is, no *special* grace is required. When such a special grace is given, the soul enters into deeper prayer: what is known as 'passive recollection', when God takes over more fully in our prayer. However, the recollection which Teresa is speaking about here – also known as 'active recollection' – is something that everyone can practise, with effort, faithfulness and readiness to move beyond words, thoughts and images into silence and listening. But she is particularly anxious that we should still dispose ourselves for this special grace of deeper recollection. Indeed, she seems convinced that anyone who perseveres in the habit of recollection *will* receive it. Teresa sees a special advantage for us in the prayer of active recollection, in that it 'prepares us to enter more deeply into the mystery of prayer: '[the] divine Master comes more quickly to teach [us]…than He would through any other method [we] might use' (WP 28:4).

A praying community of love

There are many models of church in the New Testament (cf. LG 6–7). Vatican II devotes an entire chapter of one of its documents to the scriptural image of the church as the new 'people of God' (cf. LG 9–17),[13] emphasising the human and communal aspect, rather than the institutional and hierarchical. To be a friend of Jesus, at one with him in the community of believers, is to be the members at one with the Head – the whole body of Christ spread out in the world. It is to be a friend of his friends, too.

This kind of sharing between friends is *community* as we find it in John's Gospel, a communion or fellowship described in the allegory of the vine: 'Remain in me, and I in you… I am the vine, you are the branches' (Jn 15:4–5). It is about a *fruitfulness* that is not possible apart from Jesus: 'Those who remain in me, and I in them, bear much fruit, because apart from me you can do nothing' (Jn 15:5). It is about *love*: 'remain in my love' (Jn 15:9). It is an invitation to *joy*: 'that my joy may be in you, and that your joy may be complete' (Jn 15:11). It is a community all the more *apostolic* and fruitful the more it is rooted in love of Christ and of others – and it is a fruit-bearing community that *gives glory to God*: 'By this my Father is glorified, that you bear much fruit' (Jn 15:8); that fruit is *service of others*, expressed in love. It is a *community of prayer*: 'If you remain in me,…ask whatever you will, and it shall be done for you' (Jn 15:7; cf. 15:16).

This marvellously fresh gospel vision of a praying community of friends heralds a new springtime for the church of today and of the future: a communion of love with Jesus and with one another, which gives glory to God in a joyful life of prayer; a community with a mission, not necessarily to 'go, therefore, and make disciples of all nations' (Mt 28:19); but, perhaps especially, to 'bear fruit' in love and to do so by loving one another as Christ has loved us in his passion and death (cf. Jn 13:34; 15:12).

Teresa shared this gospel vision of church. As foundress of the reformed Carmel, she wanted each of her Carmelite communities to be a 'college of Christ' (WP 27:6): a replica, in miniature, of the community of the early church. 'They devoted themselves to the apostles' teaching and fellowship,' we are told, 'to the breaking of bread and the prayers… with glad and generous hearts, praising God…' (Acts 2:42.46–47). Deeply imbued with the ancient Marian tradition of the Carmelite Order, Teresa writes: 'If there should be anything good in this work [*The Way of Perfection*], may it be for the honour and glory of God and the service of His most Blessed Mother, our Lady and Patroness, whose habit I wear despite my being very unworthy to do so.'[14] It is hardly surprising that under her inspiration and guidance, her newly-founded Carmelite monasteries, like the first Christian communities, 'with one accord devoted themselves to prayer, together with…Mary the mother of Jesus…' (Acts 1:14).

Teresa stamped her communities with her own delightful and human touch. For her, every community structure was designed to enhance, not to cripple, personal development. Or, as Vatican II reminds us: 'the beginning, the subject and the goal of all social institutions is and must be the human person' (GS 25).[15] She urges all to holiness and would draw others to

Carmel with a winning smile: 'be affable and understanding in such a way that everyone you talk to will love your conversation...and not be frightened and intimidated by virtue... the holier [the sisters] are the more sociable they are' (WP 41:7). She wanted her communities relaxed and flexible, a real family, a true home: 'Understand...that I am a friend of intensifying virtue, but not rigour, as will be seen in our houses.'[16]

Teresa always defended tolerance in applying rules and regulations, since 'a weighed-down soul cannot serve God well'.[17] Her human approach was her challenge to her sisters always to focus their eyes, with love, on the humanity of Christ and the community he founded, bonded in love: 'The Lord doesn't look so much at the greatness of our works,' she writes, 'as at the love with which they are done' (IC VII:4:15). Her challenge to her communities could be expressed using this phrase from St Paul: that their lives may be 'rooted and grounded in love' (Eph 3:17).

'By this we know love'

Teresa also stresses the importance of love for one another as a prerequisite for prayer. She envisaged each of her communities as a gathering of Christ's friends: 'All my longing was and still is that since He has so many enemies and so few friends that these few friends be good ones' (WP 1:2). So important, for Teresa, is fraternal love that she does not hesitate to devote three chapters to it when she shares informally with her sisters about prayer in *The Way of Perfection* (cf. WP 4.6–7; cf. 36). Jesus leaves his incomparable commandment – of loving others as he has loved them – as his parting gift to his disciples. This is, as we have seen, a 'new commandment...my commandment' (Jn 13:34; 15:12),[18] and he explains that there is no greater love than 'to lay down one's life for one's friends' (Jn 15:13). 'By this we know love, that he laid down his life for us,' John writes, 'and we ought to lay down our lives for one another' (1Jn 3:16). This dying to self, for others, out of love, is itself a form of martyrdom. Or, as Teresa writes: 'the life of a good religious who desires to be one of God's close friends is a long martyrdom' (WP 12:2). We know that we have passed out of death and into life, because we love our brothers and sisters in Christ (cf. 1Jn 3:14).

Significantly, when Teresa speaks of love for one another in community, she dwells at great length on forgiveness. Well did she remark that 'to be forgiving is a virtue difficult for us to attain by ourselves' (WP 36:7). She writes:

> how the Lord must esteem this love we have for one another! Indeed, Jesus could have put other virtues first and said: forgive us, Lord, because we do a great deal of penance or because we pray much and fast or because we have left all for You and love You very much… But He said only, 'forgive us because we forgive.' (WP 36:7)

For Teresa, forgiveness is the acid test of authentic prayer. She explains that if 'there doesn't arise in the soul a very resolute desire to pardon any injury however grave it may be and to pardon it in deed when the occasion arises, do not trust much in that soul's prayer' (WP 36:8). It is remarkable how Jesus, too, links his teaching on prayer with forgiveness: 'When you stand in prayer, forgive' (Mk 11:25). It is, of course, there at the heart of the Lord's Prayer: 'forgive us our debts as we also have forgiven our debtors' (Mt 6:12; cf. 18:23–35). Jesus reinforces this lesson when teaching the Our Father: 'if you do not forgive others their trespasses, neither will your Father forgive your trespasses' (Mt 6:15). Teresa has known many persons of prayer favoured with the gift of contemplation, but she says tellingly that even though she has seen other faults and imperfections in them, she has never seen any true contemplative unwilling to forgive (cf. WP 36:13). She explains why, in a nutshell: 'I cannot believe that a person who comes so close to Mercy itself, where he realises what he is and the great deal God has pardoned him of, would fail to pardon his offender immediately' (WP 36:12).

At the service of the Church

Equally important for Teresa is what she designates as the fruit of all prayer and especially of the highest union: good works.

'This is the reason for prayer…,' she says, 'the purpose of this spiritual marriage: the birth always of good works, good works' (IC VII:4:6).[19] Carmelites must 'be occupied in prayer…so as to have…strength to serve' (IC VII:4:12). They must 'be occupied in prayer for those who are the defenders of the Church and for preachers and for learned men who protect [the Church] from attack' (WP 1:2).

This was Teresa's special affirmation of an apostolic dimension to contemplative prayer. On her deathbed, she often repeated full of gratitude: 'I am a daughter of the Church'.[20] She wanted her Carmelite communities of prayer, penance, silence and enclosure to be groups of strong and close friends of one another in the service of their great Friend, his mission and his Church. For Teresa, to love Christ is to love his friends: the whole Christ, Head and members – the Church. To recall once more these words of hers: 'All my longing was and still is that since He has so many enemies and so few friends that these few friends be good ones' (WP 1:2).

Notes

1. LG = *Lumen Gentium* (*Dogmatic Constitution on the Church*).
2. See the discussion in my *The Carmelite Charism, op. cit.*, pp. 41–3.
3. For a good introduction to vocal and mental prayer in Teresa, see E W Trueman Dicken, *The Crucible of Love: A Study of the Mysticism of St Teresa of Jesus and St John of the Cross*, London: Darton, Longman & Todd, 1963, pp. 80–115.
4. Shakespeare, *Hamlet*, Act III, Scene 3, ll. 97–8.
5. MC = *Marialis Cultus* (*On Devotion to the Blessed Virgin Mary*).
6. See my *Captive Flames: A Biblical Reading of the Carmelite Saints*, Dublin: Veritas, 2005, p. 44.
7. In Sister Geneviève of the Holy Face (Céline Martin), *My Sister St. Thérèse*, Rockford, IL: Tan Books and Publishers, 1997, p. 109.
8. Benedict XVI, Homily at his Inaugural Mass, April 24, 2005.
9. This is a translation based on the Vulgate and quoted in *Divine Office*, vol. I, p. [466].
10. Office for the Promotion of Causes [OCD] (ed.), *Elizabeth Still Speaks… – In the Processes of Beatification and Canonization: Words of the Servant of God Reported by Witnesses*, Eugene, OR: Carmel of Maria Regina, 1982, p. 7.

11. See my *The Carmelite Charism, op. cit.*, pp. 18–20.

12. For a fuller treatment of the prayer of recollection, see P Marie-Eugène, OCD, *I Want to See God – A Practical Synthesis of Carmelite Spirituality*, vol. 1, Cork: The Mercier Press, 1953, pp. 198–213; Eugene McCaffrey, OCD, 'Praying with St Teresa – 3: The Prayer of Companionship', in *Mount Carmel*, vol. 46/4, 1999, pp. 9–14.

13. That is, Chapter II of *Lumen Gentium*. On the importance of this image of the church as 'the people of God', see the explanation by Avery Dulles, SJ, in *The Documents of Vatican II*, London & Dublin: Geoffrey Chapman, 1966, pp. 24–5, n. 27.

14. From her later Foreword to *The Way of Perfection*: see *The Collected Works of St. Teresa of Avila*, vol. 2, Washington, DC: ICS Publications, 1980, p. 38.

15. GS = *Gaudium et Spes* (*Pastoral Constitution on the Church in the Modern World*).

16. From a letter of Teresa to Fr Ambrosio Mariano de San Benito Azzaro, December 12, 1576 (Letter 161:8).

17. From a letter of Teresa to Fr Jerónimo Gracián, February 21, 1581 (Letter 376:3).

18. See Chapter 1, sections 'Loving in deed and truth' and 'Is this love possible?', pp. 53–5; see also my *Captive Flames, op. cit.*, pp. 189–90.

19. For a discussion of the nature of 'Teresian works' in the light of the apostolate of enclosed Carmelite nuns, see Emmanuel Renault, OCD, *The Apostolate of Contemplatives according to St Teresa of Avila*, Darlington Carmel, n.d., especially pp. 65–105.

20. See Tomás Álvarez, OCD, *Estudios Teresianos*, vol. 3, Burgos: Editorial Monte Carmelo, 1996, Chapter 6, 'Santa Teresa y la Iglesia: Sentirse Hija de la Iglesia', pp. 211–86, especially pp. 285–6.

Chapter 3

THE PRIESTLY PRAYER OF JESUS

A mirror of the soul

The priestly prayer of Jesus marks a transition between Jesus as a witness to prayer and the story of his passion, and as such it has been given a chapter apart. But another reason why this book is giving special focus to the priestly prayer is that it is deeply embedded in our Carmelite tradition throughout the ages, making a vast impact on Teresa of Avila and John of the Cross, and continuing to inspire our saints of modern times. The invitation is always there for us to contemplate it, assimilate it, and reflect on it as best we can. Indeed, reflect it. For the priestly prayer is like a 'mirror', Teresa tells us, 'where our image is engraved' (IC VII:2:8).[1]

Teresa shares with us her understanding of this prayer when she speaks about the highest peaks of prayer known to her: the mystical marriage of the soul with God. She writes:

> while Jesus our Lord was once praying for His apostles...
> He said that they were one with the Father and with Him,
> just as Jesus Christ our Lord is in the Father and the Father
> is in Him. I don't know what greater love there can be than
> this. And all of us are included here, for His Majesty said: *I
> ask not only for them but for all those who also will believe in me*;
> and He says: *I am in them.* (IC VII:2:7; cf. Jn 17:20.23)

She then exclaims:

> Oh, God help me, how true these words are! And how well
> they are understood by the soul who is in this prayer and
> sees for itself. How well we would all understand them if it
> were not for our own fault, since the words of Jesus Christ,

91

our King and Lord, cannot fail. But since we fail by not dis-
posing ourselves and turning away from all that can hinder
this light, we do not see ourselves in this mirror that we
contemplate, where our image is engraved. (IC VII:2:8)

Expressing the inexpressible

John of the Cross turns to the priestly prayer in his attempt
to express the soul's search for God when it culminates in the
experience of transforming union. He firstly describes the soul
in this state:

> There you will show me
> what my soul has been seeking...
>
> the breathing of the air,
> the song of the sweet nightingale;
> the grove and its living beauty
> in the serene night,
> with a flame that is consuming and painless. (SC, stanzas
> 38–39)

But even John's sublime lyrical poetry seems to fail him. The
Mystical Doctor is almost at a loss to describe this deep and
mysterious union with God: 'No knowledge or power can describe
how this [union] happens' (SC 39:5), he tells us. He confesses
that the 'spiration of the Holy Spirit in the soul, by which God
transforms her into himself, is so sublime, delicate, and deep
a delight that a mortal tongue finds it indescribable, nor can
the human intellect, as such, in any way grasp it' (SC 39:3). We
can almost feel him grappling with the inarticulate... until at
last comes his final 'Eureka!' – 'I have found it!' He discovers
the inexpressible expressed in the priestly prayer, and he simply
quotes an extract from it, on the oneness of believers with each
other and with God (Jn 17:20–24; cf. SC 39:5). No wonder that
John of the Cross ends his treatment of the priestly prayer with
the words of 2 Peter on our sharing in the divine nature (cf.
2Pt 1:2–4) and with this exclamation:

O souls, created for these grandeurs and called to them! What are you doing? How are you spending your time? Your aims are base and your possessions miseries! O wretched blindness of your eyes! You are blind to so brilliant a light... (SC 39:7)

Significantly, one of John's companions on his journeys, Brother Jerónimo de la Cruz, testifies that the saint used to repeat, quietly and with great devotion, the priestly prayer of Jesus.[2] His constant pondering on Scripture – the call to *lectio divina* that lies at the heart of the Carmelite *Rule* – unlocked for John the hidden treasures of this profound prayer.

Our prayer

At the end of *Story of a Soul*, Thérèse recalls the words of the Song of Songs: 'Draw me, we shall run after you in the odour of your ointments' (Sg 1:3; cf. SS, p. 254).[3] In these few words she found the solution to a problem which had perplexed her: she was troubled by her deep desire to remember the needs of all those entrusted to her prayer. 'For simple souls,' she says, 'there must be no complicated ways' (SS, p. 254). So her solution is simple: 'I dare to borrow the words [Jesus] addressed to the heavenly Father, the last night which saw [Him] on our earth' (SS, p. 254); and then, like John of the Cross but even more extensively, she repeats almost in its entirety the priestly prayer of Jesus and makes it her own. 'Perhaps this is boldness?' (SS, p. 255), she asks straight afterwards. But no, she replies, in words from another Gospel: 'EVERYTHING *that is mine is yours*' (SS, p. 256; Lk 15:31). So, for Thérèse, the priestly prayer of Jesus is *her* prayer, too. It is the prayer of intercession *par excellence*; and, as we shall see, she understands intercession in the precise biblical sense of the term.

The writings of Elizabeth of the Trinity abound with references to the priestly prayer of Jesus, and they are invariably linked with her central teaching on the indwelling of the Blessed Trinity. Her mind echoes to the words of the priestly prayer when she writes: 'It seems to me that I have found my Heaven on earth, since Heaven is God, and God is [in] my soul... I would like to whisper this secret to those I love...so this prayer of Christ might be fulfilled: "Father, may they be made perfectly one!"' (L 122; cf. Jn 17:23). And again – knowing, like Thérèse, that the prayer of Jesus is *our* prayer – she writes: 'Since Our Lord dwells in our souls, His prayer belongs to us, and I wish to live in communion with it unceasingly... "I sanctify myself for [souls] that they also may be sanctified in the truth." Let us make these words of our adored Master all our own, yes, let us sanctify ourselves for souls...' (L 191; cf. Jn 17:19).

The mystery of the inner life

Understandably, it is Edith Stein who directs our attention to the Old Testament background to the priestly prayer. A Jewess by birth, she was steeped in the life, religion and culture of her own people. She was born on the Jewish Day of Atonement, and the ritual of the celebration was deeply etched in her memory; so after she became a Christian, the links between the prayer of the high priest in Leviticus 16 and the priestly prayer of Jesus easily sprang to mind for her. Also, as a true Carmelite in the spirit of John of the Cross, she saw the priestly prayer as a springboard into the mystery of God's indwelling in our soul. She writes:

> We call these words Jesus' great high priestly prayer, for this talking alone with God also had its antecedent in the Old Covenant... This solitary dialogue took place in deepest mystery... the high priest descended from Aaron foreshadows the eternal high priest... [Christ] unlocks the mystery of the high priest's realm. All who belong to him may hear how, in the Holy of Holies of his heart, he speaks to his Father; they are to experience what is going on and are to learn to speak to the Father in their own hearts. The Saviour's high priestly prayer unveils the mystery of the inner life: the circumincession of the Divine Persons and the indwelling of God in the soul. In these mysteri-

ous depths the work of salvation was prepared and accomplished itself in concealment and silence. And so it will continue until the union of all is actually accomplished at the end of time. (HL, pp. 11–12)

Then Edith goes on to expand and gives a number of examples, from salvation history, of the inner life as a continuation of the priestly prayer – a passage worth quoting at length:

> The decision for the Redemption was conceived in the eternal silence of the inner divine life. The power of the Holy Spirit came over the Virgin praying alone in the hidden, silent room in Nazareth and brought about the Incarnation of the Saviour. Congregated around the silently praying Virgin, the emergent church awaited the promised new outpouring of the Spirit that was to quicken it into inner clarity and fruitful outer effectiveness. In the night of blindness that God laid over his eyes, Saul awaited in solitary prayer the Lord's answer to his question, 'What do you want me to do?' In solitary prayer Peter was prepared for his mission to the Gentiles. And so it has remained all through the centuries. In the silent dialogue with their Lord of souls consecrated to God, the events of church history are prepared that, visible far and wide, renew the face of the earth. (HL, pp. 12–13; cf. Lk 1:35; Acts 1:14; 9:9; 10:9–16)

As a climax, Edith returns to Mary, whose prayer life she shows to be the ultimate exemplar of the priestly prayer in the church. Edith writes:

> The Virgin, who kept every word sent from God in her heart, is the model for such attentive souls in whom Jesus' high priestly prayer comes to life again and again. (HL, p. 13)

Teresa, John of the Cross, Thérèse, Elizabeth, Edith Stein, and many other Carmelite men and women of prayer, all rank among these 'attentive' souls. And in them the priestly prayer lives on, embedded in our Carmelite tradition of prayer.

A timeless prayer

The priestly prayer has a perennial quality all of its own. One reason, as Teresa reminds us, writing of this prayer, is that 'the words of Jesus Christ, our King and Lord, cannot fail' (IC VII:2:8); and here, she is echoing the assurance of Jesus to his disciples: 'whatever you ask the Father in my name, he will give it to you' (Jn 15:16). But more even than this: the priestly prayer in itself has a timeless dimension, for past, present and future seem to fuse in it and blend almost imperceptibly. Present: 'I am no longer in the world... I am coming to you'; past: 'I have glorified you on earth, having accomplished the work which you gave me to do... I have made known to them your name...'; and future: 'I will make it known' (Jn 17:11.4.26). The prayer seems to hover over the flow of human history as a kind of still-point from which all time takes its value in God's unfolding plan of salvation from the beginning of creation until the dawn of eternity – an abiding presence.

The setting of the prayer itself confirms this timeless aspect. It is linked to the immediate context, which is timeless, as the evangelist introduces the prayer by saying: 'When Jesus had spoken these words...' (Jn 17:1). What words are these? They refer to what Jesus has just said to his disciples: 'I have overcome the world' (Jn 16:33). In the original language of the prayer, as in the English, this does not refer solely to a past action (in the sense of 'I overcame') but to one still present in its effects ('I *have* overcome') – an action finished and complete, but now permanently present. The prayer embodies the victory of Jesus through his passion-resurrection – the fruits of the paschal mystery.

This in turn is confirmed by the first words of Jesus himself in his prayer: 'The hour has come.' It is the 'hour' of his passion-resurrection. This 'hour' is mysteriously present, here and now – the same 'hour' that runs all through the Gospel of John. At Cana, we are told that this 'hour' has not yet come (cf. Jn 2:4). No explanation of the 'hour' is given. As the drama unfolds, we are told that the enemies of Jesus did not lay hands on him because his time had not yet come (cf. Jn 7:6).

Jesus prays to be saved from this 'hour': 'Father, save me from this hour' (Jn 12:27), he cries. This is John's version of the Gethsemane prayer, but with a difference. It is not necessarily a prayer in which Jesus asks the Father to save him *from* his 'hour' – that is, to spare him the painful ordeal of his passion, the way he prays in the other Gospels that 'if it were possible, the hour might pass from him' (Mk 14:35; cf. 14:36; Mt 26:39; Lk 22:42). The 'hour' of Jesus in John embraces both the passion *and* the resurrection. Here, Jesus is asking his Father to save him 'out of' this hour[4] – that is, to bring him safely *through* his passion to the glory of the resurrection. 'I have glorified you on earth' (Jn 17:4), Jesus says in his priestly prayer. In this sense, the resurrection is already past and also ever present here and now in this prayer.

Across the threshold of eternity

As we have seen, Edith Stein, with a remarkable and original insight, links the priestly prayer to the ritual of the high priest on the Jewish Day of Atonement: 'Once a year,' she writes, 'on the greatest and most holy day of the year, on the Day of Atonement, the high priest stepped into the Holy of Holies before the face of the Lord' (HL, p. 12). Again, as a Carmelite, Edith is highlighting the relationship with God, as she emphasises Jesus *standing before the face of the Father.* She writes: 'He stands, always and everywhere, before the face of God; his own soul is the Holy of Holies' (HL, p. 12); and she calls his priestly prayer a 'secret dialogue' (HL, p. 11).

This ritual of the high priest on the Day of Atonement repeats itself in the priestly prayer of Jesus. In this prayer Jesus says, 'I am no longer in the world' (Jn 17:11). But if he is not in the world, then where is he really? Jesus explains when he says to his Father, 'I am coming to you' (Jn 17:13). That is, he is *journeying towards* his Father in the new passover of his passion-resurrection: 'his hour had come' and is already present for him 'to pass out of this world to the Father' (Jn 13:1). The author of Hebrews captures this same perspective: 'But when Christ appeared as a high priest of the good things to come, then through the greater and more perfect tent (not made with human hands, that is, not of this creation), he entered once and for all into the Holy Place,…thus securing an eternal redemption' (Hb 9:11–12). This more perfect *tent*, 'not made with human hands', refers to the body of Jesus transformed by his passion and death into the new temple of his risen and glorified body.

This same perspective dominates not just the priestly prayer but the parting discourses of Jesus at the Last Supper: 'In my Father's house there are many rooms' (Jn 14:2), he says.[5] Here, Jesus is speaking of the *heavenly* temple, his Father's dwelling place, and he adds: 'I go to prepare a place for you' (Jn 14:2) – that is, to render it accessible in his transfigured and glorified body. He is on his way through his passion-resurrection into the eternal sanctuary, and this 'preparation' is precisely the transformation of his body through his passion-resurrection into the new temple of his risen body, just as Jesus had foretold it: 'Destroy this temple, and in three days I will raise it up' (Jn 2:19); and the evangelist makes clear: 'He was speaking about the temple of his body' (Jn 2:21). In the priestly prayer, Jesus is striding across the threshold of eternity and entering the heavenly temple of his Father through his passion-resurrection. The ritual of the Day of Atonement is fulfilled in a new, remarkable and mysterious way.

A prayer of at-one-ment

But what is atonement? In the biblical sense it is quite literally 'reconciliation'; in English, it is 'at-one-ment': uniting people with God, making them *one* with him. In this sense, the priestly prayer is clearly a prayer of at-one-ment, a prayer for unity. We notice the ever deepening mystery of this oneness as the prayer unfolds. Jesus prays: 'Holy Father, keep them in your name which you have given me, that they may be one, even as we are one' (Jn 17:11). Here, Jesus is speaking of a simple unity modelled on that between himself and his Father. Later in the prayer, we see the depths of this revealed as Jesus prays 'that they may all be one; even as you, Father, are in me and I in you, that they also may be in us' (Jn 17:21). So this is not just a simple unity modelled on that between the Father and the Son. It is a relationship of mutual indwelling – the indwelling of the Father in the Son, and the Son in the Father – into which believers are plunged, called to a mutual indwelling in God; it is a reciprocal oneness intimately uniting Jesus in the Father and the Father in Jesus.

Edith Stein, too, expresses the mystery in this way when she writes: 'The Saviour's high priestly prayer unveils the mystery of the inner life: the circumincession of the Divine Persons and the indwelling of God in the soul' (HL, p. 12); 'circumincession', a very technical term, literally denotes a circular movement of life in the heart of God. The mystery of the Trinity implies sharing life in an unending self-giving. It is captured beautifully for us in Rublëv's icon of the Trinity: the mutual exchange of a reciprocal sharing between Father and Son in the infinitely outpouring Love which is the Holy Spirit.

The priestly prayer is a marvellous prayer for unity. Teresa returns to the reciprocal union described in it, when she wants to provide 'the sure sign' that the one who prays is united with God, in what she calls the prayer of union in the fifth mansions of her *Interior Castle*:

> God so places Himself in the interior of [the] soul that when it returns to itself it can in no way doubt that it was in God and God was in it. This truth remains with it so firmly that even though years go by without God's granting that favour again, the soul can neither forget nor doubt that it was in God and God was in it... I would say that whoever does not receive this certitude does not experience union of the whole soul with God, but union of some faculty, or that he experiences one of the many other kinds of favours God grants souls. (IC V:1:9.11)

Jesus as mediator

In this oneness, Jesus is the link or intermediary between the Father and believers. He prays: 'The glory which you [Father] have given me I have given to them, that they may be one, even as we are one, I in them [believers] and you [Father] in me, that they may become perfectly one, that the world may know that it was you who sent me and that you have loved them even as you have loved me' (Jn 17:22–23). A oneness between ourselves and God, in that the Father is in Jesus, and Jesus is in us.

So Jesus is the mediator between God and believers; he is a bridge. No wonder the Latin word for 'priest' is 'pontifex': literally, 'bridge-maker' – from 'pons', meaning 'bridge', and 'facere', meaning 'to make'. Jesus is the great High Priest, and all believers are one with him in his own eternal love for his Father. This unity of love is what Jesus pleads for explicitly as the goal of his priestly prayer: 'I desire that those also, whom you have given to me, may be with me where I am, so that they may see my glory, the glory which you have given me in your love for me before the foundation of the world' (Jn 17:24). Elizabeth of the Trinity was much struck by this, saying: 'Such is Christ's last wish, His supreme prayer before returning to His Father. He wills that where He is we should be also, not only for eternity, but already in time, which is eternity begun and still in progress' (HF 1).

The final goal of the priestly prayer is ours *here and now*. Or, to borrow Elizabeth's phrase, 'heaven in faith': we can live this union with Jesus, this life of heaven, already here on earth through faith. So, too, the eternal glory of our final destiny is already ours in faith, to recall these magnificent words of St Paul: 'We all, with unveiled face, reflecting the glory of the Lord as in a mirror, are being changed into his likeness from one degree of glory to another. This is the work of the Spirit who is the Lord' (2Cor 3:18). And God's eternal love is already ours now in faith, for his love has been 'poured into our hearts through the Holy Spirit who has been given to us' (Rm 5:5). St Thérèse captures this insight for us – this union and identification with Jesus – in her prayer of self-offering to Merciful Love. Here, she begs the Father: 'look upon me only in the Face of Jesus and in His Heart burning with *Love*' (SS, p. 276).

A sacrificial prayer

Essential to the rite of atonement is sacrifice, just as it was for the high priest in Leviticus. Nor was this just any sacrifice, but one in which *everything* was offered to God. This was known in the Old Covenant as the 'holocaust', literally a 'wholly burnt offering' – from 'hólos', meaning 'whole', and 'kaustós', meaning 'burnt'. It was a sacrifice that was completely burnt, entirely consumed. So, too, is the sacrifice at the heart of the priestly prayer of Jesus. He prays: 'For their sake I sanctify myself, so that they also may be sanctified in the truth' (Jn 17:19) To 'sanctify' means to 'take out of profane usage and hand over to God' (cf. Lv 20:26; 1Pt 2:9–10). But it can also have a sacrificial import (cf. Dt 15:19–21; 1Pt 2:4–5).[6] Jesus sanctifies himself by *handing himself over in sacrifice* to his Father in his passion-resurrection.

Earlier in his Gospel, John gives us a glimpse into the soul of Jesus responding with his total self-offering, giving himself in love to his Father's love. This is intimately linked with his free surrender to his Father in his passion-resurrection: 'For this reason the Father loves me, because I lay down my life, that I may take it up again. No one takes it from me, but I lay it down of my own accord. I have power to lay it down, and I have power to take it up again; this command I have received from my Father' (Jn 10:17–18).

This is his 'holocaust', repeated again in his priestly prayer – total, free and unconditional. It resides at the heart of our Carmelite charism of prayer and sacrifice. Edith Stein, impatient to lead the life of a Carmelite, wrote of the necessity of her own 'holocaustum' (cf. SP, p. 60), borrowing the Latin word either from her breviary (cf. Ps 39:7; Hb 10:6) or from Thomas Aquinas, who describes religious as those who offer themselves as a 'holocaust' to God.[7] She was familiar with the Hebrew word for 'holocaust' – *'ōlā*, meaning 'that which ascends' – and this

would surely have resonated for her with the Carmelite over-
tones of the 'ascent' of Mount Carmel.[8] Thérèse, too, speaks
of prayer as an ascending movement: as 'an aspiration of the
heart,...a simple glance directed to heaven' (SS, p. 242) – that
is, a raising up of our eyes to God just as Jesus 'lifted up his eyes
to heaven' (Jn 17:1) to begin his priestly prayer. Thérèse herself
speaks of her own 'holocaust' and links her sacrifice inseparably to her total surrender to love: 'I offer myself as a victim of
holocaust to your Merciful Love' (cf. SS, p. 277), she prays to
the Blessed Trinity. Her reason, as she says: in order that her
life may be an act of perfect love. And she adds: 'consume me
incessantly' (SS, p. 277).

The holiness of God

Inseparable, too, from the ancient rite of atonement was the
sacrifice of a victim as an offering to make atonement for the
sins of the people: 'for on this day shall atonement be made for
you, to cleanse you,' the people are told; 'from all your sins you
shall be clean before the Lord' (Lv 16:30). Again, Edith Stein
highlights this aspect of the priestly prayer. She writes:

> on the Day of Atonement, the high priest stepped into
> the Holy of Holies before the face of the Lord 'to pray for
> himself and his household and the whole congregation of
> Israel'. He sprinkled the throne of grace with the blood of
> a young bull and a goat, which he previously had to slaugh-
> ter, and in this way absolved himself and his house 'of the
> impurities of the sons of Israel and of their transgressions
> and of all their sins'... The ram that is slaughtered for the
> sins of the people represents the spotless Lamb of God (so
> did, no doubt, that other – chosen by lot and burdened with
> the sins of the people – that was driven into the wilderness).
> And the high priest descended from Aaron foreshadows the
> eternal high priest. (HL, p. 12; cf. Lv 16:17.16)

Paul reminds us of this when he writes: 'We appeal to you, on
behalf of Christ, be reconciled to God. For our sake he made

thc sinless one a victim for sin' (2Cor 5:20–21; cf. 1Pt 2:24). One biblical scholar has commented on that last phrase: 'God made Christ one with sinful humanity in order to make the human race one with his obedience and saving justice'; and at the same time, he links this passage with Paul's exhortation to us to surrender ourselves to uprightness, 'which is to result in sanctification' (Rm 6:19).[9]

To 'sanctify', as we have seen, does not just mean to hand something over to God in sacrifice. It also implies, as a consequence, removing it from profane usage, from anything at variance with the holiness of God. So in Johannine language, to sanctify the disciples means to take them out of the 'world' in the pejorative sense of the word. The 'world' has various meanings in John. It refers to the world God sent his Son to save – that is, all people: 'God so loved the world that he...sent his only Son into the world' (Jn 3:16–17). It also designates the created world, the universe: Jesus speaks of the glory which he had with his Father 'before the world was made... before the foundation of the world' (Jn 17:5.24). But 'world' also has distinctly negative connotations: it is the world of darkness, sin and evil. Jesus is 'the Lamb of God, who takes away the sin of the world' (Jn 1:29) – sin, not sins. Ultimately, for John there is only one sin: refusal to accept the light. It is from this world, the world of darkness which is totally at variance with the holiness of God, that Jesus prays to his Father to transfer his disciples into the world of light and truth: 'Sanctify them in the truth; your word is truth' (Jn 17:17).

Out of darkness into light

In his priestly prayer Jesus says explicitly, 'I am not praying for the world' (Jn 17:9) – that is, the world of darkness deliberately closed to the light. He reminds us that his disciples are 'not of the world' (Jn 17:16) just as he himself is 'not of the world' (Jn 17:16). He pleads that his Father 'should keep them from the evil one' (Jn 17:15), the world where the devil, the prince of darkness, reigns supreme. There can be no fellowship between light and darkness; two contraries cannot exist in one subject: 'God is light and in him is no darkness' (1Jn 1:5). This contradiction between light and darkness is basic to the radical nature of our Carmelite ascetical teaching. Teresa had an abhorrence for all sin. 'There is nothing...that deserves this name "evil",' she tells us, 'except mortal sin' (IC I:2:5); 'there's no darker darkness nor anything more obscure and black' (IC I:2:1). Those who walk in serious sin, she adds, 'have become total darkness' (IC I:2:2). She reminds us that the 'cornerstone' of the spiritual life must be 'a good conscience', and that we must strive with all our strength to free ourselves even from lesser sins (cf. WP 5:3).

John of the Cross is no less demanding; in fact, he appears to be even more so. His recurring antithesis 'ALL-NOTHING' (cf. 1A 13:11) reaffirms Teresa's radical demands: 'ALL' requires a total and exclusive embracing of the light; 'NOTHING' challenges us to shun the darkness of evil in all its ugly forms. This is what Jesus prays for to his Father in his priestly prayer: the removal of all believers, in the words of 1 Peter, 'out of darkness into [God's] marvellous light' (1Pt 2:9).

A prayer of intercession

The priestly prayer of Jesus is the great prayer of intercession. There is no intercessory prayer comparable to it elsewhere in the Gospels, not even the Our Father, although there are striking resemblances to it in two other Gospels.[10] The intercession of Jesus in the priestly prayer has, as we have seen, its antecedent also in the high priestly prayer of Leviticus. It is intercession as Paul understands it when he speaks of 'Christ Jesus...who indeed intercedes for us' (Rm 8:34), or the author of Hebrews when speaking of Jesus who 'always lives to make intercession' (Hb 7:25). Here, the Greek word for 'make intercession', 'entunchánō', has a precise meaning. It is not merely a question of Jesus making petitions for us – of using words on our behalf – but rather of an encounter: *being with someone on behalf of another.*[11] Or *representing* that other, as Edith Stein would say: 'I keep having to think of Queen Esther who was taken from among her people precisely that she might represent them before the king' (SP, p. 291).[12]

Such is the intercession of Jesus for us as the great high priest. He is the new Moses, himself also a priest (cf. Ps 98:6), as he leads the new people of God in the new exodus of his passion-resurrection, out of slavery and into the promised land, carrying all believers in his heart (cf. Nb 11:12). Or like Aaron of old who went into the Holy of Holies in the tent of meeting, wearing a breastplate designed to represent the tribes of Israel whose priest he was (cf. Ex 28:29): he stood before the face of God carrying all the people in his heart. Jesus, too, carries all believers in his heart: he stands before the Father, in the Father's *presence*, and presents them to the Father in union with himself; 'all mine are yours,' he prays, 'and yours are mine' (Jn 17:10).

This is how Thérèse understood the priestly prayer when she turned to it, anxious to know how best to pray for those entrusted to her. As mentioned earlier, she links the priestly prayer to these words of the Song of Songs: 'Draw me, we shall run after you in the odour of your ointments' (Sg 1:3; cf. SS, p. 254). And she exclaims: 'O Jesus... This simple statement: "Draw me" suffices' (SS, p. 254). All the souls whom she loves, she explains, follow in her train: 'this is done,' she says, 'without constraint, without effort.' It is a natural consequence of her attraction for Jesus. And she continues: 'Just as a torrent, throwing itself with impetuosity into the ocean, drags after it everything it encounters in its passage, in the same way, O Jesus, the soul who plunges into the shoreless ocean of Your Love, draws with her all the treasures she possesses' (SS, p. 254). Then, at this point, she makes her own the whole of the priestly prayer and comments: 'Your words, O Jesus, are mine, then, and I can make use of them to draw upon the souls united to me the favours of the heavenly Father' (SS, p. 256).

Before the face of God

When we are at one with the priestly prayer of Jesus, we combine our Carmelite calling to a life of watchfulness in prayer with service of others. Watchfulness, alertness, is the attitude that Carmel's saints recommend to us in prayer – a prayer of loving attention, of quiet waiting, of listening to what God is saying to us in our times. We are called to be like the prophet Habakkuk standing on the watchtower. He reflects on the way things are – the evil, wickedness, tyranny that abound – and turns to the Lord in his perplexity: 'Why do you look on while people are treacherous, and stay silent while the evil swallow those better than them?' (Hab 1:13). Then he reflects to himself: 'I will stand on my watchtower, and take up my post on my battlements, watching to see what he will say to me, what answer he will make to my complaints' (Hab 2:1). Habbakuk gets his answer, enigmatic enough but ending in a phrase that applies to us all: 'See how they flag, they whose soul is not at rights, but the upright will live by their faithfulness' (Hab 2:4). It is also the lesson of the Psalmist who says: 'The just man will never waver... He has no fear of evil news; with a firm heart he trusts in the Lord. With a steadfast heart he will not fear; he will see the downfall of his foes' (Ps 111:6–8).

As Carmelites, we are called to bring before the Lord, with confidence, no matter how bleak the outlook, the problems and confusions of our day and of all people. In this intercession, we enter into the peace and stillness of the inner life of God opened up to us in the priestly prayer, which is at the same time a reaching out in service to others where they live in the rough and tumble of the world of time and change; and we draw them with us in our prayer before the face of God. Indeed, as Edith Stein expresses it so well: 'To stand before the face of the living God – that is our vocation... it is our vocation to stand before God for all' (HL, p. 1; SP, p. 178).

Being quiet before God becomes contemplation, and holding God's people in our hearts becomes compassion for others as we carry their struggles and anxieties with us into our prayer of intercession for them. Our father in Carmel, the prophet Elijah, stood before the face of God (cf. 1Kgs 17:1). And here we join the prophetic element in our Carmelite charism, helping and strengthening others through our prayer.[13]

A missionary prayer

But the priestly prayer does not involve helping others only through the intercessory aspect of prayer. In the priestly prayer, Jesus speaks of the mission of his disciples, whom he is sending out into the world to proclaim the message of his gospel. This mission is intimately linked to his own mission, and indeed modelled on it: 'As you [Father] have sent me into the world, so I have sent them into the world' (Jn 17:18). It is important to realise that mission requires from us an intimate union with Jesus, just as he was intimately united with the Father.

The universal embrace of that mission becomes clear as the prayer unfolds. It has a significant threefold division resembling the gradual expanding movement of the prayer at the Dedication of the Temple. There, Solomon prayed for himself and for the people of Israel (cf. 1Kgs 8:52). But he also included 'foreigners' (cf. 1Kgs 8:41–43) in his prayer – those who did not belong to the people of Israel. The sweep of his prayer, then, reached far beyond the national confines of God's people. In similar manner, the high priest stepped into the Holy of Holies before the face of the Lord on the Day of Atonement, to intercede 'for himself and his household and the whole congregation of Israel' (Lv 16:17). The gradual all-embracing thrust of the priestly prayer follows the same pattern. At first Jesus prays for himself (cf. Jn 17:1–5); then for his own disciples (cf. Jn 17:6–19); and thirdly he adds: 'I do not pray for these only, but also for those who believe in me through [the disciples'] word' (Jn 17:20).

Jesus will proclaim before Pilate: 'For this I was born, and for this I have come into the world, to bear witness to the truth' (Jn 18:37); and in his priestly prayer he makes this prayer to his

Father for his disciples: 'Sanctify them in the truth; your word is truth' (Jn 17:17). So the disciples are sent, like Jesus, as witnesses to proclaim the truth of the gospel message: 'what we preach,' Paul tells his converts, 'is not ourselves, but Jesus Christ as Lord, with ourselves as your servants for Jesus' sake. For it is the God who said, "Let light shine out of darkness" who has shone in our hearts to give the light of the knowledge of the glory of God in the face of Christ' (2Cor 4:5–6). As we have seen, Jesus had already said to his disciples, 'I am the light of the world' (Jn 8:12), and had reminded them: 'You are the light of the world. A city built on a hill top cannot be hidden. No one lights a lamp and puts it under a bushel, but on a stand, and it gives light to all in the house. So let your light shine before others, that they may see your good works and give glory to your Father who is in heaven' (Mt 5:14–16). We shine with the borrowed light of Christ.

Re-presenting Jesus

In Hebrew, there is a word, *shaliah*, which means a 'person who is sent'.[14] In English, the word 'mission' often implies a journey abroad, as when one is sent on a mission; or it suggests an impressive achievement – 'mission accomplished!' But it does not have to be a calling to spread the gospel on foreign soil or a challenge to accomplish something great. It may be; it sometimes is; but it is not necessarily so. The word *shaliah* denotes one who *re-presents the master*, making the one who sends present in the one he has sent. This is exactly the case with Jesus sending his disciples, as it is with the Father sending his Son: 'Truly, truly, I say to you, whoever receives anyone whom I send receives me,' Jesus says to his disciples, 'and whoever receives me receives him who sent me' (Jn 13:20). From now on, Jesus has no other hands or feet or mouth but ours.

Mission is a movement emanating from the centre of our union with Jesus. As Carmelites, we are called to a mission emanating from our centre-point: 'the inner room' (cf. Mt 6:6) of prayer. How well Teresa learnt that lesson. She writes: 'let us desire and be occupied in prayer not for the sake of our enjoyment but so as to have this strength to serve' (IC VII:4:12). And she comments, as we have seen: 'This is the reason for prayer,... the purpose of this spiritual marriage: the birth always of good works, good works' (IC VII:4:6). Then, in the closing lines of this, her final masterpiece, she observes significantly: 'let us offer the Lord interiorly and exteriorly the sacrifice we can. His Majesty will join it with that which He offered on the cross to the Father for us' (IC VII:4:15).

This is exactly what Jesus is doing for us in his priestly prayer: offering himself to the Father in anticipation of his sacrifice on the cross. So Teresa concludes: 'Thus even though our works are small they will have the value our love for Him would have merited had they been great' (IC VII:4:15). When we are in union with the priestly prayer of Jesus, the saving power of the passion is ours to spread throughout the world by means of our prayer and sacrifice, including the sacrificing of our lives in our work for others. 'As the Father has sent me,' the risen Jesus says to his disciples, 'so am I sending you.' And when he had said this, 'he breathed on them, and said to them, "Receive the Holy Spirit"' (Jn 20:21–22). With these words the church, all disciples in union with the risen Jesus, is launched on a mission to the world impelled by the Spirit. The mission of Jesus, entrusted to his disciples in his priestly prayer, is fulfilled and will continue – present in the church until the end of time.

At one with the priestly prayer

The priestly prayer is an invitation to enter into the presence of Jesus praying in us, and with us, to the Father. Jesus prays, towards the end of the prayer: 'I desire that those also, whom you have given to me, may be with me where I am' (Jn 17:24). Elizabeth of the Trinity illustrates this marvellously when she repeats the request of Jesus for the disciples to be with him where he is, and asks herself where she might find him. 'It is important then to know,' she says, 'where we must live with Him' (HF 1). She discovers the answer in John of the Cross, whom she now quotes: 'The place where the Son of God is hidden is the bosom of the Father, or the divine Essence' (HF 1; SC 1:3). And she expands: 'The Trinity – this is our dwelling, our "home", the Father's house that we must never leave' (HF 2).

John tells us forcefully, in the same chapter of his *Spiritual Canticle*, that God is present in our soul: 'you yourself are his dwelling and his secret inner room and hiding place' (SC 1:7). And true to the Carmelite charism, as well as to her understanding of her name as 'House of God', Elizabeth found her 'home', her place of prayer, within the cell of her heart – her 'little Bethany' (IN 5; cf. Lk 10:38–42), as she called it. She expresses this in many inspiring ways throughout her writings: 'the divine Adorer is within us, so we have His prayer; let us offer it, let us share in it, let us pray with His Soul!' (L 179); 'I'm never alone: my Christ is always there praying in me, and I pray with Him' (L 123); 'Since Our Lord dwells in our souls, His prayer belongs to us' (L 191). Even before entering Carmel she exclaimed: 'It is so good, isn't it, to think that, except for the fact that we do not see Him, we already possess Him [here below] as the blessed possess Him above' (L 62). We are never alone: the praying Jesus is always in us, and we have only to pray at one with him (cf. L 123).

A presence in faith

But when Elizabeth speaks of the prayer of Jesus present in her, she is speaking of a presence *in faith* – a presence 'invisible to every mortal eye, unattainable by every human intellect' (HF 1; cf. SC 1:3), she says, borrowing once more from John of the Cross. It is a watching in faith enlivened by the action of the Holy Spirit; it is being 'wholly present', 'wholly vigilant' to God, as she writes in her *Prayer to the Trinity*. It is the faith of which Jesus speaks repeatedly in his priestly prayer: an openness to receive the word of God. He prays to the Father: 'I have given them the words which you gave to me, and they have received them... and they have believed...' (Jn 17:8). In the words of John of the Cross: 'pure contemplation lies in receiving' (LF 3:36) – and it is a receiving in faith.

Faith, though, is never static. Revealingly, John the evangelist never uses the noun 'faith'; it is always the verb 'believe'. Nor does he speak of believing 'in'; it is always about believing 'into'. Faith is something powerful and dynamic which allows the priestly prayer of Jesus to penetrate more deeply into us, and likewise enables us to penetrate more deeply into the priestly prayer. It is a faith open to God's word – this word described by the author of Hebrews as 'living and active, sharper than any two-edged sword, piercing to the division of soul and spirit, of joints and marrow, and discerning the thoughts and intentions of the heart' (Hb 4:12). Elizabeth herself asks for that living faith: 'may each minute carry me further into the depths of Your Mystery... May...my faith [be] wholly vigilant, wholly adoring, and wholly surrendered to Your creative Action' (PT).

Through the power of the Spirit

This is a faith quickened by the action of the Holy Spirit – a 'consuming Fire' (cf. Hb 12:29), the 'Spirit of Love', the two names by which Elizabeth calls it in her *Prayer to the Trinity*. She implores the Spirit to come upon her and reproduce in her 'another humanity' of the Word in which he may renew his 'whole Mystery'. It is the Holy Spirit alone who can guide us deeply into the mystery of the priestly prayer. For John of the Cross, this 'consuming Fire' is the 'living flame of love', which is the name he gives to the Holy Spirit: 'This flame of love is the Spirit of [the soul's] Bridegroom,' he tells us, 'who is the Holy Spirit' (LF 1:3).

John compares this action of the Spirit in transforming union – where the soul is transformed into God and united with him – to the 'breathing of the air' (SC 39:3); and he explains, in a quotation we have already encountered, and which is quoted by Elizabeth to a future priest (cf. L 185): 'By his divine breath-like spiration, the Holy Spirit elevates the soul sublimely and informs her and makes her capable of breathing in God the same spiration of love that the Father breathes in the Son and the Son in the Father. This spiration of love is the Holy Spirit himself' (SC 39:3).

This is the very love which Jesus promises to all believers at one with him in his priestly prayer – a share in 'the glory which you [Father] have given me, in your love for me before the foundation of the world' (Jn 17:24). The priestly prayer of Jesus concludes with the promise of the presence of Jesus and the eternal love of the Father in all believers: 'I have made known to them your name, and I will make it known, in order that the love with which you [Father] have loved me may be in them, and I in them' (Jn 17:26). These are the last words of the priestly prayer. The rest is silence.

Notes

1. At this point, it would be well to read once more the text of this prayer in John 17: see Appendix 1b.
2. See *The Collected Works of Saint John of the Cross, op. cit.*, p. 624, n. 1; cf. Ruiz Salvador, *Introducción, op. cit.*, p. 82.
3. This translation and verse numbering of the quotation from the Song of Songs is taken from the Vulgate.
4. This is the translation in the *Jerusalem Bible*: 'he offered up prayer and entreaty, aloud and in silent tears, to the one who had the power to save him out of death' (Hb 5:7). See also these relevant words of one biblical scholar, David Stanley: 'it seems more plausible to understand that Jesus is represented here as petitioning the Father to bring him to salvation out of his hour, *not* to deliver him from the hour': in David M Stanley, SJ, *Jesus in Gethsemane: The Early Church Reflects on the Suffering of Jesus*, New York & Ramsey, NJ: Paulist Press, 1980, p. 241.
5. See my *The House with Many Rooms: The Temple Theme of Jn. 14,2–3* (*Analecta Biblica* 114), Rome: Editrice Pontificio Istituto Biblico, 1988.
6. Commenting on John's Gospel, St Cyril of Alexandria writes: '[Christ] said, "I make myself holy", meaning "I consecrate and offer myself as a spotless sacrifice with a sweet savour"': in *Divine Office*, vol. II, p. 551.
7. He writes: 'those are called religious…who give themselves up entirely to the divine service, as offering a holocaust to God' ('religiosi dicuntur illi qui se totaliter mancipant divino servitio, quasi holocaustum Deo offerentes'): in *Summa Theologica*, II-II q. 186 a. 1.
8. See the discussion in Mosley, *Edith Stein, op. cit.*, pp. 51–2.

9. See *The New Jerusalem Bible: Standard Edition*, note j to 2 Corinthians 5:21. Also pointed out here is that 'victim for sin' (2Cor 5:21) should perhaps be taken as meaning 'sin', since the same Hebrew word *hatta't* can have both senses (cf. Lv 4:1–5:13).

10. Matthew and Luke. This is when Jesus prays: 'I thank you, Father, Lord of heaven and earth, for hiding these things from the wise and the learned and revealing them to mere children; yes, Father, for such was your gracious will. All things have been given to me by my Father; and no one knows the Son except the Father, and no one knows the Father except the Son and anyone to whom the Son chooses to reveal him' (Mt 11:25–27; cf. Lk 10:21–22).

11. This aspect of Jesus' prayer of intercession is well treated by Michael Ramsey, in his *The Christian Priest Today*, London: SPCK, 1985, pp. 13–14.

12. For a discussion of the relationship between Queen Esther and the prayer of intercession, see Mosley, *Edith Stein*, *op. cit.*, pp. 96–104.

13. See the discussion 'Prophecy in our charism', in Anne Henderson, OCD, 'So Simple a Root: Some Strands of Spirituality in the Carmelite Rule', in *Mount Carmel*, vol. 50/1, 2002, pp. 13–14.

14. For a splendid treatment of the significance of this term in the Scriptures, see Peter G Van Breeman, SJ, *The God Who Won't Let Go*, Notre Dame, IN: Ave Maria Press, 2001, Chapter 6, 'I have chosen you to go out and to bear fruit', pp. 71–9.

Chapter 4
JESUS AND THE MYSTERY OF HUMAN SUFFERING

The treasure of the church

The Gospels were not written like any ordinary books. They record the traditions of the early church, oral and written, transmitted over many decades. In these traditions there is growth and development, and we can distinguish three stages. The first may be called the 'Christ-event': the life and teachings of Jesus prior to the Ascension. The next stage followed on from this when the early church, under the action of the Holy Spirit, penetrated ever more deeply with the passage of time into the mystery of the person of Jesus, his words and his actions, and expressed it in both a written and an oral tradition. As we are told by Vatican II: 'after the ascension of the Lord the apostles handed on to their hearers what [Jesus] had said and done. This they did with that clearer understanding which they enjoyed after they had been instructed by the events of Christ's risen life and taught by the light of the Spirit of truth' (DV 19).

Then comes the third stage: that of the Gospels, written by the four evangelists. 'The sacred authors,' we are told, 'wrote the four Gospels, selecting some things from the many which had been handed on by word of mouth or in writing, reducing some of them to a synthesis, explicating some things in view of the situation of their churches, and preserving the form of proclamation but always in such fashion that they told us the honest truth about Jesus' (DV 19). The originality of the evangelists' approach to the life of Jesus in no way lessened their total fidelity to the gospel traditions. The Gospels are not purely the literary work of individual writers. They are proclamations of the church.

The passion of Jesus, for example, is the treasure of the church, and it is the church that gives it to us. The narratives of the passion, like the rest of the Gospels, are based on the apostolic preaching and expressed by disciples fully authorised to do so: 'This is the disciple who is bearing witness to these things, and who has written these things,' we are told by way of conclusion to the Gospel of John, 'and we know that his testimony is true' (Jn 21:24). And Luke begins his own Gospel by pointing out that his sources of Jesus' life include 'eyewitnesses' (Lk 1:2) and that he aims to recount the 'truth' (Lk 1:4) concerning these things.

But this witness of the inspired authors of the Gospels in no way impeded the personal touch of each evangelist. Luke, for example, brings into his account of the passion many observations which are proper to his narrative alone and which, often enough, are related to the gospel traditions expressed in John. Matthew and Mark are very close to one another. Each one, however, has elements which pertain to him alone. The individual evangelist has his own proper emphasis and his own specific perspective on the life – and passion – of Jesus.

A unified whole

The passion narratives were born in the heart of the church.[1] Significantly, they appear to have been the first part of the Gospels to have taken on a unified shape. The public life or ministry of Jesus, for example, is made up of a sequence of events in all four Gospels which can easily be separated from one another. Not so the story of the passion. It was already the object of special attention and regarded as a unified whole, with its main parts intimately and inseparably connected in the early church tradition.

A comparison of all four Gospels bears this out. Regarding the ministry of Jesus, it is clear that, in general, the Fourth Gospel differs considerably from the other three Gospels and provides us with a great deal of facts which are not included in the others; John mentions, for example, a number of Jesus' stays in Jerusalem, and this completely transforms the arrangement of the ministry from how it is presented in Matthew, Mark and Luke. However, when we look at the passion accounts, we find they are remarkably similar. All four Gospels agree on the broad outline of events and their general order: the arrest of Jesus, the Jewish trial, the Roman trial, and the crucifixion. There is no variation by any of the evangelists in this sequence of events. It seems, then, that an account of the passion, beginning with the arrest of Jesus in Gethsemane, had been formed early on in the tradition of the early church; or that there was at least an arrangement which fixed the essential lines of the passion story before ever the Gospels were written.

'Witnesses of the resurrection'

Clearly, the passion story took on special importance in the eyes of the first Christians. This is significant – because at first sight this is, to say the least, surprising. We know that the passion accounts were written in retrospect: that is, with hindsight, in the full light of the resurrection. They help us to reflect on the importance of the passion in the perspective of the early church, where the passion holds not just an important place but, in a sense, a disproportionately large place in the understanding of the first Christians. Thanks to our familiarity with the Gospels, we accept this unquestioningly. But this should not be taken for granted.

The Gospels were written by authors who lived in the full light of the triumph of the resurrection and who were aware that they themselves were 'witnesses to the resurrection' (cf. Acts 1:22; 2:32; 3:15; 1Cor 15:14; Rm 10:9). Why, then, such insistence on the painful scenes of the passion? Why not place greater stress on the more 'positive' aspects of Jesus' life? In his ministry, Jesus is the great wonder-worker and popular preacher, captivating the crowds with his teaching (cf. Jn 7:46; Lk 4:22); and during his ministry, we are told of his *triumph* over death (cf. Jn 14:30–31;

16:33). All these 'positive' aspects, not to mention his resurrection appearances and the birth of the church launched on its mission to the world in the power of the Spirit (cf. Jn 20:21–23), might reasonably be expected to occupy a more prominent position in the Gospels – and the passion could then have been seen as an unfortunate interlude. Or so it would seem. But such was not the case.

A baffling mystery

Indeed, nothing could be further from the truth. Christianity is not a religion of evasion; it does not minimise the bruising aspects of the life of Jesus and the baffling mystery of human suffering, especially of innocent suffering. Between the passion and the resurrection, we perceive a stark contrast: it would seem that the passion is a defeat, and the resurrection a victory which overturns this defeat. The passion humiliates, the resurrection glorifies. Yet in the Christian vision, the passion and resurrection are inseparable and form an indivisible unity. There is a close bond between them: the glory of the resurrection is the fruit of the passion. And this glory shows that the passion is not really a defeat: it is a victorious event, a true fulfilment of God's design (cf. Jn 14:30–31; 16:33).

Christians have always considered the passion itself to be a light and a treasure. Far from shunning the gruesome aspects of the passion, they have pondered it and reflected on it, penetrating ever more deeply into the mystery. The length and depth of the gospel accounts, together with all their recorded details, are unassailable proof of this. The passion accounts challenge us to face the baffling and disconcerting aspects of human life, however painful they may be to bear. The resurrection gives them value. It teaches us to embrace them more fully, more confidently. The light of the resurrection reveals the value of the passion, and so invests our own life experience with a special importance and a deep spiritual meaning.

Suffering's fruitfulness

There was nothing in the traditions of the Jewish people linking the promised Messiah with suffering, pain, abasement, failure and humiliation. There is, however, a line of biblical tradition which attests to the fruitfulness of personal suffering in God's design. It has its foundation in the story of several outstanding Old Testament characters. Abraham leads Isaac to the slaughter at God's command – a passage which anticipates the Mount of Calvary: 'Take your son, your only son Isaac, whom you love, and go to the land of Moriah, and offer him there as a burnt offering upon one of the mountains of which I shall tell you' (Gn 22:2). While God intervenes to prevent the sacrifice, Abraham's faith is proved during this testing and he becomes the father of all believers[2] and receives the promise that his descendants will be as many 'as the stars of heaven and as the sand which is on the seashore' (Gn 22:17). Joseph, sold by his envious brothers to some passing merchants, becomes their eventual saviour in exile. Through him they receive this assurance: 'God will be with you, and will bring you again to the land of your fathers' (Gn 48:21).

But there are also examples where the fruitfulness of suffering is not apparent, except with the eyes of faith. Moses is rejected by the people whom he has led to freedom: 'Israel murmured against Moses… "you have brought us out into this wilderness to kill this whole assembly with hunger"' (Ex 16:2–3). Prophets are rejected as they proclaim the word of God and, with it, challenge the conscience of the rebellious Israelites. The plaintive tones of the just in their suffering fill the psalms with their sobbing music: 'How long, O Lord? Will you hide yourself for ever?' (Ps 88:47); 'This is what causes my grief; that the way of the Most High has changed' (Ps 76:11). Perhaps nobody has grappled more intensely with the problem of innocent suffering than Job – yet he concludes with a change of heart: 'I was the man who misrepresented [God's] intentions… I retract what I have said, and repent in dust and ashes' (Jb 42:3.6).

The Suffering Servant

This imposing array of biblical figures reaches its summit in Isaiah's prophecy of the Suffering Servant (cf. Is 52:13–53:12). The Servant is 'disfigured', he seems 'no longer human', 'without beauty, without majesty', 'despised and rejected', 'familiar with suffering' (Is 52:14; 53:2.3). So debased is he, in fact, that all are astonished and startled at the sight (cf. Is 52:15). He is '[without] form or comeliness... a man of sorrows... Surely he has borne our griefs and carried our sorrows... stricken, smitten by God, and afflicted... with his stripes we are healed... no deceit in his mouth... it was the will of the Lord to crush him with suffering' (Is 53:2–5.9–10).

But this should be compared with the framework of the portrait. At the outset, we are told: 'See, my servant will prosper, he shall be lifted up, exalted, rise to great heights' (Is 52:13); and at the end, we have the reassuring words: 'Hence I will grant whole hordes for his tribute, he shall divide the spoil with the mighty' (Is 53:12). The contrast between portrait and framework is striking![3] In the Suffering Servant, the depths of humiliation and degradation are united with the heights of greatness and exaltation. His humiliation and suffering are the paradoxical means chosen by God to bring about the glorification of his Servant. It is a spectacle almost beyond belief. Indeed, the question is asked: 'Who could believe what we have heard?' (Is 53:1). This is a challenge to faith.

The mystery gradually unfolds. In this weakness, there is a manifestation of 'the power of the Lord' (Is 53:1). The pain and suffering are not a punishment from God for the sins of the Servant himself: 'we thought of him as...struck by God, and brought low' (Is 53:4), Isaiah tells us. But they were wrong: the Servant is entirely blameless, without fault. 'By force and by law he was taken...though he had done no wrong and there had been no perjury in his mouth' (Is 53:8.9). Moreover, the sufferings all have a place in God's mysterious plan of redemption: 'It was the will of the Lord to crush him with suffering... through him what the Lord wishes will be done' (Is 53:10).

But if he is blameless, then why did he have to suffer? The answer for Isaiah is clear: he gave his life in sacrifice as 'an offering for sin... bore the sin of many, and made intercession for the transgressors... ours were the sufferings he bore, ours the sorrows he carried... he was bearing the faults of many... he was pierced through for our faults, crushed for our sins... The Lord burdened him with the sins of all of us' (Is 53:10.12.4–6). His sufferings are vicarious – that is, he carried them for others: 'through his wounds we are healed' (Is 53:5).

'The folly of the cross'

The Suffering Servant, portrayed in Isaiah, was not, however, the Messiah of Jewish expectations. The tradition of the Messiah and that of the Suffering Servant were never united in the Old Testament Jewish tradition. There is nothing anywhere in the traditions of God's people linking the Messiah with the pain, abasement and humiliation of God's Servant. This shattering revelation had to await the coming of Christ. The union of the two in the person of Jesus is the dazzling light that blinded the minds of his listeners, the disciples no less than the crowds. It is a central revelation of Mark's Gospel: Jesus is the *suffering Messiah*.

This was something entirely new, unexpected, astounding. Jesus had to try and stun people into accepting it. The whole arrangement of Mark shows how this Gospel pivots around this central insight. It is often said that Mark's Gospel, more than the others, is the Gospel of *proclamation*, the 'kerygmatic' Gospel. What it proclaims is the bald facts, indeed the disconcerting facts: the contradiction, rejection and misunderstanding of Jesus; his loneliness, weakness and failures. It is all part of that terrible realism and *starkness* of Mark. He is not afraid to startle us, scare us, stun us, jog us out of our complacency, and disturb us.[4] He plunges us into the darkness of human weakness and human suffering, and underlines the paradox that the cross is the scandal which reveals the Son of God.

All through the first part of Mark's Gospel, we have questions (cf. Mk 1:27; 2:6.8; 4:41; 6:2). And we note that they all have something in common: they are questions about the identity of Jesus. Who is he? We are left in suspense, waiting for an answer. Then comes the great turning-point in the Gospel, the scene at Caesarea Philippi (Mk 8:27–30). 'Who do people say that I am?' (Mk 8:27), Jesus asks his disciples. Peter answers in the name of all: 'You are the Christ' (Mk 8:29). Right answer! Jesus is the 'Christ', the 'Anointed One' – that is, the Messiah. But not a victorious wonder-worker expected to restore the political power of Israel. So Jesus now reveals that he is to be the *suffering* Messiah. He foretells his passion: 'The Son of man must suffer...be rejected...and killed, and after three days rise again' (Mk 8:31). Peter is appalled. He remonstrates with Jesus. But Jesus rebukes Peter harshly: 'Get behind me, Satan!' (Mk 8:33). There must be no mistaking his message. This is a hard saying, a profound mystery: the *suffering* Messiah. We are challenged to an act of faith – to finding light in the darkness. It requires submission to this mystery: that *Jesus saves through suffering.*

Through darkness to the light

Mark will arrange the entire second part of his Gospel around three predictions of the passion and resurrection (cf. Mk 8:31; 9:31; 10:32–34). It is within the framework of this triple foretelling that Mark gives us his teaching on discipleship, which is clearly linked to the mystery of suffering. After the first prediction, we hear the words: 'If any want to become my followers, let them deny themselves and take up their cross and follow me. For those who want to save their life will lose it, and those who lose their life for my sake, and for the sake of the gospel, will save it' (Mk 8:34–35). After the second prediction, we are told that Jesus turns to his disciples and asks, 'What were you discussing on the way?' (Mk 9:33). There is a momentary pause. 'They were silent,' Mark tells us, and adds that they were discussing 'who was the greatest' (Mk 9:34). Then Jesus takes a little child and sets the child in their midst. *Here*, he tells them with this eloquent gesture, they have true greatness! When, after the third predic-tion, we find the sons of Zebedee asking for the places of honour in the kingdom, Jesus replies, 'Are you able to drink the cup that I drink, or to be baptised with the baptism with which I am bap-tised?' (Mk 10:38). Immediately, Jesus gives us his great lesson on discipleship: 'For the Son of man came not to be served but to serve, and to give his life as a ransom for many' (Mk 10:45).

This is total service unto death, and it is the same road for every follower of Jesus: the way of Jesus himself, through his passion and death to the resurrection – a dying and a rising. It is the way of the paschal mystery, through the darkness to the light.

A journey of faith

This is the journey of faith in Mark – out of the darkness and into the light. Significantly, he introduces the ascent of Jesus to Jerusalem – to his passion and resurrection – with the account of the cure of a blind man (Mk 8:22–26). And he ends this journey with the cure of another blind man: Bartimaeus, the blind beggar (Mk 10:46–52). Both these episodes illustrate the movement of faith in Mark's Gospel. The first of these cures is worth quoting in full:

> They came to Bethsaida. Some people brought a blind man to him and begged him to touch him. He took the blind man by the hand and led him out of the village; and when he had put saliva on his eyes and laid his hands on him, he asked him, 'Can you see anything?' And the man looked up and said, 'I can see people, but they look like trees, walking.' Then Jesus laid his hands on his eyes again; and he looked intently and his sight was restored, and he saw everything clearly. (Mk 8:22–26)

This is a miracle in slow motion. We see the blind man groping his way out of the darkness and into the light. At first, things are still blurred, not yet in focus; until finally, he comes gradu-ally to clear vision. Out of the darkness and into the light – this is a meaningful image of faith in Mark's Gospel. It is an action symbolic of the painful challenge for every follower of Jesus who has to grope gradually in faith to accept the mystery of human suffering. It is never easy.

The cure of the other blind man, Bartimaeus, at the end of Jesus' journey to Jerusalem, is also highly important. Especially so the last verse of the story: 'Jesus said to him, "Go; your faith has made you well." Immediately he regained his sight and followed him on the way' (Mk 10:52). On the way! We know that Jesus is 'on the way' to his passion, death and resurrection (cf. Mk 10:32). Here again, at the heart of Mark's teaching on discipleship, we have the challenge of seeing with the eyes of faith inseparably linked with the paschal mystery. These two miracles express the whole movement of Mark's Gospel where light shimmers through, even in the thickest darkness. They also illustrate the journey of faith as a continual groping through the night towards the first streaks of dawn. It is a following of Jesus in faith along the way of his dying and his rising.

Even the whole thrust of Mark's Gospel is a movement out of the darkness and into the light – a movement that emerges ever more clearly as the ministry of Jesus unfolds. We see this illustrated beautifully for us in one of Jesus' parables. It is found only in Mark (cf. Mk 4:26–29), so it clearly has a special significance for the evangelist. It tells how the seed sprouts and grows in the depths of the earth, without the sower being aware of it. It edges its way, imperceptibly, towards the light while 'the earth produces of itself, first the stalk, then the head, then the full grain in the head' (Mk 4:28). Mark's Gospel has rightly been called 'a Gospel of veiled epiphanies' – shrouded in general darkness, but at the same time filled with revelations and manifestations of light. Even in moments of thickest darkness, brightness always seems to shimmer through.

'Out of the depths'

In Mark, the earliest of the Gospels, we see how the early church, right from the outset, valued the teaching of Jesus on prayer and reverently contemplated the example of Jesus himself at prayer. From among Mark's references to prayer, we might say that he distils the essence of his understanding of prayer into a few brief sentences spoken by Jesus about faith:

> Have faith in God. Truly, I say to you, if you say to this mountain, 'Be taken up and cast into the sea', and if you do not doubt in your heart, but believe that what you say will come to pass, it will be done for you. Therefore I tell you, whatever you ask for in prayer, believe that you have received it, and you will. (Mk 11:22–24)

This teaching of Mark on prayer is embodied for us in the story of Bartimaeus (cf. Mk 10:46–52), which we have just encountered. There, we have not just a teaching on trust and confidence, but many other dimensions of Mark's teachings on faith. We are told that Bartimaeus is a *blind* beggar – blind, sightless, *in the dark*. A beggar *in need*. Apparently, there is *no human remedy* for his affliction. It is an impossible situation. It is like saying to a mountain, 'Be taken up and cast into the sea'. But we are told that Jesus is passing by, so there is a chance for an *encounter with Jesus*. That is what prayer is: an encounter with Jesus, a meeting with him in faith.

Bartimaeus has faith in God. Out of the darkness of his own weakness and suffering, he cries for help. It is a *cry of faith*: 'Jesus, Son of David, have mercy on me!' (Mk 10:47). We notice, though, that Bartimaeus also has a *determined and persevering faith* – or, to use other words from Mark about prayer, he 'does not doubt in his heart, but believes that what he says will come to pass' (cf. Mk 11:23). And it *is* done for him. He will not be discouraged in his efforts. Many of the bystanders, we are told, rebuke him, telling him to be silent. But he cries out even more loudly, 'Son of David, have mercy on me!' (Mk 10:48).

What Bartimaeus has asked for in prayer, he believes that he will receive, and he does. Out of the darkness comes the light. Jesus stops and calls him, discovering him in his need. And Jesus asks him: 'What do you want me to do for you?'

(Mk 10:51). The blind man replies, 'Teacher, let me see again' (Mk 10:51) – *a cry for light in the darkness.* Jesus says to him, 'Go; your faith has made you well' (Mk 10:52). Immediately, the man regains his sight and follows Jesus 'on the way' – which, as we have seen, also means the 'way' of the *passion, death and resurrection.* Bartimaeus is drawn out of his human suffering, misery and weakness through the power of his prayer – *out of the darkness and into the light.*

Gethsemane prayer

Finally, we have the powerful example of Jesus himself at prayer in the garden. The whole of Mark's teaching on prayer is exemplified in his portrayal of Jesus in Gethsemane (cf. Mk 14:32–42).[5] Here, the evangelist is at pains to underline for us the weakness of Jesus in the garden, his sheer physical exhaustion. He tells us that Jesus falls on the ground (cf. Mk 14:35). But the word that he uses describes a repeated action: it implies that Jesus keeps on falling, again and again. Mark also tells us that Jesus 'began to be distressed and agitated. And he said to them, "I am deeply grieved, even to death"' (Mk 14:33–34). Jesus is seized with horror and distress. The *New English Bible* captures well his strong emotions at prayer, his surprise and terror and grief. It translates them with these words: 'Horror and dismay came over him, and he said to them, "My heart is ready to break with grief."'

However, the original language used by Mark is even more graphic: Jesus begins to be 'utterly dismayed' – the 'ekthambeîsthai' of the original has the crushing impact of a sudden clap of thunder – and, literally, 'to be out of his mind' ('adēmoneîn') with grief. Still his disciples fail to understand. Jesus finds them asleep: 'the spirit indeed is willing,' he tells them, 'but the flesh is weak' (Mk 14:38). We are then told that Jesus again left his disciples 'and prayed, saying the same words' (Mk 14:39). The 'same words' can undoubtedly refer to the previous prayer of Jesus: 'Abba, Father, all things are possible for you; remove this cup from me; yet, not what I want, but what you want' (Mk 14:36).

But not necessarily so. These 'words' can also be a prayer referring directly to what Jesus has just said: 'the spirit indeed is willing, but the flesh is weak' (Mk 14:38) – something which Jesus himself was experiencing while at prayer. As one scholar expresses it: Jesus 'has realized his own weakness.'[6]

Jesus had warned his disciples at the outset: 'remain here, and keep awake' (Mk 14:34). Now, he warns them again to keep awake, but this time he adds the word 'pray': 'Keep awake and pray that you may not come into the time of trial' (Mk 14:38). The message is: keep on watching, keep on praying. Jesus himself, at prayer in the garden of Gethsemane, is an example of this. For the disciple of Jesus, there will be a time of testing. Determination will be needed – strength for the battle. Survival is the fruit of persevering prayer.

Mark also stresses the loneliness of Jesus, his deep need for human companionship. We may remember that Jesus withdraws from his disciples three times in that scene and returns to them again three times. Matthew stresses the fact that Jesus *withdraws* from the disciples three times (cf. Mt 26:39.42.44). Mark does not tell us, at least not explicitly, that Jesus goes away three times; but significantly he stresses the fact that Jesus *returns* three times (cf. Mk 14:37.40.41). Jesus – in his prayer, in his anguish – needs the companionship of his disciples. He is lonely.

Moreover, Jesus prays not just once, but over and over again 'that, if it were possible, the hour might pass from him' (Mk 14:35). He says, 'Abba, Father, all things are possible for you; remove this cup from me; yet, not what I want, but what you want' (Mk 14:36). He means it. This 'cup' is the chalice not just of intense pain and death, but also of failure. The one thing that Jesus has come to accomplish is to unite and gather around himself a community. Yet the one effect of his passion and death will be to scatter that very community, as foretold in this prophecy, of which Jesus had reminded his disciples when they were on their way to Gethsemane: 'I will strike the shepherd, and the sheep will be scattered' (Mk 14:27; cf. Zech 13:7). But Jesus struggles in prayer, through darkness and human weakness, to discover the light of God's will: 'yet, not what I want, but what you want' (Mk 14:36).

Calvary anticipated

In these terrible circumstances, it is a real battle for Jesus to discover God's will and to surrender to it. He does so in the desolation of darkness; and finally he submits. Jesus is devastated by fear in Gethsemane. He looks for comfort from friends and an escape from death. He finds neither. In his total identification with human weakness, Jesus certainly knows the fear of extreme suffering and dying, but there is never any denial of that fear. He has to struggle with it in the garden – sorrow, confusion, anguish, loneliness. 'Remove this cup from me' (Mk 14:36), he prays – and we might think his prayer is not heard. Yet we are told that 'he was heard for his humble submission' (Hb 5:7). Yes, he comes to accept fully the mystery of evil and suffering; and in it he surrenders to the mystery of love: 'Abba, Father,...not what I want, but what you want' (Mk 14:36).

Gethsemane anticipates Calvary – for Jesus will die in abandonment and isolation: 'My God, my God, why have you forsaken me?' (Mk 15:34). *Why?* We will never know fully why. But through this experience of abandonment, Jesus does plunge more deeply into the mystery of God's love. The pain is part of that mystery. Jesus recoils from pain with every fibre of his natural being. But he surrenders in the mystery of it to the mystery of love. Or, to express it with these oft-quoted, profound words by Paul Claudel: 'God did not come to eliminate suffering, he did not come to explain it, but he came to fill it with his presence.'

A different dimension of suffering

John's presentation of the passion stands out in striking contrast to that of Mark, and indeed to that of Matthew and Luke. The sufferings of Jesus do not seem to take on the same importance as they do in the other Gospels where the physical sufferings are sharply emphasised. Somehow or other, the details of Christ's *physical sufferings* seem to matter much less to John. The crucifixion itself is described in the fewest possible words: 'And he went out, bearing his own cross, to the place called the place of the skull, which is called in Hebrew Golgotha. There they crucified him, and with him two others, one on either side, and Jesus between them' (Jn 19:17–18). This great saving event is told in the simplest of words: 'they crucified him'. There is a lessening of the effects. And the same is true of John's whole passion narrative. There are, of course, some details given in John – details, interestingly, which the other evangelists do not give: the opening of Christ's side, for example; the division of his garments; the presence of Mary at the foot of the cross. But the physical sufferings are passed over, or at least they are not emphasised.

This is all very strange. Still, there must be some reason for it. Why then, we may ask, did John pass over the terrible details of Christ's physical sufferings? We could, of course, say that the sufferings of Jesus were indescribable, so John took refuge in silence. But then, why did the other evangelists not do the same? No, there must be some other reason. The fourth evangelist must want us to pass over the *physical sufferings* and dwell on something else: *a different dimension of the reality of suffering.*

'Full of grace and truth'

Reading John's Gospel is very much like reading a play. The evangelist gives us an extended prologue (cf. Jn 1:1–18). And with this, we immediately enter into a new world of the unknown – a world of mystery, a world of wonder, a world of eternal truths: 'In the beginning was the Word, and the Word was with God, and the Word was God' (Jn 1:1). The origin of John's Gospel is born of eternity, far back in the timeless life of God. But everything then moves forward to an astounding revelation: eternity touches earth! 'The Word was made flesh…,' we read, 'full of grace and truth' (Jn 1:14) – that is, full of God's abiding love, his covenant love revealed to us in the God-made-man: 'a God merciful and gracious, slow to anger, and abounding in steadfast love and faithfulness, keeping steadfast love…' (Ex 34:6–7). The eternal relationship between Father and Son is revealed to us as *love*, and John will explore and expand this love-relationship as his Gospel unfolds: 'the Father loves the Son, and has given all things into his hands... The Father loves the Son, and shows him all that he himself is doing...' (Jn 3:35; 5:20).

Jesus in turn reciprocates that love. In anticipation of his passion and death, he unveils the inner relationship between himself and his Father in terms of love: 'For this reason the Father loves me, because I lay down my life, that I may take it up again... this command I have received from my Father' (Jn 10:17–18). And as he enters into his passion, he tells us: 'I do as the Father has commanded me, so that the world may know that I love the Father' (Jn 14:31). John invites us to think of the passion as the ultimate and supreme expression of God's love in Jesus: 'God so loved the world that he gave his only Son' (Jn 3:16); '[Jesus] loved his own who were in the world, he loved them to the end' (Jn 13:1). These significant words, 'to the end' ('eis télos'), point us forward to the final utterance of Jesus on the cross (Jn 19:30; cf. 19:28): 'It is ended' ('Tetélestai'). Love's last words were uttered in pain. His pain, freely accepted, was the completion of his love. This is the truth that dominates the whole passion narrative in John.

A world of darkness

But even in John's world of eternal truths, serene and timeless, there is a suggestion of tension. The jarring note rings out in the words: 'He came unto his own, and his own received him not' (Jn 1:11). All drama turns on conflict, and this element is already there in the prologue. Then, as we leave the prologue and turn over the pages of John's Gospel, we are still at this play. Scene after scene flashes across the mind, often with little or no obvious connection. It is no longer just a simple narrative. We are listening to dialogue. Moreover, we share in the dialogue almost without knowing it. We are actors in the drama. Nicodemus, for example, speaks, but it is we who speak together with him.

Yet even in these short scenes, so moving in their simple beauty, we find again the element of conflict. In the exchange with Nicodemus, in the encounter by Jacob's well, at the marriage feast of Cana, at the cleansing of the temple, at the scene with the woman taken in adultery, at the promise of the Eucharist, the dramatic movement repeats itself. There is tension, conflict, a climax – then acceptance or rejection. At face value, it seems to be Jesus and the Jews that clash; but at a more essential level, it is Jesus and the world; Jesus and Satan; the world of belief and unbelief; the world of light and darkness. At the Last Supper, Jesus prepares his disciples for future conflicts: 'If the world hates you, know that it has hated me before it hated you... If they persecuted me, they will persecute you... They hated me without cause... The hour is coming when those who kill you will think they are offering service to God' (Jn 15:18.20.25; 16:2). The conflict will widen to embrace the whole world and last until the end of time. It is all part of the mystery of suffering in John.

The 'hour' of Jesus

As we have seen, everything in John hurries on to an unknown 'hour'. We first hear of it at Cana: 'Woman, what is that to you and to me? My hour has not yet come' (Jn 2:4). No details are given. All through the Gospel, we are waiting for the 'hour'. Jesus keeps referring back to it; his thoughts are full of it. The disciples even urge Jesus to hasten this hour. Jesus answers quietly, calmly, serenely: 'My time has not yet come' (Jn 7:6) – there is no haste. It is, we know, an hour of danger: 'No one laid hands on him,' we are told, 'because his hour had not yet come' (Jn 8:20).

As the passion draws near, Jesus begins to shrink from this 'hour': 'Now is my soul troubled. And what shall I say? "Father, save me from this hour"?' (Jn 12:27). It is to be a terrible hour for Jesus, but it is also to be the supreme moment of his life: 'For this I was born, and for this I have come into the world' (Jn 18:37). It is a moment of *exaltation*: 'And I, if I be lifted up from the earth, will draw everyone to myself' (Jn 12:32). It is also, paradoxically, an hour of *glory*: 'Father, the hour has come; glorify your Son'

(Jn 17:1) – because the perfection of love is God's glory fully revealed. Moreover, it is a time of *judgment*: 'Now is the judgment of this world' (Jn 12:31). But most importantly of all, it is an hour of *triumph*: 'Now will the prince of this world be cast out' (Jn 12:31). And when the Last Supper is over, and the curtain rises on the trial scene of the passion, again we are watching the same dramatic movement. The tension grows and mounts to a climax. And that climax will come when Pilate leads Jesus out before the Jews for the last time and declares: 'Behold your King!' (Jn 19:14).

A new Passover

This scene is a moment of crisis, a climax. Every little detail is pressed into service to convey the impact. We are told that Pilate presented Jesus to the crowd in a place called 'The Pavement' ('Lithóstrōton'). Significantly, we are also told that the place was called, in Hebrew, 'Gabbatha' (cf. Jn 19:13). This word designates a *height* or an *eminence*. And it is on this height that Pilate proclaims the kingship of Christ. The importance of the scene deepens: this moment of crisis is a moment of *exaltation*. The circumstances of time, too, are extremely telling: 'It was the Day of Preparation of the Passover' and 'about the sixth hour' (Jn 19:14). So, the moment when Pilate exclaimed, 'Behold your King!' was the exact time when the Jews began to celebrate the Passover.

This was the feast that spoke to God's people of their escape from their terrible years of slavery. As Jesus faced his chosen people, a *new* Passover was beginning. Once again, the lamb was ready for the slaughter (cf. Ex 12:1–13) – the Lamb of God. The hand of God was reaching out in mercy to save his own people. Slavery – the slavery to sin – would soon be at an end. Liberty – the freedom of the children of God – was at hand. Israel's history had reached another climax, a turning-point. The Messiah appears before his chosen people. He is their King.

A King of mockery

There is one other important detail in John's description of this scene: it was, as some commentators have pointed out, *Jesus*, not Pilate, who sat down on the judgment seat. Translations often ignore this possible interpretation of John 19:13, where the original language can have either meaning. The English version of the *Jerusalem Bible*, for example, states that Pilate 'seated himself on the chair of judgment'; whereas the *New Jerusalem Bible*, like the French *Bible de Jérusalem*, tells us that Pilate 'seated [Jesus] on the chair of judgment'. To have Pilate sit there in judgment is to miss the deeper symbolic import of the scene.[7] Now is the Son of Man glorified: the King is seated on his throne. And this throne is a judgment seat. 'This is the judgment,' we read in an earlier scene, 'that the light has come into the world, and people preferred darkness to the light' (Jn 3:19). In fact, Jesus does not judge: God's people judge themselves – if they reject the light. Now we can see the scene in all its blinding and dazzling splendour. Jesus is sitting in judgment before his chosen people – he is their King. Not a word is spoken: he will not judge, for he has come to save his people. He is still the light of the world, but the light is shining in the darkness and the darkness cannot comprehend it.

The light of God's wisdom is streaming from the eyes of Jesus. In it, we see everything God values. That light is shining out against the so-called wisdom of the world. But God's people have no eyes for the folly of God, for the foolishness of God is wiser than human wisdom (cf. 1Cor 1:25). Worldly values crumble, new values are born – and it is a terrible birth. A man can stand in silence before a mob howling for his blood. He is making a last appeal for acceptance. He is crowned with thorns; he is the object of ridicule, the outcast of his people. Still he is a king sitting on his throne in majesty, in triumph, in power. Covered with wounds, he is a king in all his glory. We need new eyes of faith to bear the searing light of God's love. 'This is the victory which overcomes the world: our faith' (1Jn 5:4).

Love enthroned on Calvary

We can now look at the crucifixion through the eyes of John. His account is in striking contrast to that of the other evangelists. As mentioned, John does not want us to examine too closely the physical sufferings of Jesus. There is nothing harrowing about John's account of the crucifixion, nothing turbulent or spectacular. There are no passers-by in his account to taunt the Son of God; no elders to mock and deride him; no rulers to toss their heads; no soldiers to blaspheme. Nature, too, is silent. No turmoil breaks the stillness. There is no earthquake. The rocks do not split. The graves do not open and send forth their dead. The veil of the temple is not rent asunder. Darkness does not cover the earth. There is no centurion to strike his breast and proclaim Jesus as Son of God. Even Jesus himself hardly breaks the silence. We hear no prayer of forgiveness for his executioners, no sigh of anguish from his desolate soul, no word of consolation for the penitent thief. Only twice does he speak, and then quietly – never, as in the other Gospels, 'with a loud voice' (Mk 15:37; Mt 27:46; Lk 23:46). Even his last breath is drawn in peace: '"It is ended",' he said, 'and having bowed his head, he gave up the spirit' (Jn 19:30).

On the cross, Jesus is again the King on his throne: 'Jesus of Nazareth, King of the Jews' (Jn 19:19). He is making a final advance of love, pleading with his chosen people. He is silent still; he did not come to judge, he came to save. But his own receive him not. The cross is radiant with love, but people have no eyes for the light of God's wisdom, no eyes for the foolishness of the cross: 'the word of the cross is folly to those who are perishing... he was crucified in weakness, but lives by the power of God' (1Cor 1:18; 2Cor 13:4). And we who 'are weak in him... shall live with him by the power of God' (2Cor 13:4).

Beset with weakness

It was in this very weakness of Jesus in his passion that Teresa discovered a God lowering himself to share in her own weakness (cf. Ph 2:7). 'Christ is a very good friend,' she wrote, 'because we behold Him as man and see Him with weaknesses and trials' (*Life* 22:10); 'I saw that He was man, even though He was God; that He wasn't surprised by human weaknesses; that He understands our miserable make-up, subject to many falls... I can speak with Him as with a friend, even though He is Lord' (*Life* 37:5). God's self-lowering and his disguise in Jesus never ceased to touch Teresa deeply: 'He came from the bosom of His Father out of obedience to become our slave' (F 5:17), she tells us. And she reminds us that we are 'useless servants' (Lk 17:10), fortunate 'to be able to repay [God] something of what we owe Him for His service toward us'. 'I say these words "His service toward us" unwillingly,' she continues; 'but the fact is that He did nothing else but serve us all the time He lived in this world' (IC III:1:8). Teresa does not even hesitate to speak of Jesus as our slave: 'there is no slave who would willingly say he is a slave,' she explains, 'and yet it seems that Jesus is honoured to be one' (WP 33:4).

'The scene of His prayer in the garden, especially,' she tells us, 'was a comfort to me; I strove to be His companion there. If I could, I thought of the sweat and agony He had undergone in that place. I desired to wipe away the sweat He so painfully experienced... I remained with Him as long as my thoughts allowed me to... Most nights, for many years before going to bed..., I always pondered for a little while this episode of the prayer in the garden' (*Life* 9:4). But she had to pass through a number of 'conversions' before her so-called 'final conversion' in 1554.

This was not quite a Damascus experience – a once-for-all lightning transformation. It was, rather, the culmination of a gradual process. Teresa said of her early years: 'so hard was my heart that I could read the entire Passion without shedding a tear' (*Life* 3:1). But one day in the convent chapel of the Incarnation, when she was praying before the *Ecce Homo* statue of the blood-stained figure of Christ, the sight of the 'much wounded Christ' evoked in her 'what He suffered for us' in such a vivid and lifelike way that 'it seems to me,' she said, 'my heart broke' (*Life* 9:1).[8] Teresa's remarks on the self-abasement of God in the life and passion of Jesus are like a commentary on the gospel passage, 'the Son of man came not to be served but to serve, and to give his life as a ransom for many' (Mk 10:45). And they plumb the depths of these words of St Paul about Jesus: 'He emptied himself, taking the form of a slave, becoming as human beings are; and being in every way like a human being, he was humbler yet, even to accepting death, death on a cross' (Ph 2:7–8).

Lovers of the cross

It is hardly surprising that the faithful sons and daughters of Teresa are, like her, true lovers of the wisdom of the cross. Each of the saints we are considering here travelled in the wake of the Suffering Servant by way of their own painful experiences. Edith Stein, a Jewish convert, first discovered the mystery of the cross when she was still an agnostic. A good friend of hers, Adolf Reinach, had been killed in the war. He and his wife Anne were Christians, converts from Judaism. Edith wondered how she might possibly be able to comfort the bereaved widow. But she observed, in amazement, how the young woman had accepted the pain of her husband's death. And incredibly, it was Anne's strength that consoled Edith. This meeting made a deep and lasting impression on Edith who said of it, years later: 'This was my first encounter with the Cross and the divine strength that it inspires in those who bear it… It was the moment in which… Christ radiated before me: Christ in the mystery of the Cross.'[9]

Edith now faced the challenge which Paul describes: 'we proclaim Christ crucified, a stumbling block to Jews and foolishness to Gentiles, but to those who are called, both Jews and Greeks, Christ the power of God and the wisdom of God. For God's foolishness is wiser than human wisdom, and God's weakness is stronger than human strength' (1Cor 1:23–25). Here was a face of God which until then had been unknown to Edith. It impelled her to follow Christ by carrying the cross, and it revealed this to her as the special vocation of the Christian. She writes, in an article entitled, 'Love of the Cross': 'The Saviour is not alone on the way of the cross... The lovers of the cross whom he has awakened and will always continue to awaken anew in the changeable history of the struggling church, these are his allies at the end of time. We, too, are called for that purpose' (HL, p. 92).

'The hidden beauties of Jesus'

Thérèse of Lisieux entered deeply through the Servant Song of Isaiah (cf. Is 52:13–53:12) into the mystery of suffering.[10] There, she discovered the love that is both hidden and revealed in human weakness. Her own father had always radiated for her the beauty of God's love. But now, suddenly stricken with mental illness, he was beset with anguish and looked a mere semblance of his former self. At this time, Thérèse confided to her sister Pauline: 'These words of Isaias [from the Song of the Suffering Servant]...have made the whole foundation of my devotion to the Holy Face, or, to express it better, the foundation of all my piety' (LC, p. 135). Thérèse would now contemplate Jesus, the suffering Messiah, his radiant face distorted by pain, like a beautiful object reflected on rippling water. It was this image of a suffering God that opened up for her the mystery of God's love and inspired her to remove all the layers of selfishness in herself, and to give herself totally to God for others. She expressed this divesting of herself with a simple image: it was, she says, like unpetalling a rose (cf. PN 51). This expression may at first sight appear childish and sentimental. But the reality it speaks of is a total and absolute self-giving in response to love, revealed in what Thérèse calls 'the HIDDEN BEAUTIES of Jesus' (LT 108) as the Suffering Servant.

The Jesus whom Thérèse found in the Gospels was the Word made weakness: 'I must have a God who... / is able to suffer' (PN 23:4), she wrote. The Jesus of Thérèse is the Suffering Servant; he 'sweated blood' (cf. Lk 22:44) and 'offered up prayers and supplications, with loud cries and tears' (Hb 5:7). On the way to Calvary, he stumbled and fell – again and again and again. And this is what makes Thérèse remarkably original in her approach to suffering. She assures us that we do not have to suffer heroically, or even courageously. The worst kind of suffering, she tells us, is not being able to suffer *well* – though by 'well' she does not mean 'grandly'. 'What an unspeakable joy to carry our Crosses FEEBLY' (LT 82), she writes to her sister Céline. And again: 'Let us suffer...without courage!... (Jesus suffered in *sadness*! Without sadness would the soul suffer!...) And still we would like to suffer generously, grandly!... Céline! what an illusion!... We'd never want to fall?... What does it matter, my Jesus, if I fall at each moment; *I see* my weakness through this and this is a great gain for me...' (LT 89).

Contemplating the Crucified

For Elizabeth of the Trinity, as for Thérèse, God's love was inseparable from the passion of Jesus. Elizabeth longed in particular to be transformed into Christ crucified, at one with him as in these words of St Paul that she loved so much: 'to share in his sufferings, reproducing the pattern of his death' (Ph 3:10; cf. HF 28). Another passage from St Paul that was one of Elizabeth's favourites captures perfectly the abiding disposition of her heart: 'With Christ I hang upon the cross, and yet I am alive; or rather, not I; it is Christ that lives in me. True, I am living, here and now, this mortal life; but my real life is the faith I have in the Son of God, who loved me, and delivered himself up for me' (Gal 2:19–20; cf. L 214; LR 13). In her celebrated *Prayer to the Trinity*, Elizabeth distilled into a few lines the essence of her response to Love Crucified: 'O my beloved Christ, crucified by love,...I wish to love You...even unto death! But I feel my weakness, and I ask You to "clothe me with Yourself"...that I may be another humanity for [You] in which [You] can renew [Your] whole Mystery' (cf. PT; Gal 3:27).

Elizabeth does not hesitate to sum up her Carmelite vocation and its fruitfulness for the whole Church as a calling to live at one with Christ crucified, the ever-present object of her contemplation: 'A Carmelite...is a soul who has *gazed on the Crucified*, who has seen Him offering Himself to His Father as a Victim for souls and, recollecting herself in this great vision of the charity of Christ, has understood the passionate love of His soul, and has wanted to give herself as He did!' (L 133). However weak and vulnerable she felt herself to be, she knew she was united with Christ and her suffering was fruitful; and so, she could identify with Paul's words: 'I rejoice in my sufferings...' (Col 1:24; cf. GV 7). She lived out her own counsel, given to a young friend: 'a soul united to Jesus is a living smile that radiates Him and gives Him!' (L 252). Others attest to her ever-cheerful disposition: 'loveable and engaging even during the most acute sufferings of her last days... Her smile never left her lips... very forgetful of her own sufferings.'[11] Elizabeth lived Paul's teaching to the full: 'God loves a cheerful giver' (2Cor 9:7). In her, grace was the hidden smile of her soul.

Wisdom through the cross

John of the Cross was no stranger to deep suffering; and yet few, if any, have entered more deeply into the mystery of God's love concealed and revealed in the wisdom of the cross. When he has led us to the heights of holiness in his *Spiritual Canticle*, he pauses to share with us his final word on the value of pain and suffering in God's loving plan of salvation. He speaks of entering 'further, deep into the thicket' (SC, stanza 36) and explains: 'Oh! If we could but now fully understand how a soul cannot reach the thicket and wisdom of the riches of God, which are of many kinds, without entering the thicket of many kinds of suffering, finding in this her delight and consolation; and how a soul with an authentic desire for divine wisdom wants suffering first in order to enter this wisdom by the thicket of the cross!... The gate entering into these riches of his wisdom is the cross' (SC 36:13).

John also speaks of 'the high caverns in the rock / that are so well concealed' (SC, stanza 37). 'The rock mentioned here,' he explains, 'as St Paul says, is Christ' (cf. 1Cor 10:4). And he continues: 'The high caverns of this rock are the sublime, exalted, and deep mysteries of God's wisdom in Christ' (SC 37:3); they 'are so well concealed,' he adds, because there is 'much to fathom in Christ, for he is like an abundant mine with many recesses of treasures, so that however deep individuals may go they never reach the end or bottom, but rather in every recess find new veins with new riches everywhere' (SC 37:4). But then, John remarks: 'The soul cannot enter these caverns or reach these treasures if, as we said, she does not first pass over to the divine wisdom through the straits of exterior and interior suffering' (SC 37:4). No wonder Paul could cry out: 'O the depth of the riches and wisdom and knowledge of God! How unsearchable are his judgments and how inscrutable his ways!' (Rm 11:33).

At one with Mary

In one brief passage of John's Gospel, we are shown Mary as she stood at the foot of the Cross:

> Near the cross of Jesus stood his mother and his mother's sister, Mary the wife of Clopas, and Mary of Magdala. Seeing his mother and the disciple whom he loved standing near her, Jesus said to his mother, 'Woman, this is your son.' Then to the disciple he said, 'This is your mother.' And from that hour the disciple took her into his own home. (Jn 19:25–27)

Many commentaries have been written about this scene by saints and scholars, and many artists have depicted it for us – poets, sculptors and painters. But even within our own rich Carmelite Marian tradition, there is hardly any better or deeper expression of its meaning than a beautiful poem, or rather prayer, of Edith Stein entitled, 'Juxta Crucem tecum stare' – 'To stand with you by the Cross'. As we shall see, her words capture the profound significance of the scene and speak of her own tender devotion for the Mother of God, as well as her understanding of Mary's place in God's plan of redemption. It reads like a self-portrait of Edith herself, as she stands at one with Mary in sorrow at the death of Jesus.

A Pietà without the Christ

On one occasion, Edith went with a friend to a museum, to see a famous statue of the goddess Athene. Before she reached it, however, she came to a room where her attention was held by a group of sculptured figures on Calvary: Mary, John, the Magdalen and Nicodemus. These sculptures had such an over-powering effect on Edith that it was a long while before she could tear herself away. Before she did so, she observed that there was no figure of Christ in the group (cf. LJF, p. 401).

A few years after her conversion, Edith would spend many hours each Holy Week praying at the Benedictine abbey of Beuron before a statue of the Pietà. It is surely significant that when, years later, Edith was sitting and praying in the transit camp of Westerbork before her final journey to Auschwitz, she was described by one observer as 'a Pietà without the Christ'.[12] For the occasion of Edith's profession day in 1935, a friend sent her a tapestry of a Pietà. This is how Edith describes it: 'Most important, probably, is that it is a real Pietà – Good Friday evening at the Cross. The pain of the Mother of God is as great as the ocean; she is immersed in it. But it is a totally restrained pain: she lays her hand firmly upon her heart so it may not burst. The dropped jaw of the Saviour is an almost frightening symbol that he is really dead. But his head is, almost comfort-ingly, turned toward his Mother. And the cross is very light: the *lignum Crucis* [wood of the Cross] becomes the *lumen Christi* [light of Christ]' (SP, pp. 204–5).

A tender devotion

Edith's poem or prayer, just mentioned, 'Juxta Crucem tecum stare', was written on Good Friday during her retreat before taking her final vows in 1938. It was never meant for publication. So, in a real sense, we are eavesdropping on a most personal, intimate and tender outpouring of Edith's love for Mary. We also see how she understood Mary's place in God's plan of salva-tion; and this reminds us of our sharing – with Mary, and with

Edith – in the redemptive suffering of Jesus. We can reflect on the poem, section by section, knowing that Edith wrote it in the light of her own personal journey into the mystery of the cross. This is how she begins:[13]

> Today I stood with you beneath the cross
> And felt more keenly than I ever did before
> That you, beneath the cross, became our mother.

So, as Edith reminds us, Mary 'stood' beneath the cross: she did not faint; she was a woman strong and firm in her pain. And Edith 'felt' more keenly than she 'ever did before'. This is not Edith the great philosopher speaking; this is Edith the Carmelite sharing with us her own deep prayer-experience. It is, then, an experience even more intense than when she had stood with Mary so many times before – even for hours – in silent prayer at the foot of the cross.

Surrendered to his Being

> Even an earthly mother's faithful love
> Desires to carry out her son's last wish.
> Yet, you are the handmaid of the Lord,
> And surrendered in your entire being and life
> To the Being and Life of God made man.

This is Mary, the 'handmaid' of the Lord – not just Mary as mother of the incarnate God. This is the woman of faith in total surrender to her place in God's plan of salvation: 'Behold, I am the handmaid of the Lord; let it be done to me according to your word' (Lk 1:38). This is Mary, of whom Jesus is speaking in the Gospels when he says: 'Whoever does the will of my Father in heaven is my brother, and sister, and mother... My mother and my brothers are those who hear the word of God and do it... Blessed are those who hear the word of God and keep it' (Mt 12:50; Lk 8:21; 11:28).

Into her heart

> You have taken us into your heart,
> And with the heart's blood of your bitter pains
> Have purchased life that's new for every soul.

Mary has taken us into her heart: 'Woman, this is your son' (Jn 19:26), Jesus says on Calvary. These are not just bland words: they effect what they signify. With these words, then, Jesus does not simply proclaim that Mary is already our mother: he *institutes* her as our mother. And Mary responds: she makes space for all of us in her heart, and there she brings new life to birth in us. Her Son asks us, in turn, to respond by giving a special place to Mary in our hearts, too: 'to the disciple he said, "This is your mother." And from that hour the disciple took her into his own home' (Jn 19:27). This Beloved Disciple, who made a place for Mary in his heart, represents every disciple, every believer.

Hidden in God

> You know us all: our weakness and our wounds.
> You also know the spark of heaven's flame:
> Your Son's love longs to take it
> And pour it on us – an eternal blaze.

Edith is evoking here the humble woman of Nazareth, a person of flesh and blood like ourselves, at one with us in our weakness and our pain. Mary is not someone distant from us, or exalted on a pedestal; she lives the simple, ordinary life of any other housewife of her day in a remote and obscure village. She is a mother immersed in the challenge of daily living, moving calmly and quietly among the pots and the pans and the demands of domestic life. 'No rapture, miracle, or ecstasy' – to recall the expression of Thérèse (cf. PN 54:17) – marks Mary off from others in the humdrum monotony of each uneventful day. It is a life hidden with Christ in God (cf. Col 3:3).

A mother's hand

> You guide our steps with care,
> No price for you too high
> To lead us to the goal.

This is Mary who herself is guided by God, believing 'that what was spoken to her by the Lord would be fulfilled' (Lk 1:45). Mary is always close to us. And being herself guided by the Lord, she now guides us gently with a mother's love and care for all of us, her children. Through our moments of doubt and darkness and the vagaries of our lives, she stands beside us on our calvaries when the night is dark, when we are struggling in the mist of confusion, when we are still on our journey but far from home. It is then that we need her most of all – her strength, her comfort, and the reassuring pressure of a mother's hand.

Companions and heirs

> But those whom you have chosen as companions here,
> Surrounding you one day at the eternal throne,
> We now must stand, with you, beneath the cross
> And purchase, with our heart's blood's bitter pains,
> This spark of heaven for those priceless souls
> Whom God's own Son bequeaths to us, His heirs.

What a beautiful and original commentary are these final words of Edith's on St Paul's teaching, 'If we are children then we are heirs, heirs of God and co-heirs with Christ, provided that we share his suffering, so as to share his glory' (Rm 8:17). Paul even confirms the lesson with his own example: 'I rejoice in my sufferings for your sake, and in my flesh I complete what is lacking in Christ's afflictions for the sake of his body, that is, the church' (Col 1:24). And this is what the scene of Mary at the foot of the cross inspired in Elizabeth, too, as she strove to live her final illness in union with Jesus and his mother:

> [Mary] is there at the foot of the Cross, *standing*, full of strength and courage, and here my Master says to me: 'Ecce

Mater tua.' He gives her to me for my Mother... And now that He has returned to the Father and has substituted me for Himself on the Cross so that 'I may suffer in my body what is lacking in His passion for the sake of His body, which is the Church', the Blessed Virgin is again there to teach me to suffer as He did, to tell me, to make me hear those last songs of His soul which no one else but she, His Mother, could overhear. (LR 41)

This, too, is Edith's invitation to us all. She encourages us to respond with a life of surrender and sacrifice, at one with herself and with Mary, and so to share with them – at one with Jesus – in the redemption of the world. This is not a call to pain and suffering: it is a call to embrace God's plan of love for us, in all the circumstances of our daily lives. It is to stand with Edith, who was known in Carmel as 'Benedicta a Cruce' – 'Blessed by the Cross'. We can all be blessed by the cross if, like Edith, we embrace it as a special act of God's love. Everything is a grace: a gift of God's love.

All suffering redeems

But what of all the masses of suffering humanity who know nothing of Christ? Do our saints, who found purpose in uniting their suffering to his, have anything meaningful to say to us? In *The Mystery of Christmas*, Edith evokes the gentle picture of the stable at Bethlehem, where the followers of the Infant Jesus are drawn to come and be with him. Yet this is no usual crib scene: for along with the shepherds and the Magi are those whom the Child Jesus has called to take up their cross and give their lives for him. There is John, the Beloved Disciple, who followed Jesus all the way to Golgotha. There is Stephen, who was killed as he witnessed to Christ. And, most surprisingly of all: the little ones whom we know as the 'Holy Innocents'.

These are the ones who suffer without knowing why, who have no ideals about offering their life for a higher cause, but who in their innocent suffering have become the followers of

Christ. 'You children,' Edith says to them, 'who as yet cannot give of your own free will, of you these little hands [of the Child Jesus] will request your gentle life before it has even begun; it can serve no better purpose than sacrifice in praise of the Lord' (MC, p. 8). *All* suffering, then, endured willingly or not, whether we are conscious of its value or not, is a participation in Christ's redemptive work. In the end, this is a mystery – as deep and impenetrable as the paschal mystery itself. Only in heaven will it all become clear.

A joy that sustains

But already on this earth, some people are given a deeper glimpse into the mystery of human suffering. As Edith explains so well, and especially by the example of her life: the cross is laid on suffering humanity, but Christians who recognise the cross for what it is should not merely accept passively to have it laid on them but should actively offer to help Christ carry it (cf. HL, pp. 91–3; cf. SEL, p. 17). Our cross would be unbearably hard, were it divorced from the person of Christ. But in fact, our cross is *always* joined to that of Christ. As Elizabeth expresses it: 'Every soul crushed by suffering, in whatever form it may occur, can tell itself: I dwell with Jesus Christ, we are living in intimacy' (L 314). And as Edith points out: 'Voluntary expiatory suffering is what truly and really unites one to the Lord intimately' (HL, p. 92).

So, as we have seen, suffering always takes place *with* Christ, but not always *consciously* with him. To know ourselves one with Christ is what gives us the joy of intimate friendship with him, as well as the joy of knowing that we are helping our sisters and brothers – even if we never see the fruits of our labours, or ever know whom we are helping. This is what sustained Teresa, John, Edith, Thérèse, Elizabeth, and all our Carmelite saints, whose writings are an inexhaustible treasure on how to live the paschal mystery with Jesus. The cross was ever before their eyes, and the way to this is so simple. To recall the words of Elizabeth: 'Take your Crucifix, look, listen' (L 93).

Notes

1. For a splendid and scholarly treatment of how the passion narratives were formed in the early church, see Albert Vanhoye, SJ, *Structure and Theology of the Accounts of the Passion in the Synoptic Gospels*, Collegeville, MN: The Liturgical Press, 1967.

2. 'Abraham, our father in faith', we read at Mass in the first Eucharistic Prayer; see also Ecclus 44:19–21; Jn 8:56; Rm 4:16–25.

3. There is the same contrast in the prophetic Psalm about the Suffering Servant which begins, 'My God, my God, why have you forsaken me?' (Ps 21:2), and ends with him declaring God's faithfulness and deliverance of the nations: 'These things the Lord has done' (Ps 21:32).

4. We find a parallel to the stark realism of Mark's approach in some of the modern, realistic Stations of the Cross; a striking example is the 'Golgotha of Jasna Gora' by the Polish artist Jerzy Duda Gracz in Czestochowa.

5. For a comprehensive study of the Gethsemane prayer, see Stanley, *Jesus in Gethsemane, op. cit.*

6. Stanley observes: 'Usually, *the same words* are understood to refer to the articulated prayer in v. 36, and Jesus is thought to repeat the petition he had already made to be released by the Father from the drinking of *this cup*. While this is, of course, not implausible, I venture to suggest that he now prays to God about the human dilemma, which he has just voiced: *The spirit indeed is willing, yet the flesh is weak*. Jesus…has realized his own weakness.': see *ibid.*, p. 143.

7. See Ignace de la Potterie, SJ, 'Jesus King and Judge according to John 19:13', in *Scripture*, vol. 13, 1961, pp. 97–111.

8. This was not a statue of Christ bound to the column, as is sometimes thought, but an *Ecce Homo* statue – so named after Pilate's words, 'Behold the man' (Jn 19:5). It is still venerated at the monastery of the Incarnation in Avila: see *The Collected Works of St. Teresa of Avila*, vol. 1, Washington, DC: ICS Publications, 1987, p. 471.

9. In Posselt, *Edith Stein, op. cit.*, pp. 59–60.

10. For an excellent discussion of Thérèse's experience of suffering in her life, and the inspiration she took from Isaiah's portrayal of the Suffering Servant, see Vincent O'Hara, OCD, '"His face was as though hidden": St Thérèse's Understanding of Suffering', in *Mount Carmel*, vol. 48/4, 2001, pp. 25–33.

11. Curia Generalis OCD (Secretarius pro Monialibus), *To Be a Carmelite with the Blessed Elizabeth of the Trinity* [Chapter 18 of the series *Guidelines*

for study following the order contained in the Declarations], Rome: Discalced Carmelite Order, n.d., pp. 37–9.

12. In Mosley, *Edith Stein, op. cit.*, p. 55.

13. The version followed here is that by Joanne Mosley, in *Mount Carmel*, vol. 50/1, 2002, p. 64 (with two revisions in this chapter, based on another German source). See also the translations in Posselt, *Edith Stein, op. cit.*, p. 84 (by Sr M Julian, RSM), and Mosley, *Edith Stein, op. cit.*, pp. 92–3.

Chapter 5
AT PRAYER WITH THE HOLY SPIRIT

The Spirit helps us in our weakness

The Holy Spirit is fundamental for understanding the Scriptures and the mystery of Christian prayer. At prayer, we would be powerless without the Spirit. As Paul reminds us: 'the Spirit helps us in our weakness; for we do not know how to pray as we ought, but the Spirit himself intercedes for us with sighs too deep for words' (Rm 8:26). So we need to begin by considering carefully some of the insights from the New Testament into the role of the Holy Spirit, and to linger on the words that pertain directly to the Spirit's action in our lives. It is also important to discern the Spirit's action in our reading of the Scriptures. For this we can fruitfully turn not only to Scripture but also, in the second half of this chapter, to the teachings of our Carmelite saints – writings that are filled with penetrating insights into the mystery of God as revealed to our saints in Scripture and in prayer, under the action of the Spirit who guides and enlightens.

The Gospel of John contains some extremely rich texts on the Holy Spirit, especially those known as the Paraclete passages;[1] there is nothing comparable to them in any of the other Gospels. The Synoptics do, of course, refer to the Spirit, such as his role of speaking through the believer in times of trial (cf. Mk 13:11; Mt 10:19–20; Lk 12:11–12). But it is in John – the summit and climax of an extended gospel tradition on prayer – that we can enter most deeply into the profound riches of the mysterious workings of the Spirit. Little wonder that the Fourth Gospel has been rightly called the *spiritual* Gospel – a word which we should not think of solely in terms of 'spirituality' as such, but in relation to the Holy Spirit. In fact, the whole teaching of John's Gospel, as we shall see, is contained within a framework of the action of the Holy Spirit (cf. Jn 1:32–33; 20:22). Moreover, when we read this Gospel in the light of the passion-resurrection of Jesus, a still deeper spiritual sense unfolds: through the revealing action of the Spirit who, as Jesus says, 'will teach you everything, and remind you of all I have said to you' (Jn 14:26; cf. 2:22; 12:16).

Prayer books of the Spirit

The church receives the Gospels from the Spirit. He is their principal author, inspiring the evangelists. The Gospels were born and came into being under the Spirit's action in the heart of the praying church, and they express the community's lived experience of the Christ-event. As said earlier, they are the church's treasure, and it is the church that gives them to us. To approach the Gospels with the church today – open, like the first community of believers, to the action of that same Spirit – is already to pray 'in spirit and truth' (Jn 4:23.24). It is to read the word of God in the bond of love that unites all believers, and to root our experience in the community dimension of the Gospels. It is to pray at one with the community of all believers, guided by the Spirit who leads the church ever more deeply into eternal truth.

There is no such thing as *private* prayer. Personal prayer, yes – but not private prayer. Our prayer has value, not because it is *my* prayer but because it is the prayer of the *church*. John's Gospel especially – even a brief survey of it – affirms this community dimension of the Spirit's action. We find its origins when the Baptist introduces Jesus to the world with these words: 'I saw the Spirit descend *like a dove* from heaven, and it remained on him' (Jn 1:32). Straightaway, this calls to mind the image of the Spirit *hovering* like a bird over the primeval waters in the first lines of Genesis: 'Earth was still an empty waste, and darkness hung over the deep; but already, over its waters, *stirred* the breath of God' (Gn 1:2). Jesus is introduced here as the inaugurator of a new creation. He will create a new community.

The Spirit 'remains' on Jesus who in turn is to 'baptise': to make disciples 'born of water and the Spirit' (Jn 3:5; cf. 1:33). Later in the Gospel, Jesus promises the outpouring of that Spirit like 'torrents of living water' (Jn 7:38). But 'the Spirit had not yet been given, because Jesus had not yet been glorified' (Jn 7:39) through his passion-resurrection. On the cross, Jesus finally 'handed over the Spirit' (Jn 19:30) to the community, and the risen Jesus 'breathed' new life into his disciples with the words: 'Receive the Holy Spirit' (Jn 20:22). The movement of the Gospel now comes full circle, completing the framework, because the promise at the outset – to form disciples 'with the Holy Spirit' (Jn 1:33) – is fulfilled at the end. And so, the church is born through the Spirit and launched on its mission to the world. In union with that same Spirit, we pray the Scriptures within a community of faith, and bear fruit in our lives through the saving power of the word.

Our eyes fixed on Jesus

In the Paraclete passages, John specifies more precisely *how* the Spirit works as we pray the Gospels.[2] The Spirit is the 'Spirit of truth' (Jn 14:17; 15:26; 16:13), and he bears witness to Jesus who *himself* is 'the truth' (Jn 14:6). We will respond to the guidance of the Spirit in prayer if we 'look to Jesus the pioneer and perfecter of our faith' (cf. Hb 12:2), to use the expression found in Hebrews. We must never withdraw from the Word made flesh: Jesus is 'full of grace and truth... he is the way, the truth and the life...' (Jn 1:14; 14:6); 'In many and various ways God spoke of old to our fathers by the prophets; but in these last days he has spoken to us by a Son' (Hb 1:1–2).

These words are simply repeating the gospel lesson, 'Listen to him' (Mk 9:7; Lk 9:35). Each of the Gospels speaks to us about Jesus, and each of the evangelists opens up new facets on the mystery of his person. Their insights are not mutually exclusive, and they complement each other perfectly. The truth remains ever inexhaustible; glimpses of it are always partial. It is a question of emphasis. So, each of us can pray freely with our preferred gospel passages and with our favourite evangelist. The saints did. 'The Spirit breathes where it wills' (Jn 3:8) – and, led by the Spirit, each of us travels a secret path to God. It is the same Spirit who is always guiding us to the one Jesus, 'the same yesterday and today and forever' (Hb 13:8).

An indwelling presence

There are many modes of the Spirit's presence and many variations of his action. 'I will pray the Father, and he will give you another Paraclete, to be with you forever' (Jn 14:16), Jesus says. Here, he is speaking of his abiding presence in the church through the Spirit until the end of time: 'I am with you all days' (Mt 28:20). As Joan of Arc famously replied to her ecclesiastical accusers: for her, Christ and the Church are one. In John Masefield's play, *The Trial of Jesus*, the wife of Pilate asks the centurion who stood at the foot of the cross, 'Do you think he is dead?' 'No, lady, I don't,' he replies. 'Then where is he?' she asks. And the answer: 'Let loose in the world.'[3] It is only through the Spirit that we can meet the risen Jesus, present in the word of God and in the depths of our hearts: no longer limited, confined or conditioned by time and space. This is the lesson of Paul in his prayer for his first converts: 'This, then, is what I pray, kneeling before the Father... Out of his infinite glory, may he give you the power, through the Spirit, for your inner selves to grow strong, so that Christ may live in your hearts through faith...' (Eph 3:14.16–17).

But Jesus goes on to speak of another presence of the Spirit after his passion-resurrection. This companion, friend, consoler, helper and advocate with the Father will not just be *with* the disciples (cf. Jn 14:16): 'he will be *in* you' (Jn 14:17), Jesus says to them – this Spirit will be living and working deep *within* us as Jesus' disciples. So it is an *indwelling* presence, as Paul emphasises: 'Do you not know that you are God's temple and that God's Spirit dwells in you?... your body is a temple of the Holy Spirit within you... we are the temple of the living God' (1Cor 3:16; 6:19; 2Cor 6:16).

The precise nature of the Spirit's action will only gradually unfold. But Jesus does make clear the conditions for this action of the Spirit within us: to believe and to love. That is, we must come to the Gospels with the spiritual eye of *faith*. The word of God is '*not some human thinking*', it 'is still *a living power at work in believers*' (1Th 2:13). And we must receive the Spirit with an *open heart*: 'Those who love me will keep my word, and my Father will love them, and we will come to them and make our home with them' (Jn 14:23). The message of the Gospels is like 'a lamp shining in a dark place, until the day [of eternity] dawns and the morning star rises in your hearts' (2Pt 1:19). We glimpse the meaning only dimly now, as in a mirror; the full riches of God's word will take an eternity to unfold.

Promptings of the Spirit

When we pray the Gospels, the Spirit is our teacher: he 'will teach you everything' (Jn 14:26), we are told. And Jesus further explains *how*: he will '*remind you* of all I have said to you' (Jn 14:26). This action of *reminding* or *recalling* has a special significance in John. Consider the scene where Jesus cleanses the temple and says: 'Destroy this temple, and in three days I will raise it up' (Jn 2:19). There, the evangelist explains: 'When Jesus rose from the dead, his disciples *remembered* that he had said this; and they believed the scripture and the word which Jesus had spoken' (Jn 2:22). They did not merely recall *the actual words* of Jesus and the inspired texts of Scripture (cf. Ps 68:10). Enlightened by the Spirit, they realised afterwards *the deeper significance of them* – that is, *how these had been fulfilled*: that he had been speaking of 'the temple of his body' (Jn 2:21), to be transformed into the New Temple through his passion, death and resurrection. So, too, when Jesus enters Jerusalem in triumph as a 'king' (Jn 12:13.15), we are told: 'At first the disciples did not understand this, but after Jesus had been glorified, they *remembered* that this had been written about him and that this had happened to him' (Jn 12:16). Again, it is not just a simple recalling of the Scriptures (cf. Ps 117:26; Zech 9:9) and of an actual historical event. Rather, the past words and actions of Jesus become effective again, here and now, and take on significance and meaning in the light of the Spirit's teaching. Jesus' words and actions once more become present with their saving power.

Likewise, when we read the words of Jesus in the Gospels, we allow ourselves to be *read by them*. His words take on relevance and significance for us *in the concrete circumstances of our own experience*. The Spirit makes the word of God a word for *me* at this present moment. We should read the Gospels in the light of our own *personal* experience – as did Newman, who gives this moving advice: 'let [the] heart at length be ploughed by some keen grief or deep anxiety, and Scripture is *a new book*'.[4]

Jerome, in his Latin version of the Bible, the *Vulgate*, uses the term 'suggeret' to translate this 'recalling' action of the Spirit (cf. Jn 14:26). It captures the meaning beautifully. The Spirit teaches by *suggesting*. St Paul tells us not to 'grieve the Holy Spirit of God' (Eph 4:30) by refusing to accept his inspirations. The Spirit invites a response. There is no constraint, no force, no compulsion. He draws us gently and quietly with his promptings in prayer – his suggestions urging us, as it were, to a free and open acceptance. The words and actions of Jesus can suddenly become alive with new meaning, by the power of the Spirit, when something happens in our lives. This is often how the Spirit works: through our life-experiences.

Prayer of the heart

Pascal once wrote that 'the heart has its reasons of which reason knows nothing'.[5] The Psalms also speak of 'the thoughts of [the] heart' (Ps 18:15). For the author of Hebrews, the word of God is 'sharper than any two-edged sword, piercing to the division of soul and spirit, of joints and marrow, and discerning the thoughts and intentions of the heart' (Hb 4:12). The Latin rendering for the act of 'recalling' is 'recordare' – from 're'-'again', 'cor'-'heart', 'dare'-'to give' – meaning precisely: giving (handing over or entrusting) something to the heart. This is the movement of God's word from the head to the heart as it seeps into the deepest core of our being under the 'recalling' action of the Spirit. Isaiah compares the word of God to 'the rain and the snow' descending into the soil, 'making it yield and giving growth' (Is 55:10). When we read Scripture, it is destined ultimately to penetrate our hearts, the place where we commune directly with God in prayer.

The Bible speaks of the heart more than a thousand times and sees it as the perennial spring of prayer. Jesus laments, using the words of Isaiah: 'This people honours me with their lips, but their heart is far from me' (Mk 7:6; cf. Is 29:13). Prayer is indeed an affair of the heart, where the word of God sinks deep within us and is 'alive and active' (Hb 4:12) through the presence of the Spirit. This is the *new heart* promised by the prophets: 'A *new heart* I will give you, and a *new spirit* I will put *within you*' (Ez 36:26); 'I will put my law within them, and I will write it upon their hearts' (Jer 31:33). This 'new heart' and 'new spirit' foreshadow the gift of God's own love, his eternal love, his covenant love. 'The Lord, the Lord, a God merciful and gracious, slow to anger and abounding in steadfast love and faithfulness, keeping steadfast love for thousands...' (Ex 34:6–7) – Jesus prayed that this same everlasting love with which his Father loved him might be in all believers, and also that he himself might be in them (cf. Jn 17:26).

God's love is 'poured out in our hearts through the Holy Spirit who has been given to us' (Rm 5:5). Paul refers to us as 'a letter from Christ...written not with ink but with the Spirit of the living God, not on tablets of stone but on tablets of human hearts' (2Cor 3:3). Moreover, our heart, this place 'within', is for the followers of Jesus the 'inner room' where he invites his disciples to pray: 'When you pray, go into your [inner] room and shut the door and pray to your Father who is in secret; and your Father who sees in secret will reward you' (Mt 6:6). Vatican II states that 'the word of God...remains...the food of the soul, the pure and perennial source of spiritual life', and that 'in the sacred books, the Father who is in heaven meets His children with great love and speaks with them' (DV 21). Prayer accompanies a true reading of the word of God – and the Spirit releases the power of God's eternal love within us when we pray.

'Into all truth'

As we pray the Gospels, John tells us, 'the Spirit...will lead [us] into all truth' (Jn 16:13). This means, literally, 'will guide [us] along the *way* of truth'. The phrase echoes earlier words of Jesus: 'I am the *way*, the truth and the life' (Jn 14:6). Both terms – 'way' and 'lead' – recall the *way* God *led* his people on their exodus journey. In the life of Jesus, this desert journey becomes a *new exodus*. It is his passage out of this world to the Father: literally, his 'Passover' (Jn 13:1) from death to life.

This, too, is the pattern of the Spirit's action when we pray the Gospels. At one with Jesus, we are led by the Spirit along the way of the exodus through the paschal mystery, dying and rising as we journey in faith 'into all truth', revealed in the Jesus of the Gospels. Faith is not something fixed or static. It is powerful, dynamic – a movement. Significantly, as we have seen, John never uses the noun 'faith'; it is always the verb 'believe'. Nor does he ever speak of believing 'in'; it is always believing 'into' Jesus. The truth of God's word can always unfold more fully as we pray the Gospels, penetrating more deeply into them through faith. St Ephraem, one of the Eastern Fathers, expressed the idea well:

> Lord, who can grasp all the wealth of just one of your words? What we understand is much less than what we leave behind, like thirsty people who drink from a fountain. For your word, Lord, has many shades of meaning just as those who study it have many different points of view. The Lord has coloured his words with many hues so that each person who studies it can see in it what he loves. He has hidden many treasures in his word so that each of us is enriched as we meditate on it. The word of God...is like that rock opened in the *desert* that from all its parts gave forth a spiritual drink.[6]

The Spirit listens

To hear the voiceless word of God in the Scriptures, we need a listening heart. This was God's first lesson to his people: 'Hear, O Israel...' (Dt 6:4). The command is echoed repeatedly on the lips of the prophets as they recalled the people from wandering after false gods and called them back to their first allegiance, supporting and encouraging them in their times of trial. To listen is the mark of a true disciple: 'The Lord has given me a disciple's tongue,' Isaiah tells us, 'for me to know how to give a word of comfort to the weary. Each morning he wakes me to hear, to listen like a disciple. The Lord God has opened my ear and I have not resisted' (Is 50:4–5). This is a listening much deeper, even, than to the sound of words. Only a highly sensitive heart can catch the deeper resonance in another's voice, beat in unison with it, and feel the hidden pain. This is empathy. To listen like this to the noiseless promptings of the Spirit of truth is the mark of every true disciple. 'Everyone who is of the truth,' Jesus reminds us, 'listens to my voice' (Jn 18:37).

Listening opens us to the inner mystery of God. The listening heart of Jesus is always alert and attentive to the word of his Father. As he says to his disciples: 'I have made known to you all that I have *heard* from my Father' (Jn 15:15). His early years with Mary and Joseph were spent in listening: 'He went down with them and came to Nazareth, and was obedient to them' (Lk 2:51) – 'obedient' in the root sense of the word, which means literally 'to listen' (from the Latin 'ob-audire'). We find him, aged twelve, in the temple, listening to the teachers and asking them questions (cf. Lk 2:46). His were the probings of a listener waiting expectantly for an answer.

Likewise, the Spirit also listens: 'he will not speak from himself,' Jesus tells us, 'but whatever he *hears* he will speak' (Jn 16:13). When we read the Gospels at one with this listening Spirit, we are drawn into God through Jesus who is always turned '*towards* the bosom of the Father' (Jn 1:18). Jesus is not just *in* the Father, but the whole thrust of his being is a dynamic movement directed eternally *into* the heart of God (cf. Jn 1:1). He is always open so as to receive everything from the Father, and he returns everything to him in a total self-giving, just as in turn he passes on everything to others: 'All that the Father has is mine; therefore I said that [the Spirit] will take what is mine and declare it to you' (Jn 16:15). To share this eternal listening in the heart of God is to enter into a loving communion of persons – Father, Son and Spirit. It is to share in a silent dialogue, a timeless giving and receiving, an eternal exchange of love. It is to pray.

Manifestations of God

The teaching role of the Spirit is described as 'to declare'. The original Greek term for this, 'anangéllō', is given three times (cf. Jn 16:13–15). Here, though, it does not refer to a public proclamation of the message, nor does it refer to a completely new revelation. It means, rather, *to throw light on something hidden and mysterious*; to clarify an obscure saying (cf. Jn 16:25); to explain its deeper meaning. So, it is no coincidence that we find it in the Book of Daniel, in the sense of interpreting dreams and visions (cf. Dn 2:2.27; 5:15; 9:23).[7]

Revelation in John, just like faith, is never something inert or static. It is never merely about ideas. It is life-giving: 'the words that I have spoken to you are spirit and life' (Jn 6:63). It implies communication and enables the believer to penetrate into the inner life of God and to live in communion with the Father through the Spirit in the Son (cf. Jn 4:23–24). Received in faith, revelation enables us to become 'participants of the divine nature' (2Pt 1:4), sharing in an eternal exchange and dialogue of love: 'we declare to you what we have seen and heard, so that you also may have fellowship with us; and truly our fellowship is with the Father and with his Son Jesus Christ' (1Jn 1:3). It is the Spirit who quickens and activates that fellowship, releasing and enkindling the fire of God's eternal love within us when we pray.

The Spirit, we are told, will declare to believers 'the things that are to come' (Jn 16:13). In the historical setting of the Last

Supper, when Jesus announces this, these 'things' are the events of his passion-resurrection. They are repeatedly designated in John, as we have seen, as the 'hour' of Jesus.[8] The Spirit will reveal this 'hour' – not just reminding the disciples of it later, and throwing light on its true significance, but also *making it present* in the church until the end of time. It is like a still-point in the vortex of salvation history: everything pivots around it – past, present and future. The Spirit will give believers an understanding of the whole new final order of redemption ushered in by this 'hour', the new order of divine providence issuing from the passion-resurrection of Jesus – the 'eschatological age', as it is called, or the 'final days'. The Spirit will disclose the meaning of history in the light of the life and teaching of Jesus – deepening, clarifying and developing it. He will show in all things the design of God's plan of redemption (cf. Acts 20:27), shedding on every event, in every place and in every age, the radiant light of the truth revealed in Jesus. In this way, the Spirit will 'glorify' Jesus (Jn 16:14; cf. 17:1–5), releasing through the word the saving power of God's love made manifest in Jesus. 'O God, [you] manifest your almighty power above all by pardoning and showing mercy…'[9] Yes, God is glorified most of all in showing mercy.

Strength for the trial

Jesus is a witness, as he himself tells us: 'For this I was born, and for this I have come into the world, to *testify* to the truth' (Jn 18:37; cf. 18:19–20). So, too, the Spirit will be a witness. The lesson is explicit: 'he will testify on my behalf' (Jn 15:26), Jesus says – literally, he will bear witness *to* Jesus. The immediate context helps to determine the precise nature of the Spirit's witness. Jesus has just spoken about the future hostility of the world – the hatred and persecution which his followers will have to endure as his disciples: 'If the world hates you, be aware that it hated me before it hated you… Servants are not greater than their master. If they persecuted me, they will persecute you… They hated me without a cause' (Jn 15:18.20.25). Then he explains the need for the Spirit's witness: 'I have said these things to you to keep you from stumbling' (Jn 16:1) – literally, 'to keep you from being scandalised', which in gospel terms means to lose faith in Jesus (cf. Jn 6:61; Mk 6:3).

The witness of the Spirit, then, will support the disciples in their trials of faith. As the Church prays so rightly: 'Strengthen in our hearts the faith you have given us, so that no trials may quench the fire your Spirit has kindled within us.'[10] And again, in words which occur in the immediate context of a Paraclete passage about the Spirit bearing witness to Jesus in time of trial (cf. Jn 15:26–27), Jesus spells out the hostility and even danger that the disciples will have to face. 'They will put you out of the synagogues' (Jn 16:2), Jesus says, meaning that his followers will be expelled from the community; they will even be put to death, for 'the hour is coming when those who kill you will think they are offering service to God' (Jn 16:2; cf. 15:18–25).

This witness of the Spirit, like his teaching, is directed not to the world, but to the disciples: 'When the Paraclete comes,' Jesus says, 'whom I will send to *you*...' (Jn 15:26). And: 'if I do not go away, the Paraclete will not come to *you*; but if I go, I will send him to *you*' (Jn 16:7). The Spirit will strengthen, support and encourage believers, as well as enlighten them when their faith and endurance are sternly put to the test. In the midst of hostility and adversity, the Spirit will act secretly within believers and bear witness to Jesus as the truth – in opposition to the emptiness, falsity and pride of an unbelieving world that has deliberately rejected Jesus and is steeped in the darkness of its own sin: 'If I had not come and spoken to them, they would not have sin; but now they have no excuse for their sin' (Jn 15:22).

The inner witness of the Spirit

John's Gospel draws our attention explicitly to the witness of the disciples, too: 'You also are to testify' (Jn 15:27). The other Gospels, likewise, speak of the disciples' witness in a context of hostility: the world's hatred (Mt 24:9; cf. Jn 15:18–19); persecution on account of Jesus (Mt 10:23; Lk 21:12; cf. Jn 15:20); mal-treatment in the synagogues (Mk 13:9; Lk 12:11; 21:12–13; cf.

Jn 16:2). These all form part of the challenge to future witness by the disciples in times of adversity and opposition. But the Spirit will be with them. He will speak through them and in them (cf. Mk 13:11; Mt 10:20). He will also teach them what they should say (cf. Lk 12:12) when they are 'dragged before governors and kings because of [Jesus], as a testimony to them and the Gentiles' (Mt 10:18). A modern 'witness', Whittaker Chambers, describes well this *public* testimony of a disciple:

> A witness, in the sense that I am using the word, is a man whose life and faith are so completely one that when the challenge comes to step out and testify for his faith, he does so, disregarding all risks, accepting all consequences.'[11]

John's is the only Gospel in which the Spirit himself is directly presented as a witness *to Jesus*. The evangelist clearly distinguishes between the *inner* witness of the Spirit and the *external* testimony of the disciples. They are, however, closely linked. St Augustine expresses the difference well: 'Because the Spirit will bear witness, you also will bear witness; he in your hearts, you with your voices; he by inspiring, you by speaking aloud.'[12]

This applies not only to difficult situations but also to difficulties in prayer. We will have moments of doubt and discouragement, and temptations to abandon the struggle and to give up prayer; there will be times when nothing seems to happen in prayer and when there are only distractions, confusion, emptiness and dryness of spirit. Then, the Spirit as witness will act as Defender of Jesus within us, strengthening us in our faith so that, when needed, we will be able to bear public witness to the truth which we have assimilated in our moments of quiet communion with God. As Paul expresses it so well, first recalling words spoken to him by the Lord: '"My grace is sufficient for you, for my power is made perfect in weakness"... when I am weak, then I am strong' (2Cor 12:9.10). Again, Whittaker Chambers helps to illustrate this inner power of the Spirit at work, bearing witness to Jesus in the heart of the believer:

I do not know any way to explain why God's grace touches a man who seems unworthy of it. But neither do I know any other way to explain how a man like myself – tarnished by life, unprepossessing, not brave – could prevail so far against the powers of the world arrayed almost solidly against him, to destroy him and defeat his truth. In this sense, I am [a]...witness to God's grace and to the fortifying power of faith.[13]

An enlightened heart

John develops further the role of the Spirit as witness: 'he will prove the world wrong about sin and righteousness and judgment' (Jn 16:8). The standard translations do not quite capture the meaning of the original, neither the *New Revised Standard Version* as here, nor other major editions of the Bible. The *Revised Standard Version*, for example, reads: 'he will convince the world...', while the *New Jerusalem Bible* has: 'he will show the world how wrong it was...' The original term is 'elénchō'. It is found only twice elsewhere in the Fourth Gospel (cf. Jn 3:20; 8:46), and it means to 'expose', 'bring to light' or 'reveal'. Jesus says, when speaking to Nicodemus: 'For all who do evil hate the light and do not come to the light, so that their deeds may not be exposed ['elenchthê']' (Jn 3:20). In the verse that immediately follows, it is used in exact parallel with the term 'phaneróō', which means to 'expose', 'manifest' or 'make clear': 'But those who do what is true come to the light, so that it may be clearly seen ['phanerōthê'] that their deeds have been done in God' (Jn 3:21).

So, in John's final teaching on the Spirit as witness, we are told explicitly that the Spirit will *bring to light* the world's sin, righteousness and judgment. There is no question here of the Spirit convincing or converting *the world*. The witness of the Spirit is not directed to the world, for in this context the world is still the sphere of darkness and 'cannot receive' the Spirit, 'because it neither sees him nor knows him' (Jn 14:17). As we have seen, the Spirit works secretly *in the heart of the believer*. It is there that he will reveal the truth about everything – showing sin, righteousness and judgment for what they really are.

A critical decision

The Spirit will expose to believers the truth about *sin* – showing it to be essentially unbelief because, in the words of Jesus, those who are of the world 'do not believe in me' (Jn 16:9). This statement is emphatic, indicating that they *refuse* to believe in Jesus – a free, deliberate choice (cf. Jn 14:17). Just as all the commandments can, in John, be reduced to one – 'a new commandment' (Jn 13:34), 'my commandment' (Jn 15:12) of love – so, too, in his Gospel, there is ultimately only one sin. The Baptist exclaims that Jesus 'takes away the sin of the world' (Jn 1:29) – he does not say: 'sins'. All sin is rooted in the refusal to accept Jesus, who is 'the light of the world' (Jn 8:12; 9:5).

The Spirit will show *righteousness* clearly for what it truly is – that is, showing *who is in the right*: Jesus, not the world. Again, Jesus explains why: 'because I am going to the Father,' he says, referring to his victorious return through his passion-resurrection (Jn 16:10; cf. 14:31; 16:33). And he adds, 'you will see me no longer' (Jn 16:10) – by which he means: in his mortal flesh. He will be invisible to the naked eye, but visible to the eyes of faith (cf. Jn 14:17).

The Spirit will also bring to light the true meaning of *judgment* – 'because the ruler of this world,' Jesus explains, 'has been condemned' (Jn 16:11; cf. 12:31). The phrase used here is, literally, 'has been judged' ('kékritai'). Jesus had already promised, in anticipation of his passion-resurrection: 'Now is the judgment of this world; now the ruler of this world will be driven out' (Jn 12:31). And earlier, he had clarified the meaning of 'judgment': 'this is the judgment, that the light has come into the world, and people loved darkness rather than light' (Jn 3:19).

In John, judgment is *self-judgment*, or more precisely self-condemnation: a *choice* for darkness in preference to the light. Jesus says, 'I have come as light into the world, so that everyone who believes in me should not remain in the darkness. I do not judge anyone who hears my words and does not keep them, for I came not to judge the world, but to save the world. The one who rejects me and does not receive my word has a judge; on the last day the word that I have spoken will serve as judge' (Jn 12:46–48). Indeed, Jesus came for division (cf. Lk 2:34; 12:51) – that is, 'decision' ('kríma') on our part (Jn 9:39) – with a challenge freely to accept or to reject the truth of his word. To reject him is to condemn oneself, to embrace willingly the darkness of untruth. To accept him is to be drawn by the Spirit of truth 'out of darkness into his marvellous light' (1Pt 2:9).

The challenge for everyone who wishes to pray is to make a *critical decision* (cf. 'kríma') or honest judgment to turn away from the darkness of sin and reach out towards the One who is the splendour of light and truth – Righteousness itself. The Spirit, as witness to Jesus in the depths of our hearts, is always there to help us.

A deeper, 'spiritual' sense

Our Carmelite saints provide us with their own original insights into these teachings of the Scriptures on the action of the Spirit. Moreover, they invite us to explore more deeply, from their own experience, the mysteries revealed and concealed in the word of God. John of the Cross reminds us that the deeper, 'spiritual' sense has a solid basis in the Scriptures, and he rightly finds support for it in the promise of the Paraclete who will guide the Church into 'all truth':

> God usually affirms, teaches, and promises many things, not so there will be an immediate understanding of them, but so that afterward at the proper time, or when the effect is produced, one may receive light about them. Christ acted this way with his disciples. He told them many parables and maxims the wisdom of which they did not understand until the time for preaching had come, when the Holy Spirit descended on them. The Holy Spirit was to explain to them, as Christ affirmed, all that he had taught them during his life... (2A 20:3; cf. Jn 16:13; 14:26; 2:22; 12:16).[14]

Thérèse repeats this lesson in her own simple way when, speaking of Scripture, she says: 'a single word uncovers for my soul infinite horizons' (LT 226). She is echoing with her own original touch the teaching of Paul who writes: 'What no eye has seen, nor ear heard, nor entered into the human heart,...God has revealed to us through the Spirit. For the Spirit searches everything, even the depths of God... no one comprehends the thoughts of God except the Spirit of God' (1Cor 2:9–11). The word of God, Paul continues, is 'not taught by human wisdom but taught by the Spirit, interpreting spiritual truths to those who possess the Spirit' (1Cor 2:13).

John of the Cross does not hesitate to assure us: 'It would be foolish to think that expressions of love arising from mystical understanding...are fully explainable. The Spirit of the Lord, who abides in us and aids our weakness, as St Paul says, pleads for us with unspeakable groanings in order to manifest what we can neither fully understand nor comprehend... the Holy Spirit, unable to express the fullness of his meaning in ordinary words, utters mysteries in strange figures and likenesses' (SC Prol. 1; cf. Rm 8:26). This is in keeping with the long church tradition of mystical prayer to which Carmel belongs. No wonder Edith Stein could write:

> The mystical stream that flows through all centuries is no spurious tributary that has strayed from the prayer life of the church – it is its deepest life. When this mystical stream breaks through traditional forms, it does so because the Spirit that blows where it will is living in it, this Spirit that has created all traditional forms and must ever create new ones. (HL, p. 15; cf. Jn 3:8)

Without the noise of words

It is sometimes said that our Carmelite saints only rarely speak explicitly of the action of the Holy Spirit. To some degree this is true, though even a cursory glance at the writings of Elizabeth of the Trinity gives the lie to this. She speaks of 'a soul of silence

that remains like a lyre under the mysterious touch of the Holy
Spirit so that He may draw from it divine harmonies' (HF 43).
She assures us that a 'praise of glory' is 'under the action of
the Holy Spirit who effects everything in her' (HF 44). She also
says to her sister, a musician like herself: 'the Holy Spirit will
transform you into a mysterious lyre, which, in silence, beneath
His divine touch, will produce a magnificent canticle to Love'
(L 269). She prays for a priest: 'that the Spirit of Love…may pour
Himself out upon you in overflowing measure' (L 193; cf. 214).
And in another letter she says: 'I will ask the Holy Spirit, He
who alone knows what is in God,…to allow you to penetrate the
unfathomable depths of the Divine Being' (L 274; cf. 1Cor 2:10).

We can so easily forget that it is only through the gift of
the Spirit that the risen Jesus is present, working silently in our
hearts and in the church. It is no doubt for this reason, then,
that the saints do not always feel the need to mention the Spirit
explicitly. The Holy Spirit teaches noiselessly in a most delicate
and subtle way – inspiring, prompting, suggesting, and inviting a
free response: 'Where the Spirit of the Lord is, there is freedom'
(2Cor 3:17). So gentle, quiet and imperceptible are these inspirations of the Spirit that we may never be fully conscious of them.
Teresa herself evokes the gospel image of the Good Shepherd to
explain the delicacy of God's action through the Spirit, drawing
deeper into his mystery those who pray. The Holy Spirit, she
writes, acts like 'a good shepherd, with a whistle so gentle that
even they themselves almost fail to hear it' (IC IV:3:2).

Thérèse gives us two examples of the workings of the Spirit
without any explicit reference to his action. In one of these
classic passages from *Story of a Soul*, she writes:

> I understand and I know from experience that: '*The kingdom
> of God is within you.*' Jesus has no need of books or teachers
> to instruct souls; He teaches without the noise of words.
> Never have I heard Him speak, but I feel that He is within
> me at each moment; He is guiding and inspiring me with
> what I must say and do. I find just when I need them certain

lights that I had not seen until then, and it isn't most frequently during my hours of prayer that these are most abundant but rather in the midst of my daily occupations. (SS, p. 179; cf. Lk 17:21)

What we refer to as the 'sacrament of the present moment' could hardly be described more simply than in these few words. Moreover, Thérèse gives the same lesson in similar terms when, in another passage, she speaks of the hidden and mysterious action of God through the Spirit in the depths of her heart. She writes:

> I have frequently noticed that Jesus doesn't want me to lay up *provisions*; He nourishes me at each moment with a totally new food; I find it within me without my knowing how it is there. I believe it is Jesus Himself hidden in the depths of my poor little heart: He is giving me the grace of acting within me, making me think of all He desires me to do at the present moment. (SS, p. 165)

Longings too deep for words

In spite of our weakness and our feelings of inadequacy, Teresa insists on the importance of great desires. They are inseparably linked with her emphasis on determination and a wholehearted commitment to prayer. For her, there are wonders hidden in the human heart: powerful longings too deep for words. Or, to recall a famous passage from St Paul: 'The Spirit himself intercedes for us with sighs too deep for words' (Rm 8:26). Only the Spirit can give expression to these desires.

Teresa has rightly been hailed by the poet Richard Crashaw as an 'undaunted daughter of desires'.[15] She was astonished at just how much can be done if only we have the courage to attempt great things for God. An insatiable longing for God had been her desire from childhood when she set off with her brother Rodrigo, in the hope of being martyred by the Moors: 'I went because I want to see God,' she later explained to her distraught parents, 'and to see Him we must die.'[16] Teresa was already echoing, unwittingly, the deepest aspirations of every fragile human heart. There is a pain beyond all telling, hidden in the heart of love. It is there also in the heart of prayer – a thirst, and a longing unsatisfied, a reaching out in love.

Thérèse's teaching on prayer is also inseparably linked with these great desires inspired by the Spirit. She gives this brief, but striking, description of prayer:

> For me, *prayer* is an aspiration of the heart, it is a simple glance directed to heaven, it is a cry of gratitude and love in the midst of trial as well as joy; finally, it is something great, supernatural, which expands my soul and unites me to Jesus. (SS, p. 242)[17]

An 'aspiration of the heart'! 'To aspire' means, literally, 'to breathe towards' (from 'spirare' and 'ad') – to long, or to sigh, for *something* or *someone*. In a word, it is to *desire*. When the object is God, it is the ultimate outburst of love – a fling of the heart to the heart of God. But here, we begin to see the originality and depth of Thérèse's understanding of these deep longings for God. For her, as we shall now see, they are inseparably linked with her weakness.

Holiness in weakness

Thérèse tells us that doing great things for God actually comes from acknowledging and accepting our own littleness and weakness. This, she confesses repeatedly, is essential for all who wish to follow her 'Little Way': 'Is there a soul more *little*, more powerless than mine?' (SS, p. 193), she asks; 'I am the smallest of creatures; I know my misery and my feebleness' (SS, p. 195). All these facets of Thérèse's teaching are summed up briefly in one sentence: 'I feel that if You found a soul weaker and littler than mine,...You would be pleased to grant it still greater favours, provided it abandoned itself with total confidence to Your Infinite Mercy' (SS, p. 200).

Yet, for all her 'extreme littleness' (SS, p. 198), Thérèse experiences 'great aspirations' (SS, p. 197), 'measureless desires' (SS,

p. 197), '*infinite desires*' (LT 107), 'desires and longings which reach even unto infinity' (SS, p. 192). She was confused by this and asked the question: 'O Jesus, my Love, my Life, how can I combine these contrasts? How can I realise the desires of my poor *little soul?*' (SS, p. 192). Her 'Little Way' is not a contradiction of the greatness of her desires: it is precisely the 'Little Way' that can provide the explanation. It is a 'Little Way' of vast desires.

The remarkable thing about the 'Little Way' – and this cannot be overemphasised – is that these vast desires of Thérèse sprang from the experience of her own powerlessness and weakness. In fact, the deeper she plunged into the abyss of her own littleness, the greater and more intense her desires became. At an early age, Thérèse already felt that she was destined for '*glory*' – the glory of 'becoming a great *saint*' (SS, p. 72). One incident from her time in Carmel speaks volumes. 'Father,' she said to a visiting priest, 'I want to become a saint, I want to love the Good God as much as St Teresa.' 'What pride and what presumption!' he replied. 'Moderate your rash desires.' Undaunted, she insisted: 'But, Father, I do not regard these as rash desires, I can truly aspire to sanctity, even to a more exalted sanctity, if I wish, than that of St Teresa, for Our Lord has said, "Be perfect as your heavenly Father is perfect." You can see, Father, how vast the field is; and it seems to me that I have the right to run in it.'[18] The words which Thérèse quotes on perfection (Mt 5:48) can be understood in the biblical sense of mercy and holiness: 'Be merciful as your Father is merciful' (Lk 6:36); 'Be holy as God is holy' (cf. 1Pt 1:16; Lv 11:44–45; 19:2; 20:26). Holy as the Spirit of God.

Filled with the Spirit

By the time Thérèse came to describe her 'Little Way', her desires were virtually limitless, infinite. Technically, we might call this an experience of self-transcendence. She found that there was a longing in her that went beyond every boundary, breaking open every goal. The human heart can go to the lengths of God;

it is 'capable of God'.[19] John of the Cross speaks of the 'deep caverns' of the human spirit – its faculties of memory, intellect and will: 'They are as deep as the boundless goods of which they are capable,' he explains, 'since anything less than the infinite fails to fill them' (LF 3:18). And he observes: 'capable of infinite goods,...they cannot receive these infinite goods until they are completely empty' (LF 3:18). Augustine repeats the same lesson: 'This is our life, to be exercised by desire. But we are exercised by holy desire only in so far as we have cut off our longings from the love of the world... empty that which is to be filled.'[20] It was precisely this emptying out of herself, this entering into the profound depths of her own weakness, neediness and nothing-ness, that put Thérèse in touch with her vast desires, her sheer emptiness and capacity for God, for the infinite. And so, she could echo these words of St Paul: 'The love of God has been poured out in our hearts through the Holy Spirit who has been given to us' (Rm 5:5).

The enkindling of the Spirit

Entering into the depths of her own littleness and powerlessness, Thérèse experienced her total capacity for God released in the vast hunger and yearning of her painful desires, which only an infinite God of love could activate and fully satisfy. Her limitless capacity was at full stretch; her restless heart was in the pain of separation but not yet completely at rest in God. Thérèse expe-rienced herself as an immense and limitless capacity for God, and it was precisely her unsatisfied desires that impelled her forward in absolute confidence and trust towards the promised gift of God himself.

At first, Thérèse seemed troubled by her vast desires. But all that changed as they became highly important for her in defining her 'Little Way'. They gave meaning to her experience of endless need, revealing to her the transcendent aspect of what it means to be made for God – fully human in her endless desire and in her openness to be filled with God's love. Thérèse's 'Little Way' is, in fact, a perfect way to be fully human. The challenge is to recognise this, and to live it fully in total confidence, relying unreservedly on God's merciful love. To do this requires a trust as infinite as desire, both of which are reasonable, though they reach beyond reason – 'my own *folly* is this: to trust...' (cf. SS, p. 200), she writes.

To be fully open in order to receive God himself requires a radical self-emptying, like that of Jesus (cf. Ph 2:7) – something that is known as the divine 'kenosis'. Significantly, Thérèse describes this phenomenon as fire. She writes: 'I have found the secret of possessing Your flame... Yes, in order that Love be fully satisfied, it is necessary that It lower Itself...to nothingness and transform this nothingness into *fire*' (SS, p. 195). This is the enkindling of the Holy Spirit.

The Spirit of Jesus

The action of the Holy Spirit is centred on Jesus – for the Spirit is the Spirit of truth (cf. Jn 14:17; 15:26), and Jesus himself is the truth (cf. Jn 1:14; 14:6). To neglect the humanity of Christ, at any stage of the spiritual journey, is to withdraw from the action of the Spirit. It is, we might say, a recipe for failure. Teresa was to learn this lesson from bitter personal experience, but her mistake would prove a happy fault and would have unique significance for her later teaching. For after this experience, she never ceased to warn others against the dangers of withdrawing from the incarnate Word at any stage on the spiritual path. She advised beginners: 'The soul can place itself in the presence of Christ... This is an excellent way of making progress, and in a very short time' (*Life* 12:2). Those more advanced are told that the failure to keep Christ present as a companion and guide in prayer 'is why many souls...do not advance further or attain a very great freedom of spirit' (*Life* 22:5):

> I assure them that they will not enter these last two dwelling places [the highest states of union with God]. For if they lose the guide, who is the good Jesus, they will not hit upon the right road. It will be quite an accomplishment if

they remain safely in the other dwelling places. The Lord
Himself says that He is the way; the Lord says also that He is
the light and that no one can go to the Father but through
Him... (IC VI:7:6)

As Teresa shows, there is an essential link between the mystery
of the God-made-man and the highest form of prayer or union
with God. Indeed, the great and final grace of the spiritual marriage was given to her through the sacred humanity of Jesus. It
is no surprise, then, that one of her favourite gospel texts was:
'I am the way, the truth and the life' (Jn 14:6).

John of the Cross is no less explicit. He sums up his teaching on the centrality of Jesus in one sentence, alluding to the
'Word' or 'Logos' from the prologue of John's Gospel: 'The
Father spoke one Word, which was his Son, and this Word he
speaks always in eternal silence, and in silence must it be heard
by the soul' (SLL 100; cf. 2A 22:3; Jn 1:1; Hb 1:2). The saint's
advice is brief but telling: 'God could answer as follows:... Fasten
your eyes on [my Word] alone because in him I have spoken
and revealed all' (2A 22:5). One short phrase, repeating this
message, says everything: 'fix your eyes only on him' (2A 22:6).
Then we will be 'founded on the rock' (cf. Mt 7:24), rooted in
Christ. 'Well and good,' writes John, 'if all things change, Lord
God, provided we are rooted in you' (SLL 34). And he directs
us to Jesus as the only true model:

> have habitual desire to imitate Christ in all your deeds
> by bringing your life into conformity with his. You must
> then study his life in order to know how to imitate him and
> behave in all events as he would. (1A 13:3)

Yes, we must fix our eyes on Jesus, and especially when he speaks
these stark words from the cross: 'My God, my God, why have
you forsaken me?' (Mt 27:46). In this way, John tells us, 'those
who are truly spiritual might understand the mystery of the door
and way (which is Christ) leading to union with God' (2A 7:11).
To drive home his teaching, John heaps up quotations from the

Scriptures, such as: 'This is my beloved Son..., listen to him' (Mt 17:5; cf. 2A 22:5); 'In [Christ] are hidden all the treasures of the wisdom and knowledge [of God]' (Col 2:3; cf. 2A 22:6; SC 2:7; 37:4); '[In Christ] all the fullness of the divinity dwells bodily' (Col 2:9; cf. 2A 22:6). Jesus is the revelation of God in person. There is no other. The guidance of the Spirit always leads us ever deeper into the mystery of the Word made flesh.

Sharing the life of the Three

The Spirit 'will take what is mine and declare it to you,' Jesus tells his disciples, and he adds: 'All that the Father has is mine; therefore I said that [the Spirit] will take what is mine and declare it to you' (Jn 16:14–15; cf. 14:23). This is not solely a question of the Spirit revealing or opening up to us, in Jesus, the inner life of the Blessed Trinity. These words also speak to us of the Spirit communicating this life to us, sharing it with us and drawing us into the whole dynamic movement of the Three Persons. Our Carmelite saints, with their own personal insights, help us to understand better, and enter more deeply into, this great mystery.

In the story of her life, Teresa speaks of a mystical experience in which she 'saw the most sacred humanity' and was shown 'that the humanity [of Jesus] was taken into the bosom of the Father' (*Life* 38:17). It was a privileged insight into the truth of God's word: 'The only Son, who is in the bosom of the Father, he has made him known' (Jn 1:18). To be in Jesus is to be with him where he is – in union with his Father – and, at one with Jesus, to be drawn by the Spirit into the inner life of the Blessed Trinity. Teresa invites us to a prayerful experience of God as the Three, and to a sharing in the dialogue and ceaseless exchange of love in the inner life of God. When she speaks of the highest form of prayer, she explains it with these remarkable words, again based on a mystical experience:

> Here all three Persons communicate themselves to [the soul], speak to it, and explain those words of the Lord in

the Gospel: that He and the Father and the Holy Spirit will come to dwell with the soul that loves Him and keeps His commandments. Oh, God help me! How different is hearing and believing these words from understanding their truth in this way! Each day this soul becomes more amazed, for these Persons never seem to leave it any more, but it clearly beholds, in the way that was mentioned, that they are within it. In the extreme interior, in some place very deep within itself, the nature of which it doesn't know how to explain, because of a lack of learning, it perceives this divine company. (IC VII:1:6–7; cf. Sp Test 13; Jn 14:23)

John of the Cross compares the experience of final transformation in God to 'the breathing of the air... / in the serene night, / with a flame that is consuming and painless' (SC, stanza 39). Much of his explanation, by way of comment, will be echoed almost word for word by Elizabeth of the Trinity. John explains:

By his divine breath-like spiration, the Holy Spirit elevates the soul sublimely and informs her and makes her capable of breathing in God the same spiration of love that the Father breathes in the Son and the Son in the Father. This spiration of love is the Holy Spirit himself, who in the Father and the Son breathes out to her in this transformation in order to unite her to himself... In the transformation that the soul possesses in this life, the same spiration passes from God to the soul and from the soul to God with notable frequency and blissful love, although not in the open and manifest degree proper to the next life. (SC 39:3–4; cf. L 185)

Edith Stein lends her support to these words of John when she writes:

The flame of divine life *touches* the soul with the tenderness of God's life and *wounds* her so mightily in her innermost depth that she dissolves wholly in love... This happens in the *inmost region* of the soul where neither the devil nor sensuality can penetrate, therefore what occurs is the more secure, substantial, and delightful. (Sci Cr, p. 188)

Heart to heart

Elizabeth of the Trinity speaks of the intimate manifestation of the Holy Trinity which crowned her life of persevering recollection and ceaseless prayer – an experience which, as we have seen, was also given to Teresa of Avila (cf. Sp Test 13; IC VII:1:6–7). Elizabeth exclaimed to her prioress:

> The good God has granted me such a favour that I have lost all idea of time. Early this morning I heard within the depths of my soul the sentence: 'If anyone love Me... My Father will love him, and We will come to him, and will make Our abode with him,' and at the same instant I realized its truth. I could not tell you how the Three Divine Persons revealed Themselves, but I saw Them, holding their counsel of love within me, and I seem to see Them still. Oh! how great God is, and how He loves us![21]

In her *Prayer to the Trinity*, Elizabeth addresses the Paraclete: 'O consuming Fire, Spirit of Love, "come upon me"' (PT; cf. Lk 1:35). These words invite us to enter, like her, into a prayerful experience of God as Three, and to a sharing in their own dialogue and the ceaseless exchange of love in their inner life. The three heavenly Guests within our soul are always sharing and communing with each other in our deep heart's core. This personal exchange of love is taking place at the centre of our being – an unceasing dialogue. It is an active presence, creative, always reaching out to give, to communicate itself, and always inviting us through the Spirit to receive the outpouring of God's love and to let it flow into us. Elizabeth professes her openness to this transforming, *creative* love, asking the three Persons that she might be 'wholly surrendered to Your creative Action' (PT).

Elizabeth also reminds us, echoing the First Letter of John: 'There is a Being who is Love and who wishes us to live in communion with Him' (L 327; cf. 1Jn 1:3). In this way, she invites us to commune with God 'heart to heart' – a phrase that best sums up for her the dynamics of this exchange – and 'heart' is to be understood here as the deepest centre of our being.[22] 'I pour out my heart,' she says, 'I catch myself saying all sorts of foolish things [to Him], but He likes me to be uninhibited and to speak to Him heart to heart' (D 135). And she writes to a friend: 'may the Holy Spirit, who is Love, make your heart a little hearth that rejoices the Three Divine Persons through the ardour of its flames... Oh! how our soul needs to draw strength in prayer, doesn't it, especially in that intimate heart-to-heart in which the soul flows into God and God flows into it to transform it into Himself' (L 278).

'They will persecute you'

As mentioned before, the Spirit will be a witness in a hostile world. The seclusion of the cloister is no guarantee of exemption from public adversity, persecution and trials. In a word, from the challenge to follow Jesus on the way of his passion and death and bear public witness to it. Paul speaks for every true follower of Jesus when he writes: 'With Christ I hang upon the cross, and yet I am alive; or rather, not I; it is Christ that lives in me. True, I am living, here and now, this mortal life; but my real life is the faith I have in the Son of God, who loved me, and delivered himself up for me' (Gal 2:19–20). The Spirit as witness will give strength, support and encouragement at all times when faith in the presence of Jesus and our endurance are sternly tested. And not just at moments of doubt and emptiness in prayer, but also in the midst of adversity and opposition through the powers of evil that want to destroy goodness, beauty and truth. In all this, the Spirit will be our guide (cf. Jn 16:13).

The life of Edith Stein is a shining beacon of truth burning brightly in the darkness of a hostile world. As a Jewess, she could see that there was no place for her to exercise an active ministry in the darkening shadows of Nazi Germany. But she accepted this with a sense of mission. 'I talked with the Saviour,' she wrote, 'and told Him that I knew that it was His cross that was now being placed upon the Jewish people... I would [help carry it]. He should only show me how... I was certain that I had been heard. But what this carrying of the cross was to consist in, that I did not yet know' (SEL, p. 17). Edith had no illusions about the future. While she was not looking for death, she was, however, ready to face her Gethsemane 'as a sacrifice...for true peace' (SP, p. 305). She kept pinned in her habit a slip of paper with the words: 'When they persecute you in one town, flee to the next' (Mt 10:23). And her superiors did, in fact, send her to a convent in the Netherlands. But there came a time when it was no longer possible to flee.

As Edith, arrested by the SS, walked calmly to her destiny, she turned to her sister and said, 'Come, Rosa. We're going for our people.'[23] Edith well knew that Jesus had foretold the persecution of his followers: 'When they deliver you up, do not be anxious how you are to speak or what you are to say; for what you are to say will be given to you in that hour; for it is not you who speak, but the Spirit of your Father speaking through you' (Mt 10:19–20). Questioned by an SS officer in the camp as to who she was, she spontaneously replied: 'I am Catholic' – thus bearing witness to Christ in a profession of faith.[24] 'If the world hates you,' Jesus had warned, 'know that it has hated me before it hated you... A servant is not greater than his master. If they persecuted me, they will persecute you... They hated me without cause' (Jn 15:18.20.25). In her last days, before her death on August 9, 1942 in the gas chambers of Auschwitz, Edith was entirely supported and strengthened by the Spirit, and was at one in mind and heart with her suffering Messiah as he lived again in her the conflict between good and evil, truth and error, light and darkness.

The final testing

In a moving poem, which is also a prayer, Edith wrote these words:

> You have guided me on a long, dark road,
> Stony and hard.

At times the strength seemed to have gone from me,
And I almost lost all hope of seeing the light.
But when my heart grew numb with deepest pain,
A star rose for me, bright and clear.
Steadily it guided me – and I followed.
At first reluctantly, but more confidently as time went on.[25]

In these few lines – written for Rosa's becoming a Catholic, but clearly marked by Edith's own experience – she outlines for us a journey that goes ever more deeply into the mystery of pain and suffering. But other Carmelites, too, have walked the way of the suffering Messiah. If that path was not always visible to the eyes of the world around them, it was certainly there in the intimacy of their personal relationship with the crucified Saviour. We discover, for example, the real cost for Thérèse of total surrender to love in the great and final testing of her faith. Shortly before her death, she wrote to a priest friend: 'my way is all confidence and love' (LT 226). But soon afterwards, we find her writing about the 'thickest darkness' (SS, p. 211), the spiritual trial that had been with her since invading her soul fourteen months earlier. It was Easter. Thérèse had coughed up blood just a few days before. This was the first summons – a *'distant murmur'*, she called it, *'that announced the Bridegroom's arrival'* (SS, p. 211).

It is risky to assume that we can understand what Thérèse was experiencing at this time of spiritual darkness. She herself found it almost impossible to explain: 'One would have to travel through this dark tunnel to understand its darkness' (SS, p. 212), she wrote starkly. Or, as she expressed it again: she was covered in 'thick fog', which suddenly became 'more dense' (SS, pp. 212–3). Her torment redoubled. The Psalmist, at his bleakest, expresses Thérèse's experience only too well: 'my one companion is darkness' (Ps 87:19). This darkness borrowed the voice of sinners and said to her, mockingly, that death would not give her what she hoped for, but only 'the night of nothingness' (SS, p. 213). She confided to one of her community: 'I don't believe in eternal life, it seems to me that after this mortal life there is nothing left... Everything has disappeared for me, love is all I have.'[26] She could not discern any trace of heaven. Everything, it seemed, had vanished. Even her own 'Little Way' seemed lost, swallowed up in its own littleness.

Surrender and peace

A month before Thérèse died, her sister Pauline was sitting by her bed. Thérèse pointed to the chestnut trees near the cemetery and said, 'Look! Do you see the black hole where we can see nothing; it's in a similar hole that I am as far as body and soul are concerned. Ah! what darkness! But I am in peace' (LC, p. 173). Near the end, she confided that the pain was enough 'to make her lose her reason' (LC, p. 162). She asked her sister not to leave any poisonous medicines around her and said, 'If I had not had any faith, I would have committed suicide without an instant's hesitation' (LC, p. 196; cf. pp. 162–3). Earlier that summer, Thérèse had said, quoting Job: 'Although he should kill me, I will trust in him' (LC, p. 77; cf. Jb 13:15).

That trust was tested in so many ways, not least by the uncertainty concerning her illness. Her doctors had given conflicting views. Thérèse was bewildered. Was death imminent? Or would this excruciating pain last for years? However, she refused to submit to anxiety. Her phrase 'everything is a grace' (LC, p. 57), a gift of God's love, sums up her response at all times. When she felt she could take no more, she said to the prioress who was at her bedside, 'I assure you, the chalice is filled to the brim!... But God is not going to abandon me, I'm sure... He has never abandoned me' (LC, p. 205). These words were uttered the day of her death – the ultimate trust. No wonder one eyewitness could write of her final moments:

> For more than two hours, a terrible rattle tore her chest. Her face was blue, her hands purplish, her feet were cold, and she shook in all her members. Perspiration stood out in enormous drops on her forehead and rolled down her cheeks. Her difficulties in breathing were always increasing... (LC, p. 206)

This reads like a description of the crucifixion itself. Her death was like that of Jesus on the cross, in abandonment and total surrender to love – a stark reminder of the hidden workings of the Spirit – bearing witness to Jesus still living in Thérèse, and strengthening and supporting her faith in the Son of God who loved her and delivered himself up for her (cf. Gal 2:20).

With Christ on the cross

Elizabeth of the Trinity wrote her *Prayer to the Trinity* two years before her death. But she had not yet lived out fully its request, 'help me to forget myself entirely'.[27] These words give expression to her whole ascetical teaching: her desire to follow Jesus as his disciple on the way of his passion and death, in order to share in the joy of the resurrection. God was to bring that longing to fulfilment in her final illness and death from the then incurable Addison's Disease.[28] In her *Prayer to the Trinity*, she had also asked for support 'through all nights, all voids, all helplessness'. Her intrepid faith never wavered, even as her physical strength weakened and the complications of her illness multiplied. Just as for Thérèse, the severity of her sufferings grew ever more intense. On one occasion, Elizabeth, now terminally ill, pointed to the window and said to her superior, 'My Mother, are you at peace leaving me all alone like this?' She then added, in response to the surprised expression of the prioress: 'I'm suffering so much that I now understand suicide. But be at peace: God is there, and He protects me' (L 329, n. 2). Elizabeth did not desire suffering like this, any more than did Jesus on the cross. She recoiled from it, as he did. But she well knew that fear and anguish, every pain and human suffering, even death itself, can be transfigured by trust and love.

Elizabeth longed for what Jesus desired: the unfolding of God's plan of love for his people and her place at one with him, through suffering, in the redemption of the world. Towards the end of her life, she wrote: 'He wants to associate His Bride in His work of redemption' (LR 13); 'Before I die, I dream of being transformed into Jesus Crucified, and that gives me so much strength in suffering' (L 324). To a world where euthanasia is often thought of as 'mercy killing', Elizabeth's message is clear and relevant: we can do much more than just put up with suffering; we can, in fact, transform it by love and allow ourselves to be transformed by it. What Elizabeth said of her desire to love Christ 'even unto death' (PT) extends to his whole Body spread out in the world. Faced with death and the excruciating agony of her final illness, she could say: 'O Love! Love!... Spend all my substance for Your glory, let it distil drop by drop for Your Church.'[29] This is Elizabeth's way of identifying totally with Paul's words, 'Now I rejoice in my sufferings for your sake, and in my flesh I complete what is lacking in Christ's afflictions for the sake of his body, that is, the church' (Col 1:24).

'Eternal Love!'

Edith Stein gives expression to the silent conviction of our Carmelite saints: that the strengthening power of the Spirit still bears witness to Jesus, who in our pain and trials is living again the mystery of his saving love. Edith writes, in this poem which she wrote as a prayer in preparation for Pentecost:

Who are You, Kindly Light, who fill me now,
And brighten all the darkness of my heart?
You guide me forward, like a mother's hand;
And if You let me go, I could not take a single step alone.
You are the space embracing all my being, hidden in You.
Loosened from You, I would fall into the abyss of
    nothingness from which You raised me to the Light.
Nearer to me than I myself am,
And more within me than my inmost self,
You are outside my grasp, beyond my reach.
And no name can contain You:
    You, Holy Spirit,
        You, Eternal Love![30]

Notes

1. Jn 14:16–17.25–26; 15:26–27; 16:7–11.12–15. See Appendix 1c for the text of these passages.

2. For an excellent discussion of this theme, see the chapter 'The Paraclete', in Lyonnet, SJ & de La Potterie, SJ, *The Christian Lives by the Spirit, op. cit.,* pp. 57–77.

3. Masefield, *The Trial of Jesus, op. cit.,* pp. 95–6.

4. John Henry Newman, *An Essay in Aid of a Grammar of Assent,* Garden City, NY: Image Books, 1955, p. 80; italics mine.

5. From his *Pensées,* IV, 277 (Brunschvicg numbering).

6. From St Ephraem, *Commentary on the Diatessaron,* quoted in *Divine Office,* vol. I, p. 518; italics mine.

7. Although English translations of Daniel use a variety of terms for his interpretation of the dreams, the Greek version of the Old Testament, the Septuagint, specifically uses 'anangéllō': the same term as used by John for the Spirit's teaching role (cf. Jn 16:13–15).

8. See Jn 2:4; 4:21.23; 7:30; 8:20; 12:23.27; 13:1; 16:2.4.32; 17:1.

9. From the Collect prayer at Mass, 26th Sunday in Ordinary Time (Year B).

10. In *Divine Office,* vol. III, p. [115].

11. From Whittaker Chambers, *Witness,* New York: Random House, 1952, p. 5.

12. St Augustine, *In Joannis Evangelium Tractatus* (*Treatise on John's Gospel*), 93, 1.

13. In Chambers, *Witness, op. cit.,* p. 6.

14. For a masterly treatment of these Johannine texts on the action of the Spirit, see n. 2 above.

15. In Cathleen Medwick, *Teresa of Avila: The Progress of a Soul,* London: Duckworth, 2000, p. 254. The appendix (pp. 251–4) contains the third poem of Crashaw's Teresa cycle.

16. In P Marie-Eugène, OCD, *I Want to See God, op. cit.,* p. 16.

17. The first half of this passage has been included in the *Catechism of the Catholic Church* as its opening definition of prayer (cf. # 2558).

18. In Sr Cécile, OCD & Sr Geneviève, OP (eds.), *La Bible, op. cit.,* p. 158. See also Guy Gaucher, OCD, *The Spiritual Journey of St Thérèse of Lisieux,* London: Darton, Longman & Todd, 1987, p. 107. The visiting priest was Fr Blino, SJ.

19. Thomas Aquinas, commenting on the writings of Augustine, describes the human person as 'capax Dei' ('capable of God' or 'fit to receive God'):

see *Summa Theologica*, I-II q. 113 a. 10; cf. St Augustine, *De Trinitate*, 1.14 c. 8. See, too, *Catechism of the Catholic Church*, section 'Man's Capacity for God', # 27–43. Augustine also writes that 'by delaying the fulfilment of desire God stretches it, by making us desire he expands the soul, and by this expansion he increases its capacity': from his treatise on the First Letter of St John, in *Divine Office*, vol. I, p. 538.

20. Again, from the treatise of St Augustine on the First Letter of St John, in *Divine Office*, vol. I, p. 538. See also, on desire as exercised in prayer, his letter to Proba, in *Divine Office*, vol. III, pp. 661–2.

21. In [Mother Germaine de Saint-Seine, OCD], *The Praise of Glory*, *op. cit.*, pp. 182–3.

22. See my *The Carmelite Charism*, *op. cit.*, pp. 20–2.

23. In Waltraud Herbstrith, OCD, *Edith Stein: A Biography*, San Francisco: Ignatius Press, 1992, p. 180.

24. See Ambrose Eszer, OP, 'Edith Stein, Jewish Catholic Martyr', in John Sullivan, OCD (ed.), *Carmelite Studies*, vol. 4 (*Edith Stein Symposium / Teresian Culture*), Washington, DC: ICS Publications, 1987, p. 317.

25. From Edith's poem 'For Rosa's Baptism: Holy Night'; my translation. Cf. SEL, p. 59.

26. A confidence made by Thérèse to Sr Teresa of Saint Augustine: quoted in *The Poetry of Saint Thérèse of Lisieux*, Washington, DC: ICS Publications, 1996, p. 184.

27. Thérèse, too, wrote her own important prayer, the *Act of Oblation to Merciful Love*, two years before her death, and had yet to live it out to the full.

28. For a description of the symptoms of Addison's Disease, see Jennifer Moorcroft, *He is My Heaven: The Life of Elizabeth of the Trinity*, Washington, DC: ICS Publications, 2001, pp. 110–11.

29. In Office for the Promotion of Causes [OCD] (ed.), *Elizabeth Still Speaks...*, *op. cit.*, p. 39.

30. From Edith's poem 'Seven Rays from a Pentecost Novena'; my translation. Cf. HL, pp. 140–1; SEL, pp. 84 & 92–3.

Chapter 6

PONDERING THE WORD:
A CARMELITE SLANT

Love letters from Christ

As the understanding of the Carmelite saints has shown us
again and again, the Scriptures are love letters from God to
his children. This, too, is the message of Vatican II: 'in the
sacred books,' we are told, 'the Father who is in heaven meets
His children with great love and speaks with them' (DV 21).
St Thérèse always carried a copy of the Gospels on her heart
– and she carried them *in* her heart, too, which is reminiscent
of what St Paul said of his converts: 'You yourselves are our
letter of recommendation, written on your hearts, to be known
and read by all; and you show that you are a letter from Christ
delivered by us, written not with ink but with the Spirit of the
living God, not on tablets of stone but on tablets of human
hearts' (2Cor 3:2–3).

Moreover, as we have seen before, Vatican II takes great
pains to remind us, in the words of St Augustine, that the focus
of our reading of any part of Scripture must always be Christ:
because 'the New is hidden in the Old and the Old is made
manifest in the New' (cf. DV 16).[1] And as St Jerome points out
so rightly: 'ignorance of the Scriptures is ignorance of Christ'
(cf. DV 25).[2] We must never withdraw from Christ or his sacred
humanity. In words which we have again already encountered:
'It is common knowledge that among all the Scriptures, even
those of the New Testament, the Gospels have a special pre-
eminence, and rightly so, for they are the principal witness
of the life and teaching of the incarnate Word, our Saviour'
(DV 18).

Take up and read

The message of the gospel, Paul reminds us, is to be found by accepting and entering into God's word, so that it may have an effect on our lives: 'We thank God constantly for this,' he says, 'that when you received the word of God which you heard from us, you accepted it for what it really is, God's word and not some human thinking, and it is still at work in you believers' (1Th 2:13). Edith Stein echoes this important point: that the word of God has a power all of its own to influence our lives; and as she also points out, we need to take time to open ourselves to this action: 'We need hours for listening silently and allowing the Word of God to act on us until it moves us to bear fruit in an offering of praise and an offering of action' (HL, p. 16).

How, then, can we do this? In his Chrism Mass of Holy Thursday, 2006, Pope Benedict tells us how to read the word of God: 'Listening to [Jesus] – in *lectio divina*, that is, reading Sacred Scripture in a non-academic but spiritual way...we learn to encounter Jesus present, who speaks to us. We must reason and reflect, before him and with him, on his words and actions.' And the Pope continues: 'The reading of Sacred Scripture is prayer, it must be prayer – it must emerge from prayer and lead to prayer.' John of the Cross, quoting the Carthusian Guigo II, gives this very telling comment on the gospel words 'seek and you will find; knock and it will be opened to you' (Lk 11:9). He explains: 'Seek in reading and you will find in meditation; knock in prayer and it will be opened to you in contemplation' (SLL 158).[3] It is easy to catch an echo, in his words, of the four stages of the age-old monastic tradition to which Pope Benedict refers: *lectio divina*. This method of prayer, worked out by saintly men and women of the past, is quite simply, as we shall now see, a helpful way of praying the Scriptures by reading and pondering, praying and contemplating. But before exploring the main stages of *lectio divina*, and examining them in the light of Carmelite teachings, we might begin by considering a fundamental disposition which we need: a listening heart.

'Hear, O Israel'

This was God's first command to his people (cf. Dt 6:4). To be a true disciple is to hear what God is saying – it is to *listen*: 'Each morning he wakes me to hear, to listen like a disciple. The Lord God has opened my ear and I have not resisted' (Is 50:4–5). To listen is nothing less than to share deeply in the inner life of the Blessed Trinity. For the Son listens to the Father: 'I have made known to you [disciples] everything that I have heard from my Father' (Jn 15:15); and the Spirit listens to the Son: 'whatever [the Spirit] hears he will speak' (Jn 16:13).

A true disciple listens to the Spirit of Jesus, the Spirit of truth: 'Everyone who is of the truth,' says Jesus, 'listens to my voice' (Jn 18:37). Little wonder that Elizabeth of the Trinity could sum up her Carmelite life as listening: 'O Eternal Word, Word of my God, I want to spend my life in listening to You, to become wholly teachable that I may learn all from You' (PT).

Reading attentively

While all true prayer, then, stems from a deep listening, St Ambrose tells us specifically that when we *read Scripture* we 'listen' to God (cf. DV 25).[4] We read the word of God with a listening heart, as did Mary of Bethany when she 'sat at the Lord's feet and listened to his teaching' (Lk 10:39). We must read his teachings in Scripture slowly and attentively, with a lingering pace, with reverence, and with a relaxed mind. We also need to listen in deep inner silence. John of the Cross understood this so well: 'The Father spoke one Word,' he tells us, 'which was his Son, and this Word he speaks always in eternal silence, and in silence must it be heard by the soul' (SLL 100). If we think of the Virgin Mary at the Annunciation, we remember that she was troubled at first when the angel spoke God's word to her; but she *listened* to his reassurance that she had found favour with God – that she was the object of God's love.

When, in our reading, we listen to the word like Mary, we hear that we, too, are the object of God's love: we will 'know and believe the love God has for us' (1Jn 4:16). We also need to read the word of God with our life's experience. The Bible was not, of course, written just for scholars, for those wanting only to study it: the Scriptures were written to give meaning to our lives and to help us towards closer intimacy with God in prayer.

One reading alone will never suffice. St Ephraem asks: 'Lord, who can grasp all the wealth of just one of your words?... For your word, Lord, has many shades of meaning...'[5] Or, as Teresa expresses it in her commentary on the Song of Songs: 'one word of [God's] will contain within itself a thousand mysteries' (M 1:2). And Thérèse repeats the same lesson in her own beautiful way, when she says of Scripture: 'a single word uncovers for my soul infinite horizons' (LT 226). It is no wonder that John of the Cross on his journeys throughout Spain used to repeat, over and over again, quietly and with great devotion, the priestly prayer of Jesus. If we, too, read a passage repeatedly, a word or phrase will surface and strike us. We do not need to go in search of it; we let it come unbidden and we stay with it. We need to be patient and give it time – so as to listen, ready to respond, just as Mary listened to the angel and responded to God's word.

'Pondering day and night'

A Carmelite is called to *meditate* continually on the word of the Lord – to be occupied in 'pondering the Lord's law day and night', as we read in our *Rule* (# 10). The Carmelite *Rule* also recalls this lesson from St Paul: 'the word of God must abound in your mouths and hearts' (# 19; cf. Col 3:16; Rm 10:8). We ponder the word as Mary pondered and treasured the word of God in her heart (cf. Lk 2:19.51). Her faith was not a blind faith – it was a questioning faith. She probed in search of deeper meaning and explanation: 'How can this be, since I am a virgin?' (Lk 1:34). This was not an expression of doubt but a genuine searching.

The Scriptures form a complete whole. The various words and phrases, however separate they may seem, are all linked to each other and tell us about Christ. For, to recall once more these words of St Jerome – and we can never recall them enough:

'ignorance of the Scriptures is ignorance of Christ' (cf. DV 25). As Mary listened to the angel's explanation about the future destiny of her Son, other words of Scripture, too, must have echoed in her heart: 'The Lord God will give him the throne of his ancestor David; he will reign over the house of Jacob forever and his kingdom will have no end' (Lk 1:32–33; cf. Ps 88:4–5; Dn 2:44). So we let our hearts resonate to other parts of Scripture as we listen to the word of God, our hearts always focused on the person of Mary's Son. As we ponder the word of God, we will find that it journeys from the head to the heart and that the Spirit opens our eyes of faith. There is great truth in these words from Hebrews: 'The word of God is living and active, sharper than any two-edged sword, piercing to the division of soul and spirit, of joints and marrow, and discerning the thoughts and intentions of the heart' (Hb 4:12).

Aspirations of the heart

The word of God nestles in the human heart and, touched into life by the action of the Spirit, bears fruit in love. For this, we need the solitude of *prayer*: 'When you pray, go into your [inner] room, shut the door, and pray to your Father who is in secret; and your Father who sees in secret will reward you' (Mt 6:6). Jesus is speaking of the inner room of the human heart. It is the new heart promised to us by God as a new covenant: 'A new heart I will give you, and a new spirit I will put within you; and I will take out of your bodies the heart of stone and give you a heart of flesh... I will put my law within [my people], and I will write it upon their hearts' (Ez 36:26; Jer 31:33). This law is God's love – which, as Paul assures us, 'has been poured into our hearts through the Holy Spirit who has been given to us' (Rm 5:5). This is the love that Jesus asks his Father to give to all who believe. He prays, in his priestly prayer, 'that the love with which you have loved me may be in them, and I also in them' (Jn 17:26).

Releasing this eternal love of God in our hearts is essentially what prayer is all about. Prayer, Teresa tells us, 'does not lie in thinking much but in loving much' (cf. F 5:2; IC IV:1:7), and

in many other ways she tells us this again and again. Prayer is
a dialogue of love as the heart reaches out to the heart of God
– this God who, quite simply, as Teresa tells us, 'loves us' (*Life*
8:5). Here, she is echoing the words of the First Letter of John:
'God is love... In this is love, not that we loved God but that
he loved us... God is love... We love, because he first loved us'
(1Jn 4:8.10.16.19). It is out of the abundance of the heart that we
give voice to our aspirations in prayer. As we have seen, Thérèse
tells us that prayer is 'an aspiration of the heart' (SS, p. 242). It
is a fling of the heart to the heart of God; it is a communion of
love, a heart-to-heart with God. No wonder Teresa calls prayer
'an intimate sharing between friends' (*Life* 8:5). With this, she
anticipates the lesson of Vatican II: 'the invisible God out of
the abundance of His love speaks to people as friends and lives
among them, so that He may invite and take them into friendship with Himself' (DV 2). As our hearts burn within us, aspirations of the heart pour out, spoken or unspoken. The Gospels
are full of these cries of the heart: 'Lord, that I may see... My
Lord and my God... I believe; help my unbelief... God, be merciful to me, a sinner...' The list is endless; the choice is ours.

A silent glance of love

As prayer deepens, even words fail. Then, 'the Spirit comes to
help us in our weakness; for we do not know how to pray as we
ought, but the Spirit himself intercedes for us with longings too
deep for words' (Rm 8:26). Jesus calls us to remain in his love
(cf. Jn 15:9) – a request both simple and profound. And there,
we have only to look at him (cf. *Life* 13:22), as Teresa instructs us.
This looking on God is *contemplation*; and, as John of the Cross
explains, it 'fires the soul in the spirit of love' (1DN 10:6).

This is the silent love of Mary as she stood wordless at the
foot of the cross, gazing on the disfigured body of her Son. We
are all invited by John in his Gospel to share in Mary's contemplation: 'They shall look on him whom they have pierced' (Jn 19:37;
cf. Zech 12:10). For Elizabeth of the Trinity, a Carmelite is 'a
soul who has *gazed on the Crucified*' and who, in doing so, 'has

understood the passionate love of His soul, and has wanted to give herself as He did!' (L 133). The faith, the hope and the love are all in the glance towards God in wonder, bewilderment and awe at the ineffable mystery, the grandeur and beauty of God's infinite and unconditional love. I am reminded of this deathbed conversation of Thérèse with her sister Céline: 'You should try to sleep,' Céline said to Thérèse. 'I can't sleep... I am praying,' Thérèse replied. 'And what are you saying to Jesus?' asked her sister. 'I say nothing to Him,' Thérèse replied, 'I love Him!' (LC, p. 228) – a simple, wordless glance of love towards Jesus.

The Psalmist writes beautifully of resting in God: 'Truly I have set my soul in silence and peace as a child at rest in its mother's arms' (cf. Ps 130:2). As Teresa advises us: 'one should... just remain there in [God's] presence with the intellect quiet', and 'if we are able we should occupy ourselves in looking at Christ who is looking at us' (*Life* 13:22). Often it may seem as though nothing is happening. Yet, as Edith Stein assures us: 'No human eye can see what God does in the soul during hours of inner prayer.' We can be sure it is something marvellous, beyond words, as Edith continues: 'It is grace upon grace' (HL, p. 6). St Paul even tells us that we are all 'being changed into [Christ's] likeness from one degree of glory to another; for this is the work of the Lord who is the Spirit' (2Cor 3:18).

God is 'like a refiner's fire...,' the prophet Malachi tells us; 'he will sit as a refiner and purifier of silver' (Mal 3:3). An artisan of silver once said that he knew his work was complete when he saw his own image reflected in the metal. Suddenly, then, this biblical image has a wonderful meaning: God is the divine Artisan – and he knows his work is complete when he sees his own image reflected in *us*! An inner change is taking place, a transformation fashioning us into the likeness of Christ. Thérèse understood this well when she prayed to the Father: 'look upon me only in the Face of Jesus and in His heart burning with *Love*' (SS, p. 276).

'Doers of the word'

Our listening to God's word must be translated into *action*. We are not meant to be listeners merely, but also 'doers of the word' (Jas 1:22). The word of God is always an invitation to conversion – indeed, to continual conversion. It is a challenge to a life of perpetual beginnings. In the gospel sense of the word, 'conversion' is a change of mind and heart that translates into action. '[God's] word is a lamp for my steps and a light for my path' (Ps 118:105), the Psalmist writes. Jesus challenges us: 'Let your light so shine before others, that they may see your good works and give glory to your Father who is in heaven' (Mt 5:16).

Good works are the fruits by which all will know that our prayer is genuine. 'Do whatever he tells you' (Jn 2:5), Mary said at the marriage feast of Cana. She herself had already practised this, as we can see from her response to the angel: 'let it be done to me according to your word' (Lk 1:38). This surrender to God's will was not just one isolated moment in Mary's life. Her surrender to the demands of God's word pervaded her entire life. As the handmaid of the Lord, she accepted with confidence her littleness, her dependence on him. Her hope rested firmly on the assurance of the angel: 'with God nothing will be impossible' (Lk 1:37).

As mentioned before, Teresa tells of how an elderly sister came to her one day in deep distress because she could not pray any other way than vocally. Teresa, however, was convinced that the sister was experiencing perfect contemplation (cf. WP 30:7). How? She knew it by the fruits of that sister's prayer: her life was exemplary. And Teresa concludes *The Interior Castle* with this vital message: 'This is the reason for prayer,...the purpose of this spiritual marriage: the birth always of good works, good works' (IC VII:4:6). She also urges us: 'let us desire and be occupied in prayer not for the sake of our enjoyment but so as to have this strength to serve' (IC VII:4:12). But she has these realistic and encouraging words for all of us who may feel that we have to do great things for God, all the while knowing that we are not capable of great things: 'we shouldn't build castles in the air. The Lord doesn't look so much at the greatness of our works as at the love with which they are done... let us offer the Lord interiorly and exteriorly the sacrifice we can. His Majesty will join it with that which He offered on the cross to the Father for us. Thus even though our works are small they will have the value our love for Him would have merited had they been great' (IC VII:4:15).

'Determined determination'

At the beginning of this chapter, we looked at one of the essential dispositions for praying the word of God: a listening heart. But once we have begun practising *lectio divina*, there is also another attitude we need. Jesus told his disciples a parable, to the effect that they 'ought always to pray and not lose heart' (Lk 18:1). This does not mean that we must always be praying on our knees, or that we can pray only in church. Rather, he is telling us never to lose heart, always to persevere, always to stick at it. Praying with the Scriptures is not just a one-off. It is designed to be practised, and to support us, all through life – either during our silent prayer, or as a prayerful exercise that feeds into our prayer.

Prayer itself will often be difficult. Teresa herself learnt this lesson the hard way: 'I never dared to begin prayer,' she tells us, 'without a book' (*Life* 4:9). And still, she gave up prayer for almost two years. She called this failure the treason of Judas (cf. *Life* 19:11) and regretted it all her life. To combat this falling by the wayside, she even coined her own special phrase 'determined determination' (WP 21:2). That, she says, is what's needed if we are to remain always faithful to prayer. And if we do give up prayer, there is only one remedy: start again!

While it can be helpful to pray with a book, yet at times there will be moments of aridity, even when reading the Scriptures. This itself can be a desert experience. The page before us will not always 'speak' to us immediately. It may be that the seed of the word is still sinking into the soil of our hearts before it can yield a rich harvest: thirtyfold or sixtyfold or a hundredfold (cf. Mk 4:20). It can be a very painful journey. In this classic passage from Thérèse, which we have met in an earlier chapter, she speaks of 'the *vast field of the scriptures*' which sometimes 'seems to us to be a desert, arid and without water' (LT 165). She, too, needed what Teresa calls 'determined determination' (WP 21:2). And experience showed Thérèse that Jesus rewards our perseverance – for, she adds, 'He sees our sadness and suddenly His gentle voice makes itself heard, a voice more gentle than the springtime breeze' (LT 165).

Called to freedom

There are many ways of practising *lectio divina*. The traditional method of reading, meditating, praying and contemplating provides a broad and helpful outline for many who wish to commune with God authentically in the spirit of Carmelite prayer. It covers the whole movement of our ascent to God. But it is not meant to be a straitjacket, something rigid and inflexible. We can be praying while we read, and contemplating while we ponder; we may rest in any one of the traditional divisions of *lectio divina* for extended periods, even for the whole period of prayer. This is like the seven sets of mansions that mark the progressive journey of prayer in Teresa's *Interior Castle*: they are not stages that are mutually exclusive. In fact, they are intimately connected and complement each other beautifully.[6]

When it comes to praying the Scriptures in the spirit of Carmel, there is only one basic rule: 'where the Spirit of the Lord is, there is freedom' (2Cor 3:17). It is not for us to anticipate God's action but to wait on it patiently. We must walk at God's pace in quiet submission to the action of the Spirit, as Mary did when the angel assured her: 'The Holy Spirit will come upon you, and the power of the Most High will overshadow you' (Lk 1:35). With Mary's gentle hand to guide our steps, we 'run with perseverance the race that is set before us, looking to Jesus who leads us in our faith and brings it to perfection' (Hb 12:1–2).

Notes

1. From St Augustine, *Quaestiones in Heptateuchum*, 2, 73.
2. From St Jerome, *Commentary on Isaiah*, Prol.
3. John is quoting here from Chapter 2 of the Carthusian Guigo II's *Scala paradisi* (*Ladder of Paradise*).
4. From St Ambrose, *On the Duties of Ministers*, I, 20, 88.
5. From his *Commentary on the Diatessaron*, I.18, in *Divine Office*, vol. I, p. 518.
6. For a guided exercise in *lectio divina* following the various stages, see Appendix 2a; for an outline of how to pray with Scripture cutting across the stages – that is, including them while simply immersing oneself in the word of God – see Appendix 2b.

Epilogue

ON THE ROAD TO EMMAUS

Every passage of the Gospels takes on a deeper significance when read and pondered through the eyes of the early church. Luke's Emmaus story is no exception. We can well imagine how the early readers, steeped mind and heart in the whole context of the events of the Gospels, would have drawn out the implications of the Emmaus episode for their lives as Christians; they would have taken as their starting-point the very background and context in which it was written. The Emmaus story is also a splendid example of *lectio divina* with all its traditional phases: reading or listening, meditating, praying, and contemplating. And to these we may add 'action' – that is, allowing the word of God to bear the fruit of good works in our lives.[1]

The Emmaus story comes by way of conclusion to Luke's Gospel, followed only by Jesus' taking leave of the disciples before ascending into heaven. So it is hardly surprising if other words or phrases, or even the whole thrust and movement of Luke's Gospel, still echoes in our hearts as we resonate to the full scope of the evangelist's teaching and purpose. As already mentioned, we are always enriched and enlightened by associations with other passages of the Bible sparked off by our reading of a particular passage – though these are not something to be sought for anxiously, still less as the fruit of study. We let these echoes come spontaneously as our hearts remain open to the action of the Holy Spirit who is the principal author of all the Scriptures, the Old and New Testament alike.

There is one important geographical detail which sets the Emmaus story significantly within the general setting of Luke's Gospel. Two of the disciples of Jesus, we are told, 'were going to a village named Emmaus, about seven miles from Jerusalem'

(Lk 24:13). We should remember that Luke is the author not just of his Gospel, but also of the Acts of the Apostles. Together, they form two complementary volumes of his story of salvation history (cf. Lk 1:1–4; Acts 1:1–2). That story begins in Jerusalem (cf. Lk 1–2), it invites us on a long journey with Jesus to Jerusalem (cf. Lk 9:51 ff.), and it ends with the passion-resurrection of Jesus in Jerusalem (cf. Lk 22:47 ff.). Jesus leaves his disciples with these parting words: 'And behold, I send the promise of my Father upon you; but stay in the city [Jerusalem], until you are clothed with power from on high' (Lk 24:49). At the end of the Gospel, we are told that the disciples 'returned to Jerusalem with great joy, and were continually in the temple blessing God' (Lk 24:52–53).

When we open the first page of Acts, we find the disciples still in Jerusalem (cf. Acts 1:1–5). We see that Luke links back with the concluding words of his Gospel as the risen Jesus promises his disciples once again, in almost identical terms, the gift of the Holy Spirit: 'You shall receive power when the Holy Spirit has come upon you; and you shall be my witnesses in Jerusalem and in all Judea and Samaria and to the ends of the earth' (Acts 1:8; cf. Lk 24:49). Acts ends with Paul, the 'Teacher of the Nations' and 'Apostle of the Gentiles', in Rome – the centre of the then-known world. There, he proclaims the same message preached around the Sea of Galilee – a message now spread by his missionary journeys to distant countries washed by the Mediterranean Sea. 'Let it be known to you then,' he says, 'that this salvation of God has been sent to the Gentiles' (Acts 28:28). Clearly, the whole movement of Luke's Gospel is towards Jerusalem, which is the place of the passion-resurrection of Jesus and the centre of God's loving plan of redemption. And from Jerusalem, it spreads out to embrace the whole world.

This point has been emphasised here because of its importance for the Emmaus story. Given that Luke stresses the centrality of Jerusalem in God's plan of redemption, it is highly significant that when we meet the two disciples on their Emmaus journey, they are moving *away* from this centre, wandering aimlessly in search of meaning and purpose in their lives. But even in their quest, God is searching for them much more intently than they are looking for him: unrecognised, Jesus joins the two disciples. Like the Good Shepherd, he leaves the ninety-nine in the green pastures and sets out to search among the hills and the crags for these two straying sheep that are lost.

Jesus speaks. The disciples *listen* attentively as they continue walking on the way to Emmaus. They listen to him in the light of their own experience. They are sad, downcast. They had hoped, but now they hope no longer; they are teetering on the brink of despair. Their world is shattered. These disciples relate to Jesus just as they are – no frills, no façade, no affectation, no pose. How should I relate to Jesus in prayer? Just as I am. And listening attentively, like the disciples on the road to Emmaus.

These disciples are seeking to understand the meaning of what is happening in their lives. They are *meditating* – pondering, reasoning and reflecting on the signs of the times, 'talking with each other about all these things that had happened' (Lk 24:14). Jesus himself draws near and walks with them on their journey, while they are discussing together. He takes the initiative as he did with the Samaritan woman by Jacob's Well (cf. Jn 4:7), and he asks them: 'What is this conversation which you are holding with each other as you walk?' (Lk 24:17). One of the disciples replies: 'Are you the only visitor to Jerusalem who does not know the things that have happened there in these days?' (Lk 24:18). Still their eyes are kept from recognising him. So he leads them on, gently. 'What things?' he asks. 'Concerning Jesus of Nazareth,' they answer, 'who was a prophet mighty in deed and word before God and all the people, and how our chief priests and rulers delivered him up to be condemned to death, and crucified him' (Lk 24:19–20). But then, they comment sadly: 'we had hoped that he was the one to redeem Israel' (Lk 24:21).

The light has not yet begun to dawn. But it does, gradually. The disciples recall the things they have just heard: some women went to the tomb, they tell Jesus. They found it empty and saw a vision of angels who said that Jesus was alive. Some of the disciples also went to the tomb and found it as the women had said. On hearing them speak in this way, telling him all this news but with such sad hearts, Jesus suddenly exclaims: 'O foolish men, and slow of heart to believe all that the prophets have spoken!' (Lk 24:25).

Jesus now begins to open up for these two disciples the meaning of the Scriptures: 'Was it not necessary,' he asks, 'that the Christ should suffer these things and enter into his glory?' (Lk 24:26). Then he interprets for them the Scriptures concerning himself, beginning with Moses and all the prophets. Here, Luke is anticipating a central lesson of his Gospel that Jesus will later address to all the disciples: 'These are my words which I spoke to you, while I was still with you, that everything written about me in the law of Moses and the prophets and the psalms must be fulfilled' (Lk 24:44). Then, as we will see, 'he opened their minds to understand the scriptures' (Lk 24:45). As St Augustine said so rightly, in words we have encountered before: 'the New is hidden in the Old, and the Old is made manifest in the New.'[2]

As they draw near to the village of Emmaus, and Jesus seems about to take leave of them, the two disciples press him to remain with them. Jesus agrees and they share a meal together. During the meal he takes the bread, blesses it, breaks it and gives it to them. At this point, Luke tells us, 'their eyes were opened and they recognised him; and he vanished out of their sight' (Lk 24:31). Then they say: 'Did not our hearts burn within us while he talked to us on the road, while he opened to us the scriptures?' (Lk 24:32). And that is *prayer*: a heart burning with love, and responding to love in dialogue with God's word. For Teresa, this is the core of prayer: 'not thinking much but loving much' (cf. F 5:2; IC IV:1:7). As we see from the Emmaus episode, Jesus takes the initiative in this dialogue of love. And just as the disciples listened and spoke with him, so we see how listening to Jesus leads to prayer.

From the dialogue of prayer, we are led to prayer's highest form: *contemplation*. No single detail in Scripture is insignificant, and we note that Luke tells us that Jesus vanished from the disciples' *sight*. But most of all, to contemplate God is to see with the eyes of *faith* – for Jesus is hidden in his word, recognised only by faith. The same is true of the Eucharist: the disciples recognise Jesus, we are told, 'in the breaking of the bread' (Lk 24:35; cf. 24:30–31) – with a silent gasp of wonder, awe, amazement at this blinding ray of darkness. The mystery of it all!

Jesus is always present, always absent. Reading the Scriptures, and listening to Jesus in *lectio divina*, cannot be just an isolated moment in our lives. We have to discover him again and again in his word and in the Eucharist. He is the Unknown Stranger whom Jacob encountered on his journey (cf. Gn 32:25–31). Jacob wrestled with God in the dark until the first streaks of dawn. Then the Stranger immediately disappeared. He withdrew into the luminous darkness of his own mystery – an elusive being. So, too, does Jesus at Emmaus: for the moment the disciples recognised him, 'he vanished out of their sight' (Lk 24:31). 'He is such a fast God,' the Welsh poet R S Thomas tells us, 'always before us and leaving as we arrive.'[3] Like the disciples at Emmaus, Jacob discovered God, only to lose him again. But not before Jacob had been wounded in the struggle and been given a blessing. Renewed, refreshed and strengthened, Jacob hobbled across the threshold and into the Promised Land. Likewise, by the end of the Emmaus story, the disciples turn back to return to Jerusalem, to the centre of salvation history – they have truly listened to the word of God: they have experienced a complete conversion.

We must always read the word of God as an invitation, a challenge to change, to put on the mind and heart of Christ and to *act* accordingly. After their experience at Emmaus and their return to Jerusalem, the two men join the other disciples who proclaim their faith in the paschal mystery: 'The Lord has risen indeed, and has appeared to Simon!' (Lk 24:34), they exclaim. The Emmaus disciples now add their own testimony in the gathering of the disciples, the assembly (cf. Ps 149:1; 39:11): they 'told what had happened on the road, and how he was known to them in the breaking of the bread' (Lk 24:35). They are witnesses to the paschal mystery with the other disciples in Jerusalem; and from Jerusalem Jesus will send them out to proclaim, with the whole church, the core message of their faith in the crucified-risen Saviour.

'Thus it is written,' Jesus will tell his disciples before leaving this earth, 'that the Christ should suffer and on the third day rise from the dead, and that repentance and forgiveness of sins should be preached in his name to all nations, beginning from Jerusalem.' And he will add: 'You are witnesses of these things' (Lk 24:46–48). Their witness, as we have seen from the story of Emmaus, is ultimately the fruit of a prayerful listening to the word of God. No wonder Pope Paul VI could write of his own day, in words that are no less true of ours: 'People today listen more willingly to witnesses than to teachers, and if they do listen to teachers, it is because they are witnesses.'[4] And John Paul II would speak in similar terms:

> We need heralds of the Gospel who are experts in human-ity, who know the depths of the human heart, who can share the joys, the hopes, the agonies, the distress of people today, but who are, at the same time, contemplatives who have fallen in love with God.[5]

Notes

1. At this point, it would be worth rereading the episode of Emmaus: see the text in Appendix 1d.
2. From the Prologue to his commentary on Isaiah; cf. DV 16.
3. 'From his poem 'Pilgrimages'.
4. From Pope Paul VI, 'Address to the Members of the *Consilium de Laicis*' (October 2, 1974), quoted in his Apostolic Exhortation of December 8, 1975, *Evangelii Nuntiandi* (*Evangelisation in the Modern World*), # 41.
5. From a talk given in 1999.

APPENDICES

ANNUNCIATION

(Lk 1:26-38)

26   In the sixth month the angel Gabriel was sent from God to a city of Galilee named Nazareth,

27   to a virgin betrothed to a man whose name was Joseph, of the house of David; and the virgin's name was Mary.

28   And he came to her and said, 'Hail, full of grace, the Lord is with you!'

29   But she was greatly troubled at the saying, and considered in her mind what sort of greeting this might be.

30   And the angel said to her, 'Do not be afraid, Mary, for you have found favour with God.

31   And behold, you will conceive in your womb and bear a son, and you shall call his name Jesus.

32   He will be great, and will be called the Son of the Most High; and the Lord God will give to him the throne of his ancestor David,

33   and he will reign over the house of Jacob forever; and of his kingdom there will be no end.'

34   And Mary said to the angel, 'How can this be, since I have no husband?'

35   And the angel said to her, 'The Holy Spirit will come upon you, and the power of the Most High will overshadow you; therefore the child to be born will be called holy, the Son of God.

36   And behold, your kinswoman Elizabeth in her old age has also conceived a son; and this is the sixth month with her who was called barren.

37   For with God nothing will be impossible.'

38   And Mary said, 'Behold, I am the handmaid of the Lord; let it be done to me according to your word.' And the angel departed from her.

Appendix 1b

PRIESTLY PRAYER

(Jn 17:1-26)

1   When Jesus had spoken these words, he lifted up his eyes to heaven and said, 'Father, the hour has come; glorify your Son that the Son may glorify you,

2   since you have given him power over all people, to give eternal life to all whom you have given him.

3   And this is eternal life, that they may know you, the only true God, and Jesus Christ whom you have sent.

4   I have glorified you on earth, having accomplished the work which you gave me to do.

5   And now, Father, glorify me in your own presence with the glory which I had with you before the world was made.

6   I have manifested your name to the men whom you gave me out of the world. They were yours, and you gave them to me, and they have kept your word.

7   Now they know that everything you have given me is from you;

8   for I have given them the words which you gave to me, and they have received them and know in truth that I came from you; and they have believed that you have sent me.

9   I am praying for them; I am not praying for the world, but for those whom you have given me, for they are yours;

10   all mine are yours, and yours are mine; and I am glorified in them.

11   And now I am no longer in the world, but they are in the world, and I am coming to you. Holy Father, keep them in your name which you have given me, that they may be one, even as we are one.

12   While I was with them, I kept them in your name, which you have given me; I have guarded them, and none of them is lost but the son of perdition, that the scripture might be fulfilled.

13   But now I am coming to you; and these things I speak in the world, that they may have my joy fulfilled in themselves.

14   I have given them your word, and the world has hated them because they are not of the world, even as I am not of the world.

15   I do not pray that you should take them out of the world, but that you should keep them from the evil one.

16   They are not of the world, even as I am not of the world.

17   Sanctify them in the truth; your word is truth.

18   As you have sent me into the world, so I have sent them into the world.

19   And for their sake I sanctify myself, so that they also may be sanctified in the truth.

20   I do not pray for these only, but also for those who believe in me through their word,

21   that they may all be one; even as you, Father, are in me and I in you, that they also may be in us, so that the world may believe that you have sent me.

22   The glory which you have given me I have given to them, that they may be one, even as we are one,

23   I in them and you in me, that they may become perfectly one, that the world may know that it was you
who sent me and that you have loved them even as
you have loved me.

24   Father, I desire that those also, whom you have given
to me, may be with me where I am, so that they may
see my glory, the glory which you have given me in
your love for me before the foundation of the world.

25   O righteous Father, the world has not known you, but
I have known you; and these know that you have sent
me.

26   I have made known to them your name, and I will
make it known, in order that the love with which you
have loved me may be in them, and I in them.'

Appendix 1c

PARACLETE PASSAGES

(Jn 14:16–17; 25–26; 15:26–27; 16:7–15)

14:16–17 And I will pray the Father, and he will give you another Paraclete, to be with you forever. This is the Spirit of truth, whom the world cannot receive, because it neither sees him nor knows him. You know him, because he abides with you, and he will be in you.

14:25–26 I have said these things to you while I am still with you. But the Paraclete, the Holy Spirit, whom the Father will send in my name, will teach you everything, and remind you of all I have said to you.

15:26–27 When the Paraclete comes, whom I will send to you from the Father, the Spirit of truth who comes from the Father, he will testify on my behalf. You also are to testify because you have been with me from the beginning.

16:7–11 Nevertheless I tell you the truth: it is to your advantage that I go away, for if I do not go away, the Paraclete will not come to you; but if I go, I will send him to you. And when he comes, he will expose the world concerning sin and righteousness and judgment: about sin, because they do not believe in me; about righteousness, because I am going to the Father and you will see me no longer; about judgment, because the ruler of this world has been condemned.

16:12–15 I still have many things to say to you, but you cannot bear them now. When the Spirit of truth comes, he will lead you into all truth; for he will not speak from himself, but whatever he hears he will speak, and he will declare to you the things that are to come. He will glorify me, because he will take what is mine and declare it to you. All that the Father has is mine; therefore I said that he will take what is mine and declare it to you.

EMMAUS

(Lk 24:13–35)

13   That very day two of them were going to a village named Emmaus, about seven miles from Jerusalem,

14   and talking with each other about all these things that had happened.

15   While they were talking and discussing together, Jesus himself drew near and went with them.

16   But their eyes were kept from recognising him.

17   And he said to them, 'What is this conversation which you are holding with each other as you walk?' And they stood still, looking sad.

18   Then one of them, named Cleopas, answered him, 'Are you the only visitor to Jerusalem who does not know the things that have happened there in these days?'

19   And he said to them, 'What things?' And they said to him, 'Concerning Jesus of Nazareth, who was a prophet mighty in deed and word before God and all the people,

20   and how our chief priests and rulers delivered him up to be condemned to death, and crucified him.

21   But we had hoped that he was the one to redeem Israel. Yes, and besides all this, it is now the third day since this happened.

22   Moreover, some women of our company amazed us. They were at the tomb early in the morning

23　　and did not find his body; and they came back saying that they had even seen a vision of angels, who said that he was alive.

24　　Some of those who were with us went to the tomb, and found it just as the women had said; but him they did not see.'

25　　And he said to them, 'O foolish men, and slow of heart to believe all that the prophets have spoken!

26　　Was it not necessary that the Christ should suffer these things and enter into his glory?'

27　　And beginning with Moses and all the prophets, he interpreted to them in all the scriptures the things concerning himself.

28　　So they drew near to the village to which they were going. He appeared to be going further,

29　　but they constrained him, saying, 'Stay with us, for it is toward evening and the day is now far spent.' So he went in to stay with them.

30　　When he was at table with them, he took the bread and blessed, and broke it, and gave it to them.

31　　And their eyes were opened and they recognised him; and he vanished out of their sight.

32　　They said to each other, 'Did not our hearts burn within us while he talked to us on the road, while he opened to us the scriptures?'

33　　And they rose that same hour and returned to Jerusalem; and they found the eleven gathered together and those who were with them,

34　　who said, 'The Lord has risen indeed, and has appeared to Simon!'

35   Then they told what had happened on the road, and how he was known to them in the breaking of the bread.

SOME CHURCH TEACHINGS ON SCRIPTURE

'Hearing the word of God with reverence...' (DV 1)

The invisible God, out of the abundance of His love, speaks to people as friends and lives among them, so that He may invite and take them into friendship with Himself. (DV 2)

The plan of salvation, foretold by the sacred authors, recounted and explained by them, is found as the true word of God in the books of the Old Testament: these books, therefore, written under divine inspiration, remain permanently valuable... God, the inspirer and author of both testaments, wisely arranged that the New be hidden in the Old and the Old be made manifest in the New. (DV 14.16)

It is common knowledge that among all the Scriptures, even those of the New Testament, the Gospels have a special pre-eminence, and rightly so, for they are the principal witness of the life and teaching of the incarnate Word, our Saviour. (DV 18)

For in the sacred books, the Father who is in heaven meets His children with great love and speaks with them; and the force and power in the word of God is so great that it remains the support and energy of the Church, the strength of faith for her sons, the food of the soul, the pure and perennial source of spiritual life. (DV 21)

...as many ministers of the divine word as possible will be able effectively to provide the nourishment of the Scriptures for the people of God, thereby enlightening their minds, strengthening their wills, and setting people's hearts on fire with the love of God. (DV 23)

This cultivation of Scripture is required lest any of [the ministers of the Church] become 'an empty preacher of the word of

God outwardly, who is not a listener to it inwardly'... This sacred Synod earnestly and specifically urges all the Christian faithful, too,...to learn by frequent reading of the divine Scriptures the 'excelling knowledge of Jesus Christ'. 'For ignorance of the Scriptures is ignorance of Christ.' Therefore, they should gladly put themselves in touch with the sacred text itself, whether it be through the liturgy, rich in the divine word, or through devotional reading... (DV 25)

And let [everyone] remember that prayer should accompany the reading of sacred Scripture, so that God and people may talk together; for 'we speak to Him when we pray; we hear Him when we read the divine sayings.' (DV 25)

Listening to [Jesus] – in *lectio divina,* that is, reading sacred scripture in a non-academic but spiritual way... we learn to encounter Jesus present, who speaks to us. We must reason and reflect, before him and with him, on his words and actions. The reading of sacred scripture is prayer, it must be prayer – it must emerge from prayer and lead to prayer. (Pope Benedict XVI, Homily at the Chrism Mass, 2006)

A GUIDED *LECTIO DIVINA* IN FIVE STAGES

'Remain in my love' (Jn 15:1–9)

I am the true vine, and my Father is the vinedresser. Every branch of mine that bears no fruit he takes away, and every branch that does bear fruit he prunes, that it may bear more fruit. You are already made clean by the word that I have spoken to you. Remain in me, and I in you. As the branch cannot bear fruit by itself, unless it remains in the vine, neither can you, unless you remain in me. I am the vine, you are the branches. Those who remain in me, and I in them, bear much fruit, for apart from me you can do nothing. Anyone who does not remain in me is thrown away as a branch and withers; and the branches are gathered, thrown into the fire and burned. If you remain in me, and my words remain in you, ask whatever you will, and it will be done for you. By this my Father is glorified, that you bear much fruit, and so become my disciples. As the Father has loved me, so have I loved you. Remain in my love.

Reading

Relax. Invoke the Holy Spirit. Then read this passage slowly, attentively and reverently, with mind and heart open so as to receive the word, listening deeply and ready to respond to whatever it asks of you. Know that it is a word of love from God addressed to you personally. Reread it two or three times – calmly, quietly and without haste.

Meditation

Take any word or phrase that strikes you spontaneously. For example: 'Remain in my love.' Reflect on this, repeating it softly over and over again if necessary, as an aid to keeping your attention focused on the word or phrase. Are you at ease with it, or does it challenge you? Are you disturbed by the thought of intimacy with Jesus, or does it fill you with joy? Ponder on your reaction and give reasons for it.

Recall another use of this word in the Gospel passage. For example: 'Remain in me, and I in you.' How does this help you to understand the meaning of 'remain'? Note its lasting quality. Observe also how Jesus speaks of a mutual indwelling: 'Remain *in*'. What does this mean to you personally? Finally, consider once more your reactions to this passage.

Prayer

Pray now to Jesus in your own words, enriched by your reading and pondering of this passage. Perhaps something like the following: 'Jesus, you ask me to remain in you; may I never leave your presence, just as you never leave me. Surround me with your love as you have promised.'

Contemplation

Remain quietly in the presence of Jesus with your mind still, looking at him who is looking at you, his eyes brimming with love and mercy. Let the silence deepen; ignore anything that threatens to distract your silent gaze of love away from him. Stay in the inner silence, rest in it, listen to it (for as long as it continues), aware that the Father has forgiven you, that he is touching your heart and changing you quietly, imperceptibly, into the likeness of his Son.

Action

Jesus asks us to bear fruit and also to remain in his love. The one does not come without the other. The more we remain in this silent gaze of love, the more we will be ready in our lives to serve others and to live for God, and in this way God will be glorified, praised and honoured.

We can all lack love and be judgmental at times, picking out the little 'speck' in our neighbour's eye and ignoring the 'beam' in our own. Resolve in future to try and radiate to others the love, compassion and understanding that Jesus has just offered you in your communion with him through his word. Be assured that you can do this with the help of his grace.

Appendix 2b

LECTIO DIVINA – AN EXERCISE IN INNER SILENCE

The various stages of lectio divina, as mentioned throughout the book, are not necessarily separate in the sense of one following on from another. They can co-exist, simply when we listen to the word in inner silence and allow it to sink deep into our hearts. Then, open to the Holy Spirit, we immerse ourselves in the word of Scripture and allow it to act on us, guiding us into communion with God. The following is an example of how a group lectio session might take place, though it can just as easily be adapted for use on one's own.

Preparation

The session might begin with the leader asking the group to relax, to make themselves as comfortable as possible, and to make a mental note of how they are feeling – anxious, apprehensive, tired, sad, in pain, joyful, sorrowful, depressed... Then, once they have become aware of this, they can hand it all over to God.

The leader now begins by calling upon the Holy Spirit, asking the group to open their hearts to the action of the Spirit who guides each person ever more deeply into the mystery of Jesus who is always the focus of *lectio.* Any appropriate prayer may be chosen. For example, 'Come, Holy Spirit', 'Fill me with your light and love', or perhaps a prayer of the leader's own choosing. Some may prefer to begin with just a simple gesture of open and upturned palms, indicating a readiness to receive the inpouring of the Spirit.

First reading

At this point, either the leader or any member of the group reads the chosen Scripture passage aloud. This reading should be done slowly and attentively, with each word and phrase articulated clearly. Immediately after the reading, each person is invited to make a mental note of the word or phrase that strikes them, that opens up for them. They should not go in search of it but just let it come, spontaneously. In other words, we do not consciously choose a word or phrase; rather, it chooses us.

This first stage should end with a period of silence. Each person should remain in the stillness and listen to the silence. The length of silence should vary according to the time available, and should not be prolonged unduly; however, even if time is limited, this should not be omitted. These moments of silence are of supreme importance for a fruitful *lectio divina*.

Second reading

There then follows a second reading on the same pattern as previously, with each word and phrase read slowly and attentively, and articulated clearly. This reading may be done by the same or another member of the group. It is important that the reader or readers be carefully chosen in advance, so as to avoid unnecessary confusion and distraction during the session. As before, the reading should be followed by a time of silent listening to the word, and again the silence should not be prolonged unduly. In particular – and something which holds for all three stages – any indication of unease or restlessness should signal time to move on.

At the end of the second reading and its period of silence, the leader should invite anyone who wishes, to speak out loud the *word or phrase* that the reading has lit up for them. *But without comment.* If, for some people, nothing lights up – or if, quite simply, someone is very shy – that's fine: no one is obliged to share a word or phrase. All must feel supremely free. The group just continues to remain in the silence, listening attentively to it and to anyone who may wish to share.

Third reading

A third reading is now done, following the same pattern as before. After this reading, all should feel free to share the personal *significance* of the word or phrase that has lit up for them (instead of just the word or phrase itself). However, this should always be brief and at their own comfort level. Note, too, that it should not be material for confession or for spiritual direction; the leader should tactfully ensure that this is carefully observed. Another important point is that *lectio divina* is not the time for a homily or for teaching others – this particular stage is a time for sharing personal experience. But as before, nobody must feel constrained to share. All tension or rigidity should be carefully avoided – 'Where the Spirit of the Lord is, there is freedom' (2Cor 3:17). If no one speaks, again that's fine: the group can just remain in the silence, letting the word of God sink ever more deeply into their hearts until the session draws to a close.

After the session

Once the members have left and gone home, it can help them to recall, at intervals, the word or phrase that lit up for them during the session, and to keep it alight in their hearts. In this way, each person can tap into that word or phrase during the day or following days, and so help the word of God to continue bearing fruit in their hearts and in their lives.

It is also helpful to reflect on the continuing action of the Holy Spirit – to say to ourselves, in the words of Scripture, that the Spirit will be in us (cf. Jn 14:16-17), guiding us (cf. Jn 14:26) into all truth (cf. Jn 16:12-16) – into Jesus, who *is* the Truth (cf. Jn 1:14; 14:6) and through whom God speaks to us (cf. Hb 1:1-2). And finally, to return, throughout each day, to the inner silence in which the word of God is bathed.

ABBREVIATIONS
AND EDITIONS USED

Works by Teresa of Avila

The Collected Works of St. Teresa of Avila, 3 vols., tr. Kieran Kavanaugh, OCD & Otilio Rodriguez, OCD, Washington, DC: ICS Publications, 1987, 1980 & 1985, including:

F	*The Book of Her Foundations*
IC	*The Interior Castle*
Life	*The Book of Her Life*
M	*Meditations on the Song of Songs*
Sat Cri	*A Satirical Critique*
Sp Test	*Spiritual Testimonies*
WP	*The Way of Perfection*

Works by John of the Cross

The Collected Works of Saint John of the Cross, tr. Kieran Kavanaugh, OCD & Otilio Rodriguez, OCD, Washington, DC: ICS Publications, 1991, including:

A	*The Ascent of Mount Carmel*
DN	*The Dark Night*
LF	*The Living Flame of Love*
P	*Poetry*
R	*Romances*
SC	*The Spiritual Canticle* (Redaction B)
SLL	*The Sayings of Light and Love*

Works by Thérèse of Lisieux

LC	*St. Thérèse of Lisieux: Her Last Conversations*, tr. John Clarke, OCD, Washington, DC: ICS Publications, 1977

LT	*General Correspondence*, 2 vols., tr. John Clarke, OCD, Washington, DC: ICS Publications, 1982 & 1988
PN	*The Poetry of Saint Thérèse of Lisieux*, tr. Donald Kinney, OCD, Washington, DC: ICS Publications, 1996
Pri	*The Prayers of Saint Thérèse of Lisieux*, tr. Aletheia Kane, OCD, Washington, DC: ICS Publications, 1997
SS	*Story of a Soul: The Autobiography of Saint Thérèse of Lisieux*, tr. John Clarke, OCD, Washington, DC: ICS Publications, 1996

Works by Elizabeth of the Trinity

Complete Works of Elizabeth of the Trinity, 2 vols., tr. Aletheia Kane, OCD (vol. 1) & Anne Englund Nash (vol. 2), Washington, DC: ICS Publications, 1984 & 1995, including:

GV	*The Greatness of Our Vocation*
HF	*Heaven in Faith*
L	*Letters from Carmel [L 84–342]*
LR	*Last Retreat*
PT	*Prayer to the Trinity ['O my God, Trinity whom I adore']*

Œuvres complètes d'Élisabeth de la Trinité, vol. II, Paris: Cerf, 1985, including:

D	*Diary*
IN	*Intimate Notes*
L	*Letters from her Youth [L 1–83]*
Pm	*Poems*

Works by Edith Stein

FEB	*Finite and Eternal Being*, tr. Kurt F Reinhardt, Washington, DC: ICS Publications, 2002
HL	*The Hidden Life*, tr. Waltraut Stein, Washington, DC: ICS Publications, 1992
LJF	*Life in a Jewish Family*, tr. Josephine Koeppel, OCD, Washington, DC: ICS Publications, 1986
MC	*The Mystery of Christmas: Incarnation and Humanity*, tr. Josephine Rucker, SSJ, Darlington Carmel, 1985

Sci Cr   *The Science of the Cross*, tr. Josephine Koeppel, OCD, Washington, DC: ICS Publications, 2002

SEL   *Edith Stein: Selected Writings*, tr. Susanne M Batzdorff, Springfield, IL: Templegate, 1990

SP   *Self-Portrait in Letters 1916–1942*, tr. Josephine Koeppel, OCD, Washington, DC: ICS Publications, 1993

W   *Essays on Woman*, tr. Freda Mary Oben, PhD, Washington, DC: ICS Publications, 1996

Carmelite *Rule*

Rule of Saint Albert, in John Malley, O Carm, Camilo Maccise, OCD & Joseph Chalmers, O Carm, *In Obsequio Jesu Christi: The Letters of the Superiors General O.Carm. and O.C.D. 1992–2002*, Rome: Edizioni OCD, 2003, pp. 133–9. This edition follows the numbering of points agreed in 1999.

Psalms

Numbering and text follow the Grail version, in *The Psalms: A New Translation*, London & Glasgow: Fontana, 1963.

TERESIAN PRESS

PUBLICATIONS AVAILABLE

Elizabeth of the Trinity: The Unfolding of her Message
Volume 1: In the World & In Community
Volume 2: In the Infirmary & After her Death
Joanne Mosley
£10.00 each volume

Holiness For All: Themes from St Thérèse of Lisieux
Aloysius Rego, OCD
£7.00

Upon This Mountain: Prayer in the Carmelite Tradition
Mary McCormack, OCD
£4.00

Let Yourself Be Loved: Elizabeth of the Trinity
Eugene McCaffrey, OCD
£5.00

Teresian Press
Carmelite Priory
Boars Hill
Oxford OX1 5HB

www.carmelitebooks.com

TERESIAN PRESS
SOME FORTHCOMING PUBLICATIONS

John of the Cross: Seasons of Prayer
Iain Matthew, OCD

A Moment of Prayer – A Life of Prayer
Conrad De Meester, OCD

The Writings of St Teresa of Avila
Eugene McCaffrey, OCD

Living with God
Tomás Álvarez, OCD

St Teresa on Prayer
Jerome Lantry, OCD

What Carmel Means to Me
Edited by James McCaffrey, OCD & Joanne Mosley

Teresian Press
Carmelite Priory
Boars Hill
Oxford OX1 5HB

www.carmelitebooks.com